INFORMAL ARCHITECTURES
Space and Contemporary Culture

black dog
publishing
london uk

Anthony Kiendl

INFORMAL ARCHITECTURES

SPACE/PERCEPTION

CONSUMPTION/RUIN

MONUMENT/EPHEMERALITY

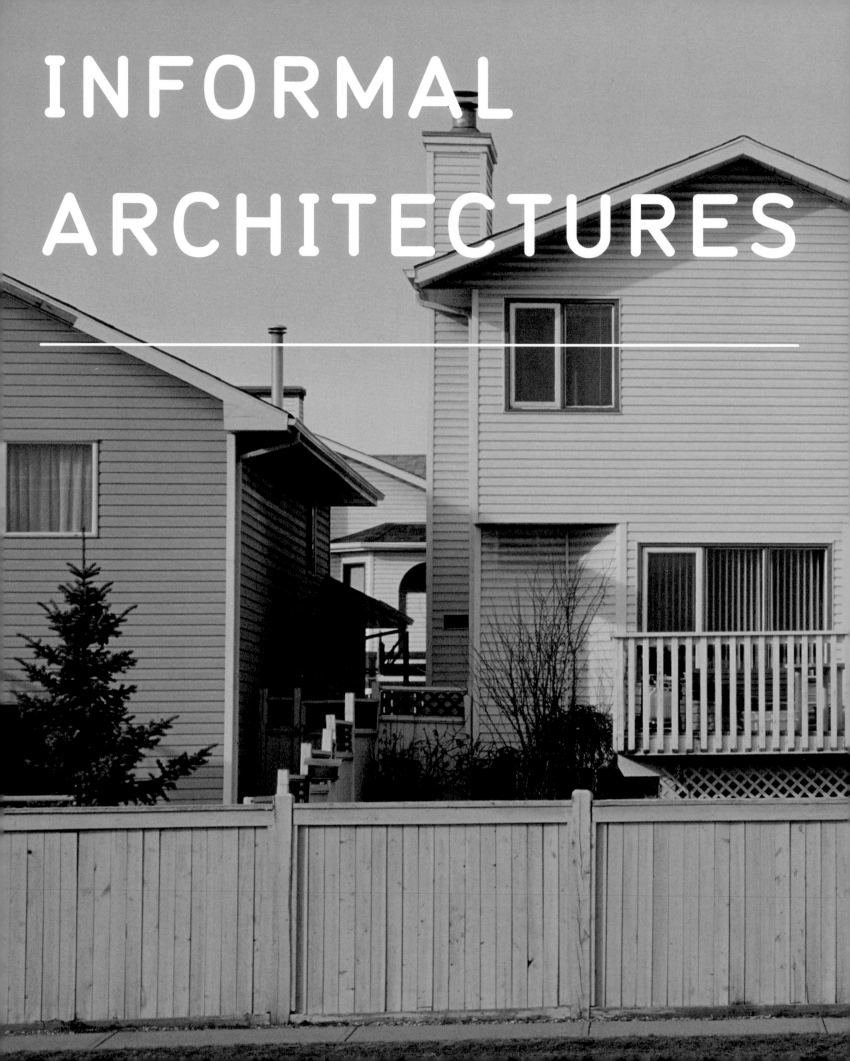

INFORMAL
ARCHITECTURES

Introduction
• Anthony Kiendl

Informal Architectures proposes several ideas that collectively constitute a re-imagining of the cultural meanings of space in contemporary Western societies. While architecture—understood in the broader sense as our entire built environment—is the subject of this book, it is analysed from interdisciplinary perspectives, particularly those found in contemporary art. This book examines several factors: the role of architecture in reflecting our culture's dominant values, the often unspoken assumptions and factors that our architectural surroundings contribute to culture and the inseparability of architecture from the broader ecology of contemporary culture; art, media, film, advertising and politics.

As a collection of images and writing, *Informal Architectures* elucidates an understanding of the culture of space that is to be defined in some way as variously social, philosophical, political and poetic. Interdisciplinarity within both visual art and architectural practices makes the distinction between these fields permeable and shifting. This intersection has engendered a kind of intermediary art that, as Anthony Vidler states, is comprised of objects which—while situated ostensibly in one practice—require the interpretive terms of another for their explication.

Moving beyond generalisable and arguably accepted ideas about how spatial culture may be represented, interpreted and created, *Informal Architectures* mobilises several other streams of thought in contemporary culture, recontextualising these ideas within spatial culture to form tenable counter narratives to dominant paradigms in architectural practices.

Informal Architectures specifically presupposes that modernity, as a socio-political ethos, is still the dominant operative paradigm in Western culture, as witnessed by war, technological imperatives and consumer capitalism. The autonomy of art from society has been revealed as a modernist myth, and postmodernism, particularly in architecture, is more of a re-assignment of formal conditions and values (a style) than a theoretical disruption of modernity's values and assumptions. Furthermore, the role of consumerism and attendant phenomena, such as advertising, are re-evaluated as primary factors governing contemporary culture, and must be reconciled in light of art's and architecture's inseparability from society as large.

This inter-textuality between art, architecture and other forms of culture can be understood, by example, through the work of artists such as Dan Graham, where strategies of shifting works between traditional categorical boundaries are key to understanding the psycho-social effects of systems and structures. The signification of objects is dependent upon how they are positioned within framing systems. This idea emphasises the dominant, but often overlooked and under-examined, role of architecture. Similarly, Georges Bataille employed a method of disrupting categorical boundaries in the journal *Documents,* by juxtaposing art with the material and products of capitalist, religious and other cultures. Bataille's influence is further considered through *Informal Architectures'* foregrounding of contemporary theories of abjection, or the formless, as seen in the work of artists such as Mike Kelley.

In this spirit, *Informal Architectures* looks at the marginal, contingent, and unmonumental to elucidate meaning in contemporary culture post-9/11. If the traditional forms of art and architecture intrinsic to twentieth century modernity have privileged the skyscraper, monument and technological progress, then alternative meanings are sought in that which is somehow ephemeral, hypothetical and even fictional.

Despite visiting scenes of various catastophes and loss, *Informal Architectures* is by no means nihilistic. Instead, it describes the means by which we may reconsider culture within modernity, finding alternative places and positions which are ultimately optimistic, if not liberating.

By considering work by artists from diverse and unconventional perspectives, the assumptions and dream-narratives of modern art and architecture may be re-imagined. The artists in *Informal Architectures* visualise economies of both excess and lack, proposing alternative strategies and criteria for the creation, representation and inhabitation of space in the (built) world.

Informal Architectures: Space in Contemporary Culture • Anthony Kiendl

The crowd is his element, as the air is that of birds and water of fishes. His passion and his profession are to become one flesh with the crowd. For the perfect *flâneur,* for the passionate spectator, it is an immense joy to set up house in the heart of the multitude, amid the ebb and flow of movement, in the midst of the fugitive and the infinite....

He gazes upon the landscapes of the great city—landscapes of stone, caressed by the mist or buffeted by the sun. He delights in fine carriages and proud horses, the dazzling smartness of the grooms, the expertness of the footmen, the sinuous gait of the women, the beauty of the children, happy to be alive and nicely dressed—in a word he delights in universal life.[1]

—Charles Baudelaire

He imagined he was watching the construction of the Great Pyramid at Giza—only this was 25 times bigger, with tanker trucks spraying perfumed water on the approach roads. He found the sight inspiring. All this ingenuity and labour, this delicate effort to fit maximum waste into diminishing space. The towers of the World Trade Center were visible in the distance and he sensed a poetic balance between that idea and this one. Bridges, tunnels, scows, tugs, graving docks, container ships, all the great works of transport, trade and linkage were directed in the end to this culminating structure. And the thing was organic, ever growing and shifting, its shape computer-plotted by the day and the hour. In a few years this would be the highest mountain on the Atlantic Coast between Boston and Miami. Brian felt a sting of enlightenment. He looked at all that soaring rubbish and knew for the first time what his job was all about. Not engineering or transportation or source reduction. He dealt in human behaviour, people's habits and impulses, their uncontrollable needs and innocent wishes, maybe their passions, certainly their excesses and indulgences but their kindness too, their generosity, and the question was how to keep this mass metabolism from overwhelming us.[2]

—Don DeLillo

Informal Architectures explores the meaning of space in culture, particularly as informed by contemporary art. This selection of gestures, ideas and images spans the late twentieth and early twenty-first centuries. It describes a culture at once still subject to the terms and ideology of modernity, and yet resistant to them. Rather than a project that is resolutely *anti-*modern, *Informal Architectures* describes numerous attempts to re-inscribe modernity with alternative values and subjectivities. In exploring contemporary art and spatial culture, we may redefine and recontextualise the terms under which we inhabit space, and understand how one may be in the world. Rather than an oppositional critique—posing the ephemeral versus the monumental or the intangible against the permanent—*Informal Architectures* is an attempt to figure out co-existent states, in the crevices of capitalism and modernity.

When Baudelaire used the term "modernity" in "The Painter of Modern Life", 1859–1960, he not only defined a term, but simultaneously redefined the sense of our place in our environment, in particular, the built, cultural and social environment of the city in modern Western culture. The figure quoted above in DeLillo's *Underworld,* surveys the modern city over a century later. It is dramatically different in scale and development, but still primarily consumed by the same systems and metabolism first described by Baudelaire.

Modernity—in the socio-political sense—may be generally characterised by the abandonment of a sacred vision of existence, and the affirmation of secularisation. The key point of secularisation is faith in progress. Faith in progress affirms the 'new' as a fundamental value. The 'new' as a dominant value suggests the imperative of consumption. The narrative of *Informal Architectures* assumes a distinction between notions of modernity in art and modernity in politics, but does not hold them to be separate. One of the abiding projects of artistic modernity was to be held apart from, and consequently impervious to social and political modernity. The notion of art's autonomy from politics and society has been exposed as a myth, so art and society must be understood in relation to each other. Whereas the art of modernity was concerned with the temporal, transient, detached, alienated—life viewed from the crowd or speeding automobile—the articulation of speed and progress through technical innovation accumulated into an edifice of capitalist values.

Walter Benjamin's often-cited project, "Theses on the Philosophy of History", was an attempt to organise the tidal waves of modernity into a cohesive architecture. In it he describes the last angel of history, in Klee's painting *Angelus Novus*:

> This is how one pictures the angel of history. His face is turned toward the past. Where we perceive a chain of events, he sees one single catastrophe which keeps piling wreckage upon wreckage and hurls it in front of his feet. The angel would like to stay, awaken the dead, and make whole what has been smashed. But a storm is blowing from Paradise; it has got caught in his wings with such violence that the angel can no longer close them. This storm irresistibly propels him into the future to which his back is turned, while the pile of debris before him grows skyward. This storm is what we call progress.[3]

At the beginning of the twenty-first century Western society comprises a system by which we understand our lived experience—a matrix of ideas, images, stories, politics, histories—a system that holds up images of technological innovation, conflict, and excess, all of which cohere into a form of monumentality. Simultaneously, however, we are haunted by collapse, weakness and entropy.

9/11 has been described as a watershed moment that changed everything. It was not so much a singular event that caused our current situation, but was rather a symptom that emerged among the matrix of history, ideas and economies—social, political, cultural—that more broadly constitute twenty-first century modernity. The attack on the World Trade Center appropriated the visual language of architecture to mobilise a broader cultural attack. It was not by coincidence or chance: Mohamed Atta, who hijacked the first plane to crash into the World Trade Center, had a degree in architecture, while Osama Bin Laden is believed to have studied civil engineering. Rather than a single moment of unquestionable historical consequence, it was an indexical moment, pointing to a discourse of modernity, consumption and spatial culture that existed pre-9/11. The architect of the World Trade Center, Minoru Yamasaki, suffering the previous destruction of his Pruitt-Igoe housing developments in St Louis in 1972, became modernity's tragic architect. Charles Jencks referred to the destruction of Pruitt-Igoe as the day that modern architecture died. This begs the question: what was the significance almost 30 years later of the destruction of the World Trade Center, if modern architecture was already dead?

As a striking social catastrophe and iconic image, the World Trade Center attack has arguably focused the popular imagination on notions of monumentality and ephemerality, yet our cultural discourse already spoke of its meanings and implications. 9/11 registered as a form of discourse because we were already aware, in countless ways, of the potential of our mass metabolism to overwhelm us.

In an installation that well preceded 9/11, *Catastrophe*, 1995, David Hoffos constructs a dream-like montage of multiple disasters, piling up consecutive events and debris. A plane crashes into a city, automobiles collide, explosions erupt, implying an earthquake and numerous other natural and man-made disasters occurring within a brief, inconceivable moment. Spectral images are projected on a curved 'cinerama' screen from projectors fabricated by the artist with found lenses and other surplus parts. The giant projection and subject matter allude to the Irwin Allen disaster films of the 1970s which played off Cold War anxieties and ecological crises. *Catastrophe* creates a built environment akin to such film sets, subsequently projecting our fears.

Prior to 9/11 one of New York City's biggest problems was the imminent closing of the Fresh Kills Landfill on Staten Island: the largest rubbish dump on the continent. The city generated 12,000 tons of residential municipal waste daily. Waste barges trolled the waters surrounding the city as solutions were sought. Following the attacks on the World Trade Center, Fresh Kills received the detritus from the site itself. As suggested by DeLillo, Fresh Kills overshadowed the World Trade Center as a site marking "the internment of our habits and impulses, our uncontrollable needs and innocent wishes, our passions, excesses and indulgences".

The measurable aftermath of 9/11—war and a concomitant and widespread malaise—tells us that Western culture is still subject to and consumed by modernity. The self-awareness expressed in postmodernism—the return of subjectivity in artistic discourse and resultant revisions of aesthetic dispositions—affect little in the context of the dominant political and social ideology. The totalising quality of modernity has remained constant over the past century, a modernity of technical innovation, consumption, and universalising values.

The byproducts of society's mass metabolism are perhaps more telling than the monumental artefacts—skyscrapers, technology and progress—of modernity are. The ephemeral, temporary, and contingent emerge in space and culture as embodying an alternative narrative to the dominant paradigms of strength, utility and permanence. In spatial terms, we may draw our attention more to the meaning of the interstitial or uncertain. In building terms we may draw our attention to the temporary, contingent, mobile and incomplete. In narrative terms we may draw our attention to the hypothetical, fictional and filmic.

The past two centuries have seen a succession of ideas evolve which, taken collectively, amount to the project of modernism. They include: the Kantian sublime, Freud's "primal scene", the rise of the 'unconscious' (a litmus paper upon which the world is a great reserve to trace our fears and desires), a prohibition on representation and mimesis in art (under the simultaneous proliferation of mechanical reproductions), the 'death of the author', the dematerialisation of the art object, and art's play in the expanded field, Minimalism, Conceptualism, and so on. These cultural transformations cannot be separated from wars, technological innovation, the bomb, an economy of scale and consumption, plastic, pharmacology, and holocausts among other catastrophes. The Nazis' programme attempted to erase all traces of unassimilable otherness, most obviously embodied by the programme of racial cleansing.

Looking back at the twentieth century, the sweep of artistic and socio-political modernity form an intertextual fabric. The processes, objects and ideas, of art are inextricably linked to historical, social and political precipitates. While events in the world hasten transformations in art and architecture, art practices are also structuring and initiating of transformations.

Art is, in part, constitutive of social imaginary, which is also made up of the media, history and politics; the broadest range of human expression and activity. While the dominant ethos in Western society remains modern, we understand culture to be dialogical and intertextual, to be understood not only within the context of other art but of society.

Art and architecture are critical in structuring, reflecting and interpreting society. Dialogism—or intertextuality—proposes that each work of art is influenced not strictly by the author's intention, but by and of other works. Meaning is created by the viewer, as well as by the artist. Not only is the meaning of a given work affected by those that precede it, but also by those that are in close proximity to it and that refer to it. Such meaning is further created by the viewer's ongoing reference to magazines, billboards, television, and other media and cultural representations.

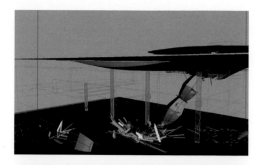

In *Philosophy of Time Travel*, 2007, an installation by Edgar Arceneaux, Vincent Galen Johnson, Olga Koumoundouros, Rodney McMillian and Matthew Sloly at the Studio Museum in Harlem, a monstrous totemic form descends through the ceiling of the gallery. The crash site, it appears, was caused by Brancusi's *Endless Column,* launched as a projectile that has come crashing down to earth and into the museum. The column, a modernist iconic monument, represents not only a missile or plane crash, but symbolically functions as a reminder that modernity's escape from classical art was accomplished through reference to African art, as well as other 'indigenous' cultures. What Brancusi encountered in African art apparently freed him from his European roots, while mediating between the present and a distant past that was positioned as somehow universal or transcendent of European values and history. *Philosophy of Time Travel* performs a critique of modernity. Further, it brings criticism into the realm of the institution, particularly museums. The launch of *Endless Column* defies rational explication but, as an event approaching science fiction, further speaks to a history of African American liberation through the adoption of science fiction narratives as a means to pursue alterity and freedom (as seen in the work of Sun Ra, Parliament Funkadelic and Samuel Delaney, to name just a few). Created post-9/11, the work does not explicitly cite the World Trade Center, but functions with the knowledge that images of such disasters predominate in the popular imagination.

Modernity has engendered the illusion of art being separate—transcendent of—the social and political context in which it is produced and received. While art could critically reflect on socio-political issues, it was prescribed a revised role which focused on the materiality of given media: painting was reduced to concern for pigment on a two-dimensional surface, further freed from mimesis in an attempt to discover the essence of painting. Music was reduced to 12 tone variations, freed from the need to be expressive of harmony. Writing was stripped of the need to relate an expressive narrative, to discover the minimal forms of tone and rhythm. As Clement Greenberg describes:

> … it developed that the true and most important function of the avant-garde was not to 'experiment', but to find a path along which it would be possible to keep culture moving in the midst of ideological confusion and violence. Retiring from public altogether, the avant-garde poet or artist sought to maintain the high level of his art by both narrowing and raising it to the expression of an absolute in which all relativities and contradictions would be either resolved or beside the point. 'Art for art's sake' and 'pure poetry' appear, and subject matter or content becomes something to be avoided like a plague.[4]

This turn was precipitated by socio-political preoccupations. Greenberg sought relief in art's potentially transcendent status because of the approaching Holocaust. In 1939 he wrote:

> The main trouble with avant-garde art and literature, from the point of view of Fascists and Stalinists, is not that they are too critical, but that they are too 'innocent', that it is too difficult to inject effective propaganda into them, that kitsch is more pliable to this end. Kitsch keeps a dictator in closer contact with the 'soul' of the people. Should the official culture be one superior to the general mass level, there would be a danger of isolation.[5]

Haunted by Fascism, this moment had, as one of its defining characteristics the attempt to resist the recuperation that more popular forms ostensibly leant themselves more readily to. As Jacques Rancière states:

> The idea of modernity would like there to be only one meaning and direction in history, whereas the temporality specific to the aesthetic regime of the arts is a co-presence of heterogeneous temporalities. The notion of art thus seems to have been deliberately invented to prevent a clear understanding of the transformations of art and its relationships with the other spheres of collective experience.[6]

The ability of art to propagate change provides an appealing counter narrative to art's aloof and neutral status under the terms of mid-century modernity: terms still deferred to under the myth of the artist as isolated, misunderstood and impoverished genius. Recent transformations in art, under the banner of Postmodernity, have revised its exclusive status to forms increasingly occupied by context, audience and society. Rancière writes:

> By drawing lines, arranging words or distributing surfaces, one also designs divisions of communal space. It is the way in which, by assembling words or forms, people define not merely various forms of art, but certain configurations of what can be seen and what can be thought, certain forms of inhabiting the material world. These configurations which are at once symbolic and material, cross the boundaries between arts, genres and epochs. They cut across the categories of an autonomous history of technique, art or politics.[5]

In *Species of Spaces and Other Pieces* Georges Perec offers further perspectives from which to consider art's positioning within the material world. Here he highlights the dialectic operation that occurs when art is perceived in space:

> I put a picture up on a wall. Then I forget there is a wall. I no longer know what there is behind this wall, I no longer know there is a wall, I no longer know this wall is a wall.

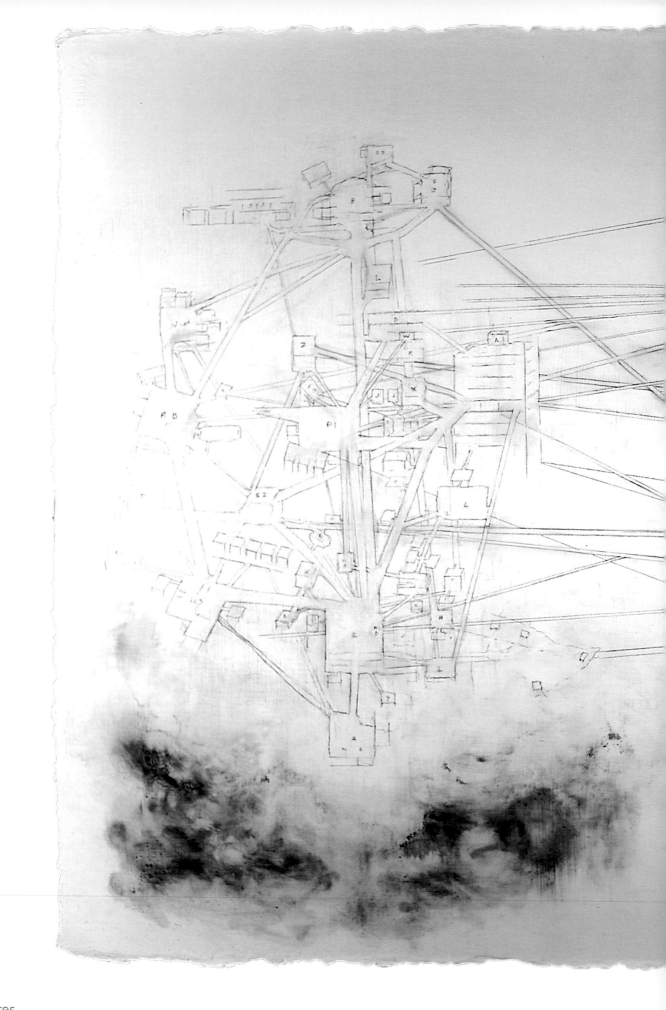

Eleanor Bond
Untitled, 2007
Mixed media on paper
55.9 x 76.2 cm
Collection of the artist.

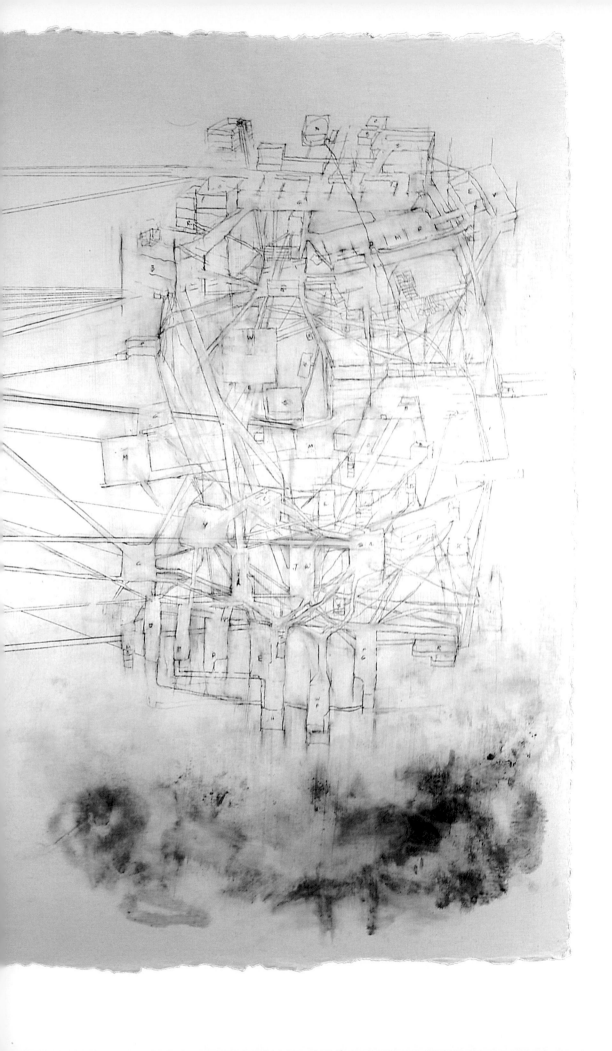

I no longer know what a wall is. I no longer know that in my apartment there are walls, and that if there weren't any walls, there would be no apartment. The wall is no longer what delimits and defines the place where I live, that which separates it from the other places where other people live, it is nothing more than a support for the picture. But I also forget the picture, I no longer look at it, I no longer know how to look at it. I have put the picture on the wall so as to forget there was a wall, but in forgetting the wall, I forget the picture, too. There are pictures because there are walls. We have to be able to forget there are walls, and have found no better way to do that than pictures. Pictures efface walls. But walls kill pictures. So we need continually to be changing, either the wall or the picture, to be forever putting other pictures up on the walls, or else constantly moving the picture from one wall to another.[8]

In the installation *Parasite Buttress*, 2005, Luanne Martineau has created a striking and disturbing form that brings into play notions regarding the relationship between art and space. Constructed out of felted wool, the piece unfurls down the wall and across the floor like a limpid protruding tongue saying "ahh". Formally, it features three great stripes—pink, white, pink—that extend vertically the length of its corporeal bulk. The top of the form curves back from the wall, drooping downward. Closer examination reveals various protuberances and mottled splotches. Even appendages—toes and fingers—are affixed to the main body. Despite its flaccid biological condition, the form also references the linearity of hard edge colour field abstraction like a mouldy Barnett Newman. The two parallel pink stripes emerge as Twin Towers if one squints their eyes enough. *Parasite Buttress* is a meditation on process-based conceptualism, and the anthropomorphism and de-neutralisation of architectural space. It is the physical space of the gallery that is complicit in creating the work's meaning. Without the wall for support, the work would not function in the same way. Martineau states:

Physically, my intent was to create a form that combines bed mattress and blanket with domestic rug, melting ice cream with liquid flesh, shed fur with dryer lint accumulation, and pork rib BBQ with spinal deformation. Normatively considered to be a pragmatic marriage of form and function, architectural spaces nevertheless incorporate cultural values and political beliefs. For example, Barnett Newman and Clement Greenberg both asserted that the Abstract Expressionist Movement was a revolution because the

paintings could not be contained within the space of the bourgeois home. Why was this? The Abstract Expressionist paintings could not be contained within the bourgeois home for two reasons: first, during 1947–1952, [such] paintings ran counter to popular taste, although this public rejection quickly ended when *LIFE* magazine came out with the article "Jackson Pollock: Is he the Greatest Living Painter?" in 1949. Secondly, the physical sizes of most of the Abstract Expressionist canvases were too large to hang in the majority of middle class dwellings. This can be seen as being an economic and social strategy: at the time a large canvas could be bought only by a museum or wealthy art patron.[9]

Furthermore, as Stephen Willats purports:

> The social consciousness on which the foundations of society are constructed is constantly presented to us all through the very physicality of our surrounding environment. This is especially apparent in city developments, where the layout of every complex of buildings, the shapes, the surfaces, materials and colours employed, have all been considered within a predetermined framework of cultural meaning. Hence, when I walk down any street I encounter a whole spectrum of physical organisations, over which I have no influence, but which are continually impressing their social message upon me. This lack of personal influence is so engrained into everyone's consciousness that it seems well nigh impossible, if one thinks about it at all, to challenge or change the composition of that environment. I am presented with what radiates from the surface; a language for me to decode, the message in the surfaces that comprise the city's physical fabric.[10]

Architecture is consumed by this ecology, creating a constellation of references and intertextual allusions. As architecture in urban settings is so structuring of our environment, we live within a matrix of signals and images. Architecture is itself loaded with meaning and references that must be taken into account when interpreting culture and our surroundings. The object-status of discrete architecture—monuments, skyscrapers, signature edifices—still resonates as a popular form of discourse; this is equivalent to the way that art and artists may still be (mis)understood in the terms outlined by Greenberg and modernity.

The roles of 'artist' and 'art' do not have a stable meaning in diverse, fragmented Western society. Since the 1960s artists have destabilised art's foundational tenets to both resist assimilation as a commodity-object, and to further its conceptual possibilities.

Above
Lida Abdul,
Clapping with Stones,
Bamiyan, 2005
16mm transfer to DVD, 4'50"
Images courtesy of the artist and
Giorgio Persano Gallery.

Opposite
Alex Morrison
Found Minimalism: Rotterdam, 2001
Colour print
69.2 x 99.7 cm
Image courtesy Catriona Jeffries
Gallery, Vancouver.

The end of the Soviet Union culminated with an iconoclastic carnival around public monuments to Soviet heroes…. The toppled statues eventually made their way to a park near the Central House of Artists and were left lying on the grass, abandoned to natural decay and casual vandalism. Here was 'grandpa Kalinin' with his eyes heavily made up in white chalk like a vampire from a Moldavian movie, Nikita Krushchev with red paint splashed over his bald skull, and Dzerhinsky's body with traces of all kinds of bodily fluids…. The monuments lying on the grass turned into picturesque ruins. If the monuments to the leaders had helped to aestheticise the ideology, their ruins revealed its perishability. No longer representing power, the monument reflected only its own fragile materiality.[11]

Theorists such as Jürgen Habermas, after the Frankfurt School, created a means by which to interpret the social dimensions of space and its construction, representation and interpretation.[12] Two of art's leading theorists of the late twentieth century, Rosalind Krauss and Lucy Lippard, while explicating art's trajectory in seemingly opposing directions, both describe art's evolution in terms related to its spatial qualities and to its relation to space. Both the disappearance and the ostensible "non-objectness" of the object under score the importance of an object's location in space as a primary factor related to its meaning. Since the late 1960s conceptions of architecture have incorporated social factors, informed by space, the body, movement, spectacle, relationships, history—in a word—culture.

Lippard described how art in the 1960s experienced a "dematerialisation" of the art object, a lasting effect of conceptual art, in which the autonomous object has become less crucial to the understanding and meaning of art than art's process of production, presentation or conceptual apparatus. This dematerialisation has the implied effect of underscoring art's position in space, even if it is intended to minimise art's material status. The conceptual art projects of the 1960s and 70s paralleled the work of 'paper architects', whose projects were never meant to be realised as built structures, but rather as hypothetical ideas that leant themselves to criticising traditional means and assumptions associated with architecture.

Lippard's dematerialisation of art seems, at first glance, almost contradictory to the "expanded field", as art was described by Krauss. She delineated the "expanded field" during the 1960s and development of minimal, installation and earth art, and its seamlessly expanded parameters became inseparable from art's surroundings (including architecture). "In the early 1960s… sculpture had entered a categorical no-man's-land: it was what was on or in front of a building that was not the building, or what was in the landscape that was not the landscape."[13]

The idea of art—and I would argue architecture—as a commodity is reinforced by periods of growth in capitalist economies which emphasises its function as an object of exchange value as opposed to an idea, language or process. The cycle of commodification also fosters a kind of historical amnesia that, in some ways, explains the cyclical nature of art's ebb and flow to and from 'objectness'.

Art is consumed by an ecology formed of electronic, film and media images, including advertising, email, virtual environments and the arena of public spaces—shopping malls, streets—and other such spaces from which art and architecture become relatively indistinguishable. It is now generally accepted that contemporary art practice precipitates transformations in and perceptions of the environment. There are direct links between culture and public spaces as sites of social communication. This interdisciplinary practice makes an active contribution to the ways in which the significance of the built environment can be questioned. Space in culture is a reflection of multiple factors, social, political, economic, aesthetic, and not the architect or urban planner alone. Like art, the social, economic and political dimensions of how we create the built environment are determined by—and inseparable from—a matrix of inputs and outputs that determine the assumptions and beliefs that are ultimately reflected in our environment.

The developments of spatial practice in art and architecture have distinct histories and often entirely different consequences. The term 'environment' in architectural practice has different sets of histories and implications than it does in art practice. Unlike the ecological connotation that is now heard in the contemporary use of environment, the environmental design movement used the term to distinguish its expanded architectural practice from an understanding of building as discrete or formally hermetic. For them, environment was used as a key term through which to sponsor a broader, urban-orientated, consideration of architecture's widest spatial and social effects. Environment thus became a polemical proposition as well as a description of architecture's social and technological complexity. While the strictest adherents of environmental design mobilised the social sciences to describe the perceptual and psychological aspects of new spatial conditions, another strata of the movement conceived of a media environment permeated by communicative impulses and electronic messages. Sometimes strategically, and sometimes as an unintended consequence, these poles of architecture's environmental theorisation threatened to dismantle its foundational stability. A counter trajectory for architecture's communicative and linguistic practice was set in play, distinct from that of the syntactic operations that gained prominence in the 1970s. As Anthony Vidler states:

> Artists, rather than simply extending their terms of reference to the three-dimensional, take on questions of architecture as an integral and critical part of their work in installations that seek to criticise the traditional terms of art. Architects, in a parallel way, are exploring the processes and forms of art, often on the terms set out by artists, in order to escape the rigid codes of Functionalism and Formalism. This intersection

has engendered a kind of 'intermediary art', comprised of objects that, while situated ostensibly in one practice, require the interpretive terms of another for their explication.[14]

Art delineates alternative strategies for understanding and critically analysing the structures—architectural, institutional, political, social—that shape and give rise to the patterns and practices which define the terms of everyday lived experience. The operation of art and the lived environment informing each other moves discursively back and forth as a feedback loop. The built environment is a space of creation and interpretation. However, the possibilities of how we choose to build, move through and interpret space are not only imagined by architects, but by artists, philosophers, filmmakers, writers, performers and others who also contemplate how to be in space. If we consider the activity of urban skateboarders, for example, the movement of their bodies through space performs a critique of architecture's meaning. Surfaces are found, analysed and re-appropriated for uses that are often contrary to their original intention.

In the 1950s the Situationist International, as they would later be called, propagated their belief that a world of permanent creativity could exist; against the backdrop of "the society of the spectacle" they were developing means to pursue that world. The Situationists conceived of contemporary consumer culture as a one-way spectacle in which the consumer is reduced to an isolated, passive receiver. They applied Marxist critiques of capital not only to political economic organisation but to everyday experience in consumer culture; an experience of alienation generated by the commodity. The name Situationism derives from the 'constructed situations' through which they proposed to experience life. For the Situationists, the city would no longer be experienced as a backdrop of received (and orthodox) information; of power relationships, consumer culture, products and of boredom. Rather, it would be an epistemology of everyday life where each 'situation' would be a setting for a play of events. Through this play, one could live life as if writing a book or making a drawing—as events happened—allowing one to transform society, to call forth new places, new buildings, new meanings.

Iain Borden describes how the physicality of skateboarding, for example, is at the centre of its representational meaning:

> [Skateboarding's] representational mode is not that of writing, drawing, or theorising, but of performing; of speaking their meanings and critiques of the city through their urban actions. Here in the movement of the body across urban space, and in its direct interaction with the modern architecture of the city, lies the central critique of skateboarding; a rejection of both the values and of the spatio-temporal modes of living in the contemporary capitalist city.[15]

It has been said that "200 years of American technology has unwittingly created a massive cement playground of immense potential, but it was the minds of 11 year olds that could see the potential".[16] Skateboarding's critique of the built environment is one that occurs liminally, as another way of knowing. Like play, this takes place in space, in crevices, gaps, and potholes; potential spaces of cultural experience. The critique of boredom, conformity, and consumer culture courses within the performance of skateboarding.

A number of works by Alex Morrison speak to the extended terms of reference employed in creating meaning with art and the built environment. These works further speak to the relationship between modernism's legacy and present day strategies to articulate a position that is reflective of one's situation within modernity. Morrison does this by articulating individual agency and subjectivity within the framework of modernity. *Teenage Runaway Campsite*, 2001, performs this action, while delineating the back and forth dialogic nature of contemporary art and culture. As a starting point, Morrison borrowed the form of what he terms "found minimalism", a sloped, pyramid-like structure abutting a low wall; in this case one he found in Rotterdam that serves as a popular skateboarding site. The form simultaneously echoes the form of Robert Morris sculptures of 1967. As

found architecture and, alternately, minimalist sculpture sharing the same formal qualities, Morrison creates a situation where, viewed alternately, the representational meaning of these two forms may be destabilised, denying all but momentary coherence. Morrison frames a photograph of the Rotterdam found minimalism on the gallery wall, and beside it places a 'life-size' white, minimalist form of the same shape. As the viewer peers at the back of the form, a cavity is discovered. The small 'hideout' is lined with photographs ripped from skateboarding magazines, alluding to a teenager's bedroom. Within the walls of the monumental structure lives an alternative space and identity. (This strategy of juxtaposing fine art and non-art artefacts and images was pioneered in Bataille's *Documents* magazine as a means to destabilise the foundations and meaning of art and other forms of culture.)

Architecture was historically ascribed a kind of foundational function in regard to all other arts, at least in the sense that it makes a place for them. This foundational role has been challenged by the medium of film which could, in reverse, make a place for architecture. The role of building sets in film has obvious analogies to architecture, and the ability of film to construct through light, sound, and movement also provides it with architectural qualities. Indeed, such is the realtionship bewteen the two that architecture itself may now be considered 'filmic':

> Out of this intersection of the two arts, a theoretical apparatus was developed that saw architecture as the fundamental site of film practice, the indispensable real and ideal matrix of the filmic imaginary, and at the same time posited film as the modernist art of space *par excellence*—a vision of the fusion of space and time.[17]

Playtime, filmed in 1967 by director, Jacques Tati, during Paris' years of post-war prosperity, features a quintessential modern city of glass and steel high-rises. The historical streetscape of Paris, including the Eiffel Tower, recedes to a reflection in its modern surfaces. Travel posters advertising various cities around the world all feature the same monolithic office tower in every city.

A satellite city was constructed for the set of *Playtime*. It was later torn down, and the land eventually absorbed by the real Paris. Some of the modern towers in the film were built on wheels to facilitate production. Where the Situationists were drifting through the city in order to re-interpret existence, Tati set the urban landscape itself on wheels. In the film, the architecture is as much a narrative element as the actors and their performances. At the end of *Playtime,* the movement of the modern city is transformed into a carnival. Traffic negotiating a roundabout implies the movement of a carousel, comically triggered when a pedestrian inserts a coin into a parking meter.

For Mikhail Bakhtin, carnival—the pre-Renaissance celebrations and spectacle of laughter and irreverence—signified the symbolic destruction of authority and the assertion of popular renewal. In a specific sense, Bakhtin's interpretation of the symbolic destruction of official culture (in Tati's film this could be read as modernity) is a lens through which to interpret *Playtime's* 'climax'. In a broader sense, Bakhtin's ideas of meaning outside the domain of art, or the organisation of life itself, deny the view of life as inert 'chaos' that is transformed into organised 'form' by art.

"Bakhtin claims that life itself (traditionally considered 'content') is organised by human acts of behaviour and cognition… and is therefore already charged with a system of values at the moment it enters into an artistic structure. Art only transforms this organised 'material' into a *new* system whose distinction is to mark new values."[18] Bakhtin delineates that art and everyday life are neither autonomous nor independent of each other.

We daily see how the use (and misuse) and the creation (and destruction) of objects, among which are works of art, play a frequent and sometimes crucial role in the transformation of societies. We may stick to the conception that sees our world as the goal of mankind and the end of history, and consider these phenomena as a temporary relapse into earlier stages of development, or we may use them to revise our understanding of ourselves and of the importance of 'symbolism' in our societies.[19]

Alex Morrison
Homewrecker, 2001
DVD 1'54"
Image courtesy Catriona
Jeffries Gallery, Vancouver.

Because they thus function in relation to the logic of representation and marking, sculptures are normally figurative and vertical, their pedestals being an important part of the structure since they mediate between the actual site and representation sign. There is nothing very mysterious about this logic; understood and inhabited, it was the source of a tremendous production of sculpture during centuries of Western art.

> But convention is not immutable and there came a time when the logic began to fail. Late in the nineteenth century we witnessed the fading of the logic of the monument. It happened rather gradually... one crosses the threshold of the logic of the monument, entering the space of what could be called its negative condition—a kind of sitelessness, or homelessness an absolute loss of place. Which is to say one enters modernism, since it is the modernist period of sculptural production that operates in relation to this loss of site, producing the monument as abstraction, the monument as pure marker or base, functionally placeless and largely self-referential.[20]

Lenin's idea in the months following the October Revolution was to install public art throughout the squares of Moscow in order to write history onto urban space. The masses would experience history—what Lenin termed "monumental propaganda"—as they went about their daily lives. Names of revolutionaries of socialism were inscribed on hastily constructed obelisks: Karl Marx, Frederick Engels, Thomas More, and others.

Today, as Stephen Willats states: "The sophistication and complexity of building language is so engrained in the fabric of our culture that there is an implicit recognition, even from the most casual observer of a building, of a whole hierarchy of relative symbolism that immediately denotes levels of social authority."[21] The implication of such a statement is that we have now so engrained authority (dominant values) into quotidian architecture, that it may function as a sort of banal, immersive, and yet effective, propaganda—eliminating the need for a monument as it has been historically understood. "Architecture", says Bataille, "is the expression of every society's being":

> [But] only the ideal being of society, the one that issues orders and interdictions with authority, is expressed in architectural compositions in the strict sense of the word.... Thus great monuments rise up like levees, opposing the logic of majesty and authority to any confusion: church and state in the form of cathedrals and palaces speak to the multitudes, or silence them. The storming of the Bastille is symbolic of this state of affairs: it is hard to explain this mass movement other than through people's animosity (animus) against the monuments that are its real masters.[22]

Foucault's conception is of an "architecture that would be operative in the transformation of individuals: it is not just a simple container, but a place that shapes matter, that has performative action on whatever inhabits it, that works on its occupant".[23] Bataille's writing on 'general' economy suggests that the heaving mass of inhalation and excretion in our culture sets the parameters and frame around which we build, move about and exist in the world. He writes:

> I will begin with a basic fact: the living organism, in a situation determined by the play of energy on the surface of the globe, ordinarily receives more energy than is necessary for maintaining life; the excess energy (wealth) can be used for the growth of a system (eg. an organism); if the system can grow no longer, or the excess cannot be completely absorbed in its growth, it must necessarily be lost without profit; it must be spent, willingly or not, gloriously or catastrophically.[24]

There is a surplus of energy on the globe that exceeds what is strictly necessary for maintaining human life. Bataille's concept of the "accursed share", is the surplus energy that any system, natural or cultural, must expend; and according to Bataille, the way in

which each society dealt with material excess most clearly defined that society. On two occasions Bataille would illustrate one of his texts in *Documents* with an image attesting to the vulnerability of architecture: the first photograph, accompanying the 'dictionary' entry *Cheminee d'usine* (Factory Chimney) and published without any other commentary than its caption, shows, "the collapse of a chimney stack, 60 metres high, in a London suburb", the second, directly corresponding to a passage in the entry *Espace*, shows the "collapse of a prison in Columbus, Ohio".[25]

The continual redistribution of elements in the world is a physical manifestation of entropy. While serving an applied function, architecture seeks to escape entropy, it is a reflection of our dreams and desires.

The contemporary shopping mall is a site where advertising and architecture intermingle, creating a new structure that is, overall, a system of consumption. Dan Graham explored this environment in *Death by Chocolate: West Edmonton Mall*, 1987–2005. The world's largest mall at the time it was constructed, it features a range of architectural features including a water park, an ice hockey rink, a zoo, a theme hotel and an amusement park. The mall is reifying of our hopes and desires; a complex of cultural messages constructed in physical space. The notion of consumption—whether in a conceptual, physical, economic, or social sense—connotes visceral, salivary and awesome spectral images, such as "death by chocolate". In *Being and Nothingness*, Jean-Paul Sartre speaks of:

> A sickly-sweet feminine revenge which will be symbolised on another level by the quality 'sugary.' This is why the sugar-like sweetness to the taste—an indelible sweetness, which remains indefinitely in the mouth even after swallowing—perfectly completes the essence of the slimy. A sugary sliminess is the ideal of the slimy; it symbolises the sugary death of the for-itself (like that of the wasp which sinks into the jam and drowns in it).
>
> … the slimy offers a horrible image; it is horrible in itself for a consciousness to become slimy. This is because the being of the slimy is a soft clinging, there is a sly solidarity and complicity of all its leech-like parts, a vague, soft effort made by each to individualise itself, followed by a falling back and flattening out that is emptied of the individual, sucked in on all sides by the substance. A consciousness which became slimy would be transformed by the thick stickiness of its ideas. From the time of our upsurge into the world, we are haunted by the image of a consciousness which would like to launch forth into the future, toward a projection of self, and which at the very moment when it was conscious of arriving there would be slyly held back by the invisible suction of the past and which would have to assist in its own dissolution in the past which it was fleeing, would have to aid in the invasion of its project by a thousand parasites until finally it completely lost itself.[26]

As Julia Kristeva points out, it is not a lack of cleanliness or health that causes abjection, but that which disturbs identity, system, order; what does not respect borders, positions, rules; the in-between, the ambiguous, the composite.

It has been described how the abject, filth and contamination were employed as a means to resist Fascism during the rise of the Nazis.[27] Those invested in forms of community opposed to that of the Fascists directed their energies to questions of otherness and the abject. Philosophers such as Bataille sought to rehabilitate fields of knowledge such as the human sciences through an ongoing challenge via a form of epistemology that took as its foundational problem the status of the abject as an object of knowledge.

> *Pica* is an appetite for earth and other non-foods. *Geophagia*, the act of eating mud, is a century-old practice, but in contemporary clinical practice may be considered an eating disorder. Yet it occupies a place between nourishment and waste: "A complicated weave of sociology... psychology... politics... and biologism.... We are in the space where culture and disease overlap.

Soil eating is poverty and hunger's most extreme outpost. It is an activity that is charged with a strangely archaic quality where a lack is miraculously turned into a surplus. In his febrile state of hunger, the soil eater transforms the bed of the river into filling food. He is set within a hallucinogenic landscape where the very ground he walks on is transformed into nourishment. For science, *geophagia* is a hard nut to crack. The phenomenon is located at the intersection of sociology, medicine and religion, and studies of soil eating need a thoroughly interdisciplinary approach.[28]

Rather than a pathology, this omnivorous capacity may be turned into a calculated radical gesture, as by artist Rita McKeough in her performance *Take it to the Teeth*, 1993, in which she masticated the walls of a museum (the walls were made of gypsum, a clay product). This implied consumption—tasting, tearing and regurgitating the walls—draws ideas of excess, waste, and landfill into a space of institutional critique. Over the course of a month, McKeough inhabited the gallery space, ripping apart the museum both literally and figuratively. The meaning of this work reflected a feminist critique of institutional systems broadly speaking, but also brought about a consideration of the human body in relation to architecture. The monstrous propensity and salivary qualities of the work bring to mind contemporary ideas of abjection. Following on, Sartre states:

> The slimy, from my first intuitive contact, appears to me rich with a host of obscure meanings and references which surpass it. The slimy is revealed in itself as 'much more than slimy'. From the moment of its appearance it transcends all distinctions between psychic and physical, between the brute existent and the meanings of the world; it is a possible meaning of being.[29]

In *Historic Building*, an installation by William Pope.L, the artist has constructed a domestic structure with four distinct faces. Approaching the structure from one side, one is confronted by a large white wall, approximately 5.5 metres in length, pierced by four holes about the diameter of a pencil. From these holes, a brown sickly sweet liquid oozes. Almost imperceptible at first, as one approaches they find that chocolate (identifiable by smell) is pooling along the base of the structure. One can just perceive the sound of crickets chirping at twilight. On an adjoining exterior wall, a multicoloured fungus appears to have grown in stripes. Upon closer inspection, the fuzzy stripes seem to have been adhered as an imprint of a Hudson's Bay blanket. (For many Canadians, the Hudson's Bay blanket is a symbol of Canadian identity; a cherished emblem of the fur trade representing exploration, wilderness survival and the birth of a nation. But Hudson's Bay blankets also allude to the decimation of Aboriginal people on the North American continent by disease. Gifts of Hudson's Bay blankets from Europeans were often tainted with infectious illnesses, such as small pox, that quickly spread death.) Around the corner is a door (there is a key in the door, but it is locked and will not open). A puddle of chocolate leaks out from underneath, forming a sticky brown puddle. In contrast to the historical allusions and title of the piece, the rest of the wall is covered in contemporary Typar-brand weather barrier with the words "Made in USA". Pope.L intercepts here by taping over "USA" and scrawling "Heaven" on top. Wrapping around the end of the wall on to the fourth side of the building is a rough, gestural hand painting representing a mountain landscape. Tins of paint are stacked against the foot of the structure. The specificity of chocolate refers to racial identity, and particularly the black subject exceeding the boundaries of authorised habitation. In another reading, the stickiness of the chocolate substance exceeding the explicit boundaries of the structure are associations of the slimy, speaking to the incapacity of technology to manage the biological; more specifically excreta.

Mike Kelley speaks of his interest in the aesthetics of ufology depicted as a "collision between a housing structure, the UFO, and an alien element that inhabits this house, in an uncommon aesthetic mixture of the abject and technological".[30] Kelley discusses how Hollywood films of the 1950s depicted aliens as totally 'other', such as one-eyed blob monsters that inhabit flying saucers.

I am fascinated by the contrast between the primordial appearance of such a being and the ultra-sophisticated device it pilots. It prompts the question of just why there should be such an overt inconsistency in design between the form of the being and its craft. The two are so unlike that they are impossible to reconcile. It's as if I were asked to believe that the pea soup, or refried beans, that inhabit a tin can designed that housing for itself and that this shell somehow represents its 'psychology'. On the symbolic level, the two forms simply cannot have similar meaning. The pleasure provoked by this incongruity evokes George Bataille's aesthetics of heterogeneity. Bataille described the similarity he felt between such abject excremental forms as sperm and shit and the 'sacred, divine or marvellous'. As a byproduct of their shared heterogeneous status as 'foreign bodies' in relation to our assimilating and homogenous culture. They are both, in a sense, equally taboo.[31]

Bataille's notion of "base matter" had its ground in his name for abject discipline: heterology. Heterology presupposed the incommensurability of the abject, its resistance to cognition and sublation. As Denis Hollier put it, heterology styled itself as the "theory of that which theory expels". Elsewhere, Bataille defined heterology more specifically as "the science of what is completely other". As such, heterology might approach its object (or abject) only via a series of statements about what it is not. Heterology dare not produce an idea of the abject, for that would defeat its purpose, but it might well develop second order ideas about the abject, about the way in which an unknowable abject works (or unworks) in a broader universe of meaning.[32] It is neither the 'form' nor the 'content' that interests Bataille, but the operation that displaces both these terms. As Stuart Brisley states:

> There are categories of order with universal meaning: shit, trash, dirt, entropy. But does order fall within definable parameters? Our existence, beginning with excrement—the most basic human production—depends on the ingestion of material sustenance and food, within its own organic continuum. It is claimed that individuals produce enough waste to recycle a lifetime's worth of food energy. We hardly glimpse what we produce, conditioned to regard it as noxious, contaminatory, extraneous. It is a constant reminder of that part of human life we have not yet managed to elude. A throwback to everything about us that is primitive and humbling. Loaded down with those fundamental pathogens: agents of contamination.[33]

Gordon Matta-Clark considered waste as architecture. In 1970 he built a wall from trash mixed with plaster and tar (*Garbage Wall*, which served as a set for a performance before being dismantled and thrown in a dumpster); in 1971, another wall, the construction of which was shot for his film *Fire Boy*, was built out of trash massed under the Brooklyn Bridge and held together by a chain-link fence; in 1972 a whole house was constructed in a trash bin, or rather a trash bin transformed into *Open House*.

Gordon Matta-Clark
Anarchitecture (hole in wall),
Anarchitecture (train derailment) and
Anarchitecture (towers: small,
medium, large WTC), 1974
Gelatin silver print
40.6 x 50.8 cm
Sucession de Gordon Matta-Clark en
dépôt au Centre Canadien d'Architecture,
Montréal/Estate of Gordon Matta-Clark
on deposit at the Canadian Centre for
Architecture, Montréal.

His first 'anarchitectural' piece—to use one of his favourite expressions—plays on the linguistic equation architecture = waste. This was *Threshole*, 1973. Under this generic term Matta-Clark designed a certain number of cutouts resulting in the removal of thresholds of apartments in abandoned buildings in the Bronx, often on several floors, opening the gloomy spaces to light. ('Threshole' is also a trash hole, a cloacal opening like that of the Paris sewers he filmed in 1977, in *Sous-Sol de Paris*).[34]

Connecting the human form with architecture is not exclusively Batailles's idea. It appears already in Vitruvius, when he found the proportions of contemporary types of humanity in the different orders of Greek architecture. He, however (and everyone after him), used this metaphor to give life to the stone, to rediscover the caryatid in the column.... Bataille makes this a demonstration of the opposite, a petrification of the organism that is reduced

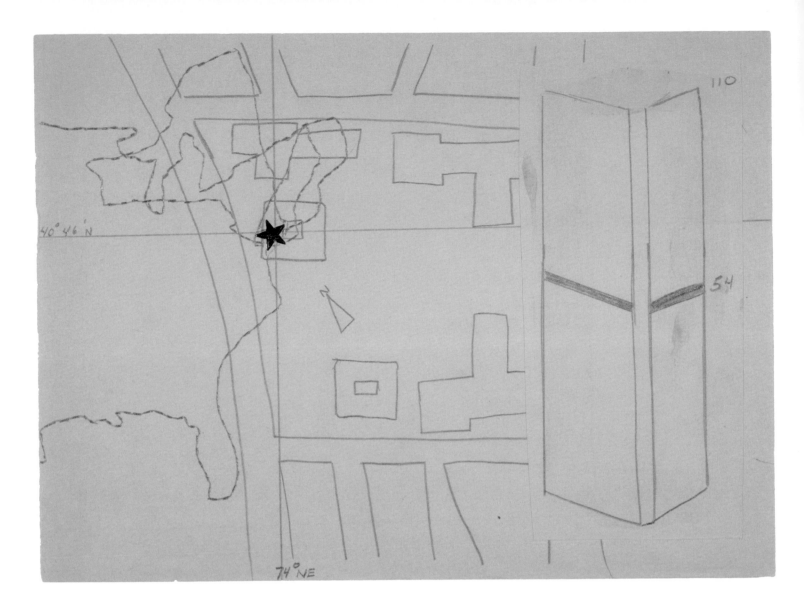

Gordon Matta-Clark
USA Map Imposed on Urban Map, c 1970
Collage with graphite and foil (metal)
22.2 x 30.2 cm
Sucession de Gordon Matta-Clark en
dépôt au Centre Canadien d'Architecture,
Montréal/Estate of Gordon Matta-Clark
on deposit at the Canadian Centre for
Architecture, Montréal.

in advance to its skeleton. With man, the dialectic of forms that constitutes natural history approaches a harmonius stability, an immoblity that architecture will have little to do to bring to completion. From human body to monument all that disappears is that which was perishable, which reamined in time's power: flesh that rots and its transitory colours. All that remains is the skeleton, the structure. Architecture retains of man only what death has no hold on.[35]

In a series of photographs, *Skull Houses*, 2004, Ryan Nordlund photographed new homes that make up the suburban sprawl of Calgary, one of North America's fastest growing cities due to revenue from oil. At first glance, the suburban sprawl seems uncanny, perhaps it is how close the houses are to each other. Perhaps it is the dominance of the garage door at the front of these new houses, making no secret of the importance of the automobile in suburban culture in North America. But upon closer inspection, the photographs reveal the literal meaning of their title. Each home projects the image of a skull. The eyes are formed of windows, and noses and mouths variously form from other architectural details such as doors or the garage. As a carrier of an image of human frailty and mortality, these skull houses speak to every aspect of *Informal Architectures:* the ratio of consumption and entropy which forms the backdrop of contemporary society, the intertextual quality of art and architecture, the reading of alternative subjectivities within the body of socio-political modernism, the quotidian and non-monumental site where meaning is found, as opposed

to authorised sites of memorial and monument. The matrix of the media environment is also alluded to in the photographs' plain documentary style. *Skull Houses* 'writes' a visual summary of *Informal Architectures* preoccupations and meaning.

Informal Architectures puts forward alternative strategies and criteria for the creation, representation and interpretation of space and its cultural implications. Institutions and the structures that frame society—government, religion and architecture, for example—assume particular practices and economies of consumption. Architecture is another word for system. During the Cold War, dreams of excess formed a consensual nightmare in nuclear power and the spectral image of atoms ceaselessly multiplying in a chain reaction—a surplus energy that would not be contained—as seen in Hiroshima, or in Chernobyl. Atomic visions seemed more palpable then, more commonly circulating in the media's representation of Cold War politics. Atomic energy is analogous to the accursed share, with limitless expenditure embodied by the chain reaction. This surplus energy, unfettered, would unleash radiation—an invisible quality that clings like slime, an invisible contamination.

Through emergent narratives among the materials of contemporary art, architecture, writing, performance and visual culture, this subjective history describes a contemporary culture that, despite the transformations of the past several decades—decades that might be generally termed postmodernity—is still subject to the terms and conditions of modernity as we saw them emerge in the development of the twentieth century. But within this system, one may find numerous possibilities to re-imagine and recontextualise one's surroundings under the terms of alternative subjectivities and possibilities. While monumentality continues to haunt contemporary art and architectural practices in Western societies, alternative strategies in spatial culture have proliferated since the 1960s. By taking into consideration the works of artists, including those from culturally diverse and unconventional perspectives, the canons of modern art and architecture may be recontextualised.

Ryan Nordlund
Skull Houses, Citadel,
Northwest Calgary, 2004
Colour photographs
Collection of the artist.

SPACE/
PERCEPTION

Popular Science
• Patrick Keiller

During the 1980s, I spent a lot of time looking out of a window of the third floor flat in which I lived and worked in London.[1] The window faced west towards Battersea Power Station, about three kilometres away. I lived in this flat for almost exactly ten years, during which the landscape that it overlooked changed in various ways. In 1983, the Central Electricity Generating Board (as it then was) ceased to operate Battersea, arguing that a relatively small power station in the middle of London was uneconomic. A competition was announced for commercial developers to propose new uses for the building and the surrounding site, which was large and extremely valuable. The winner was the owner of the most successful theme park in the UK who, with the explicit approval of the then prime minister, proposed to turn the structure into a theme park and invited her to return in two years time to open it.

Contractors gutted the building and removed the roof, installing two cranes which stuck out above the empty shell. The project then stalled amid suspicion that the long-term goal was to demolish the building and develop the site in more profitable ways. The developer sold the most successful theme park in the UK to raise funds to complete the project, but was unable to do so, and for some years the cranes remained on the site free to move in the wind. Sometimes they both faced one way, sometimes the other; sometimes they faced each other, sometimes in opposite directions. Their movements were not that frequent, and didn't seem to be much connected with the weather, but gave the impression that the building was alive, and was perhaps thinking. Inside the flat, we were thinking it would have been better if the power station had gone on working, or perhaps been replaced by a more modern one.

In its day, Battersea Power Station was exemplary. Its exterior was designed by Sir Giles Gilbert Scott, a leading architect; its flue gases were 'scrubbed' clean; its city centre position meant that energy lost in transmission was kept to a minimum and its cooling water provided heating and hot water to a large number of dwellings on the opposite bank of the river. When it was closed, a boiler house had to be constructed to replace this function. Similar joint heat and power schemes are common in other countries. In England in the 1980s none of this counted for anything, but as a monument the building's future had to be guaranteed. The nearby Bankside Power Station opposite St Paul's Cathedral, also a work of Scott, has now been converted into the Tate Gallery of Modern Art.

As we felt ourselves losing ground, both politically and economically, our sense of loss was partly mollified by observing these visible changes in the detail of the landscape as spectators at some sporting event might watch the opposition winning. We might not like the way things were going, but at least we had a good view. Satellite dishes began to appear on the houses and flats visible from the window. We would notice them for the first time in the morning when they caught the sun, so that they seemed to have grown in the night. Soon we could see about 20, then the rate of increase slowed. A couple of years later the dishes began to disappear. I began to think of the entire view as a very slow but visible movement of self-organising matter.

Apollinaire's impression of the south London suburbs, seen from the train, was of "wounds bleeding in the fog". Sometimes it seemed possible to perceive the view as an organic phenomenon. There was a Kentucky Fried Chicken outlet nearby, so there was always plenty of animal protein lying about the streets. At other times, the perception was of molecular vibration, turbulence, consciousness even. From *The Importance of Being Earnest*, I recalled: "Pray don't talk to me about the weather, Mr Worthing. Whenever people talk to me about the weather, I always feel quite certain that they mean something else." In the narration of a film, I quoted Democritus:

"According to convention, there is a sweet and a bitter; a hot and a cold; and according to convention there is colour. In truth, there are atoms and a void." Such abstraction leads to irony. I began to think it might be possible to predict the future by looking out of the window. In *The Anatomy of Melancholy* Robert Burton (who styled himself Democritus Junior, and is said to have accurately foretold the date of his own death) wrote: "Democritus... was so far carried with this ironical passion, that the citizens of Abdera took him to be mad, and sent therefore Embassadors to Hippocrates the physician, that he would exercise his skill upon him." I decided to cure myself by making a film about London. Many details of the view from the window appeared in the film. Shortly before it was finished, we moved out of the flat.

In the summer of 1989, there were several bankruptcies among London property developers. The political atmosphere in the UK began to change. At first, this change seemed rather rapid, but it slowed. With the fall of the Berlin Wall, one vague unease was replaced by another. As we now know, on average, people in the DDR lived longer than Westerners—even wealthy Westerners— because they were more equal, and it is said that in the advanced economies more people now die as a result of depression than in car crashes. In a somewhat similar way, since pure science began taking a serious interest in the weather and other indeterminate, complex phenomena, the second law of thermodynamics has lost much of its melancholy allure, but phenomena like the fluctuations of the stock market have become part of 'nature'. Everything is 'nature'. Everything that exists in actuality, perhaps even every thought, dream or fantasy, must have some material basis or it wouldn't exist at all. Probably artists have always known this, but for many people it is distressing. How can human aberrations like nuclear power stations, neo-liberal governments or uncomfortable clothing

be 'natural' in the same way as wild flowers or thunderstorms? A spoilsport might assert that though everything may be natural, not everything comes about in quite the same way, but that doesn't seem to diminish the sense of enlightenment.

In 1900, in his essay "Laughter", Henri Bergson wrote: "If reality could immediately reach our senses and our consciousness, if we could come into direct contact with things and with each other, probably art would be useless, or rather we should all be artists."[2] About 30 years later, in Prague, in the essay "What is Poetry", Roman Jakobsen wrote:

> Nowadays, the department-store mirror monstrosity and the village inn's tiny fly-bespattered window are considered to be of equal poetic worth. And just about anything can come flying out of them.... No nook or cranny, no activity, no landscape, or thought stands outside the pale of poetic subject matter.[3]

In the twentieth century, images of already-existing modern urban and industrial landscapes were involved in the production of new and influential buildings, and hence new landscapes: the photographs in Le Corbusier's *Vers une Architecture*, those in László Moholy-Nagy's *Von Material zu Architektur*; in Eric Mendelsohn's *Amerika*.

Though not realised, Archigram's proposals, similarly derived from observations of the already-existing, have diffused into much of the mainstream of international architecture in various ways, via the Centre Pompidou in Paris, for instance, or the Lloyd's building in London. OMA's buildings are accompanied by Rem Koolhaas's polemic of 'bigness' which is identified as a crucial characteristic of already-existing built environments beyond the conventional value systems of architectural criticism. In many of these modern examples, representational space—the image—and representations of space—the design—are the work of the same individual, or of practitioners of the same art form. Representational space—to use Lefebvre's term—and built environments are more usually produced by the practitioners of different art forms and often at different times. For instance, the tradition of literary urbanism—if one can call it that—which includes De Quincey, Poe, Baudelaire, Rimbaud, Apollinaire, Aragon, Benjamin and Bataille became highly influential in the architectural culture of the 1970s, so much so that many of these writers' texts are now required reading for shopping mall designers.

This division of labour is not surprising when one compares the work involved. Radical subjectivities tend to be inclusive, whereas design is ultimately a process of selection. Radical subjectivities in art, on the other hand, usually presuppose some outcome other than the artwork—"a bridge between imagination and reality must be built" (Raoul Vaneigem, in *The Revolution of Everyday Life*), and "to change life, however, we must first change space" (Henri Lefebvre, in *The Production of Space*). The *dérive* was not an end in itself—among the Situationists were architects: Constant's New Babylon was a physical proposal that offered a new built form for the society of *homo ludens*. In the UK recently there has been a remarkable revival of interest in the Situationist subjectivity of place, in psychogeography, but so far there has been little interest in the Situationists' architecture. New Babylon was based on an early recognition of the implications of information technology and automated production, which was to bring a freedom from work that has to some extent been realised, though not in quite the way it was envisaged. What has not been realised at all is any corresponding automation of the production of built structures. This has meant

that in relative terms buildings have continued to become more expensive, while other goods have become cheaper. The volume of new construction is now less than it used to be, and Western cities have not changed anything like as much as was expected in, say, the early 1960s. Most of the new landscapes which have evolved as a result of computer-driven change have been peripheral and either ephemeral and relatively insubstantial—the logistics warehouse, the container port, the business park—or, if more substantial, have been realised only because they generate very high profits: the shopping mall, the airport. It is intriguing that some of the forms of these last two examples somewhat resemble those of Constant's unrealised architecture.

I am inclined to set the growing interest in the poeticisation of experience of landscapes—typically urban landscapes, but also those of railways, airports and various other industries, even agriculture—in an economic and political context. In the UK now there is a lot of official and other thinking about ways in which the anomalous high cost of built structures can be reduced. In the 1950s, for example, a new suburban house in the UK cost about as much as three new family cars. The price of a similar house in the 1990s would probably be about that of ten new cars. These cars will be more impressive products than the cars of the 1950s, and will last longer, whereas received opinion is that the houses of the 1990s are no better than those of the 1950s, and may well not last as long. This relative increase in the cost of buildings is evident in most 'advanced' economies, but is particularly marked in the UK, where the building industry is less mechanised and more deskilled, and the supply of land for building is highly constrained.

Buildings and other infrastructure often seem surprisingly rudimentary or dilapidated to visitors from other industrialised countries, and in London especially, even relatively wealthy people often live in houses that are small, old and architecturally impoverished, but extraordinarily expensive. In a context where building—not just the building of houses, but all building—has become more expensive, so that the volume of new construction is less than it used to be, new architecture has assumed a kind of scarcity value. It has become exotic, so that its representation and discussion in various media is now much more widespread than was the case when encounters with actual built architecture were more common. For most people, in most of the landscapes of 'advanced' economies, the transformation of everyday surroundings is achieved much less by physical rebuilding than by other means. Perhaps this is why an interest in the subjective transformation of landscape has become so widespread in recent years. In London now, psychogeography leads not so much to avant garde architecture, but to gentrification.

One wonders what to make of this. For government, the encouragement of gentrification, or some euphemism for it, seems to be a central strategy both for cities and in housing policy. The great irony of the UK's psychogeography phenomenon is that its invocation of the *flâneur* only narrowly preceded an almost immediate commodification of cafe culture. Downing Street advisors just back from Barcelona marvel at the sudden appearance of aluminium furniture on the pavements of northern cities. This phenomenon, and its residential counterpart, the 'loft', is now regarded as a principal means of urban regeneration. Lifestyle magazines discover the collectable qualities of Modern Movement public-sector housing developments, as flats in them begin to change hands on the open market. This notion of regeneration, where existing physical structures are socially reconstructed through acquisition and improvement, has been a familiar feature of life in London and other cities since the 1960s, when middle class buyers 'discovered' run down districts, usually in inner cities, and in doing so increased their value, rather in the way that the Surrealists 'discovered' the bric-a-brac of the flea market.

In the UK, the subjective transformation of landscape seems to offer the individual a way to oppose the poverty of everyday surroundings. As individuals, we can't rebuild the public transport system, or re-empower local democracy, but we can poeticise our relationship with their dilapidation. Perhaps this is a legacy of the 1980s when, in London at least, large parts of the city were visibly altered by a political force that was shocking, especially after the stagnation of the 1970s.

Perhaps the impulse to poeticise landscape in this way always coincides with times of heightened political tension. In 1948, the Czech Surrealist Vratislav Effenburger made a film *Outline of a Study of a Fraction of Reality*, which survives only as a retrospective script, but apparently included "images of the Prague loading dock and other deserted corners of the city".[4] Effenberger's film was made in the same year as the Stalinist coup.

In 1974, in his introduction to *The Practice of Everyday Life*, Michel de Certeau identified the same predicament in a slightly different way:

> The purpose of this work is to... bring to light the models of action characteristic of users whose status as the dominated element in society (a status that does not mean that they are either passive or docile) is concealed by the euphemistic term 'consumers'....
>
> Increasingly constrained, yet less and less concerned with these vast frameworks, the individual detaches himself from them without being able to escape them and can henceforth only try to outwit them, to pull tricks on them, to rediscover,

within an electronicised and computerised megalopolis, the 'art' of the hunters and rural folk of earlier days....

Witold Gombrowicz, an acute visionary, gave this politics its hero... whose refrain is 'When one does not have what one wants, one must want what one has: I have had, you see, to resort more and more to very small, almost invisible pleasures, little extras....' You've no idea how great one becomes with these little details, it's incredible how one grows.[5]

Capitalism both destroys and creates places, but the places it creates seem always, at least to begin with, less substantial, less rich, than the places it destroys; as in the cases of, say, the mechanisation of agriculture and the ports, or the replacement of mining and other industries by landscapes of distribution and retailing. It is difficult to be certain about this, but judged simply by the numbers of people present in, say, a modern port, it seems a reduced phenomenon compared with the seaports of earlier times. On the other hand, modern capitalism also gives place high value, partly by making its sought after qualities scarce, partly by concentrating power in the global system in particular places—New York, Tokyo, Frankfurt, Paris, London and so on. In the interstices of all this—in more or less dilapidated domestic spaces, as 'consumers' (neither passive nor docile)—we live our lives.

The Surrealists admired Gaudi, though Surrealism itself produced no architecture until the 1940s, in New York, when Frederick Kiesler aligned himself with the movement and developed a polemic for "magic architecture", largely unbuilt but now influential. In a gesture which can be read in various ways, the Royal Institute of British Architects recently awarded its 1999 Royal Gold Medal to the city of Barcelona. A report of the award ceremony quoted Pasqual Maragall, former socialist mayor of Barcelona, comparing London under Thatcher with Barcelona under Franco: "Cities have periods in history in which they do nothing because of their politicians", and "the radical puritanism of Mrs Thatcher's government condemned the destitute to remain entrenched in their destitution". Incapable of magic architecture, we made art out of our deprivation. I hadn't realised it was quite that bad. "When one does not have what one wants, one must want what one has."

The Center for Land Use Interpretation

The Center for Land Use Interpretation (CLUI) is a research organisation that examines the nature and extent of human interaction with the earth's surface. Its stated mission is to "increase and diffuse information about how the nations lands are apportioned, utilised, and perceived". CLUI embraces a multidisciplinary approach to fulfilling this mission, employing conventional research and information processing methodology as well as non-traditional interpretive tools.

CLUI exists to stimulate discussion, thought and general interest in the contemporary landscape. Neither an environmental group nor an industry affiliated organisation, it works to integrate the many approaches to land use into a single vision that illustrates the common ground in 'land use' debates. At the very least, it attempts to emphasise the multiplicity of points of view regarding the utilisation of terrestrial and geographic resources.

Land Use Database

At the core of the CLUI's methodology is the Land Use Database (LUD). The LUD is a collection of source material and processed information on unusual and exemplary land use in America. The database is used in-house as a resource for regional and thematic programming, and is coupled with the CLUI Photographic Archive. A limited version of the LUD, over 1,000 locations, is available online.[1] This database is a free public resource, designed to inform the public about the function and form of the national landscape.

Some sites included in the database are works by government agencies involved in geo-transformative activities, such as the Department of Energy, the Bureau of Reclamation, the Army Corps of Engineers and the Department of Defence. Also included are industrially altered landscapes, such as mining sites, features of transportation systems, and field test facilities for a variety of high impact technologies. The database includes museums and displays related to land use, and one of the most thorough listings of land art sites available. It describes these sites, and offers links for more detailed information. In many cases information on how to visit these sites is provided, so that they may be directly experienced. The database is continually being updated by increasing the number of sites listed and expanding the information it contains.

Programmes and Projects

CLUI produces public exhibits for many galleries and museums and conducts various public bus tours and educational field trips. Lectures and presentations are held at CLUI's exhibit spaces, through programmes such as the Independent Interpreter Series; an ongoing series of presentations by selected artist and researchers. These presentations come in the form of lectures, films and exhibitions. Other programming includes site-specific Extrapolative Projects in the field, and special focus thematic study areas. CLUI also publishes guidebooks, catalogues, and other books addressing land use issues as well as *The Lay of the Land*, which is distributed worldwide.

CLUI engages in a number of interpretive projects that are designed to draw meaning from land use sites and phenomena. Many of these projects represent extensions of traditional interpretive techniques, and are designed to expand the methodology into new fronts. Extrapolative Projects can be ongoing or momentary, physically realised or simply design. They include outdoor displays and signage, site-specific interactions and other permanent or ephemeral activities. Some projects can be considered as a sort of R&D (research and development) of interpretive practice at CLUI.

An example of CLUI's extrapolative projects is the Event Marker Project in which a series of markers, similar to those roadside

markers installed by historical organisations, have been installed around America. Several themes are explored here, including Inundations and Denudations, Perpetual Flames, and Selected Film Location Sites.

CLUI's main exhibit space and offices in Los Angeles offers exhibits, lectures, and other resources for the public. CLUI's library and archives are accessible to researchers by appointment and lecturers/guides are available to address classes and groups. Project support facilities exist at CLUI's Wendover, Utah, complex, which houses a residency programme and at the Desert Research Station (DRS) near Barstow, California. The DRS is a research and display facility located in the Mojave Desert, acting as a satellite to the LA location, and focusing on the California Desert region.

CLUI's bus tours offer participants direct experience of the landscape. One of the many tours CLUI has conducted is a visit to the industrial city of Irwindale, east of LA, as part of the exhibit Ground Up: Photographs of the Ground in the Margins of Los Angeles. The tour, entitled Margins in Our Midst: A Journey Into Irwindale, focused on the material that makes up the ground we live on and featured visits to the gravel and aggregate mining pits that continue to provide the concrete and asphalt that is spread on LA's roads, and provides the raw material for the city's major construction projects.

Thematic Programme Areas

Thematic Programme Areas are subject categories that have been selected for extended research and examination by CLUI. Selected themes are studied in an ongoing manner, with findings periodically presented to the public in the form of publications, lectures, exhibits or other programmes.

Model Earth

An example of one of CLUI's Thematic Programmes is our interest in models, maps, globes, and other stylised representations of the earth or portions of the earth's surface that are part of the phenomenon of terrestrial miniaturisation. Such representations often say much about how we see, or want to see, the world. Some fascinating examples of this phenomena include the utilitarian models created for hydrologic studies by the American Army Corps of Engineers; the world's premier functional terrestrial model makers. The three largest hydrologic models in the world are located in America, and CLUI has developed exhibits about each one. Model of Decay: The Chesapeake Bay Model was an exhibition of images and artefacts from this miniature (working) model of the Chesapeake Bay. Now abandoned and decaying, this was once the largest indoor hydraulics model in the world. The second exhibit on this theme was Mississippi Model, an exhibition of images and artefacts from this 200 acre outdoor installation—the largest hydraulics model in the world, now abandoned and overgrown outside of Jackson, Mississippi. Our Model Limits: The San Francisco Bay Model exhibit was a photo documentary of the San Francisco Bay-Delta tidal hydraulic model, a two acre working model of the San Francisco Bay Area.

Guide Points

As a tourist one directly experiences places beyond the familiar limits of one's local community. Whether self-guided through the landscape by tour books, or on a programmatic excursion under by a tour guide, this kind of experience both enriches and confuses the traveller's sense of the places they visit. Points of interest along a tourist's route have heightened relevance, while the tourist often feels a sense of a disturbing passivity, having relinquished control to someone else. This state of being, and the industry that promotes it, is of interest to all of us who have 'been there'.

CLUI developed the theme of the guide point in an exhibit about postcard entrepreneur Merle Porter. Porter was a one-man postcard production company who produced and distributed millions of cards over a 50 year career. Nearly always about places, his cards have a distinctive style, sometimes depicting famous sites, but more often they are a celebration of the ordinary landscape: highways, abandoned buildings, and oil fields. Typically his route took him through the California, Arizona and Nevada Desert areas in winter, and the California beach areas in summer. At the height of his career, Porter was adding 1,000 miles a week to his Ford Econoline van (which served both as living quarters and portable inventory room), and circulated one million cards a year, under the name Royal Pictures of Colton, California.

Above Ground

The relationship between land use and the sky is the subject of this Thematic Programme Area. From aerial observations of the ground, to mountaintop observatories that gaze out into space, land and sky are linked in many ways, and the electronosphere—the infrastructure of the information age—is an invisible realm, often tangible only at the physical sites, such as antennas and earth stations, where waves make contact with the earth.

This theme was explored in CLUI's VORs of Texas exhibit. VOR (very high frequency omnidirectional radial) antennas are radio beacons, part of a nationwide network of navigational aids used by civil and military aviation. While their function is consistent, their shapes and colouration can vary, and their enigmatic forms hint to the all too unfamiliar parallel universe of communication technologies. The exhibit was a typological photographic research project exploring the context and form of all the VOR antennas in the state of Texas, and included a colour photograph of each of the 70 antennas in the state. This project was the product of the field research and photography of CLUI researcher and Texas Projects Coordinator, Mark Curtin.

Under Ground

Human interaction with the land often extends beyond the superficial veneer, into the underground. Whether things are located underground for spatial or climatic reasons, for secrecy or security, or simply by chance, an examination of this realm can give a sense of what lurks in the fundament of the country, and provide an indirect 'overview' of what exists on the surface.

CLUI's exhibit, Subterranean Renovations: The Unique Architectural Spaces of Show Caves, featured colour photographs of 12 of the most compelling examples of this unique form of underground architecture. Represented were the lunch rooms at Carlsbad Caverns and Mammoth Cave, light show theatres at DeSoto and Meramec Caverns, the reception room at Truitt Cave, with its working fireplace, the abandoned bandstand and dance floor, deep within Wonderland Cave and Club in Bella Vista, Arkansas, and the haunting Stalacpipe Organ at Luray Caverns, Virginia.

Mediated Space

In this media age, much of our experience of places and landscapes is through the production of the entertainment and advertising industries, such as films, television, and commercial photography. This thematic programme area examines representations of place through the lens of this mediated perspective.

Subterranean Renovations:
The Unique Architectural Spaces
of Show Caves exhibition, 1998
Image courtesy of CLUI Archive.

Two recent CLUI exhibitions, On Locations: Places as Sets in the Landscape of Los Angeles and Emergency State: First Responder and Law Enforcement Training Architecture, examined what the critic Norman Klein calls "Scripted Space". On Locations featured images, text and a multimedia display about the film location industry and how places within the public realm can be transformed, physically and contextually, by the moving image industries. Within the spectrum of facades, streetscapes, and structures that are used as locations are certain spaces that vividly embody, physically and theoretically, this paradox of place and express, subtly or otherwise, the intriguing dynamic between 'real' and 'cinematic' space. Emergency State, about police and emergency training structures, featured images taken by CLUI photographers depicting ten representative locations in Southern California.

Southern California's training villages and emergency props range from the modest to entire towns, complete with simulated convenience stores, apartments and gas stations with a level of realism one would expect in a place where movies are made and theme parks originated. The training sites depicted in this exhibit showed different characteristics of this unusual form of architecture; a form which is increasing in its sophistication and occurrence across the country, as this era of preparedness progresses.

As with several recent exhibits at CLUI, this was a digitally created and displayed production, with each of the sites described on a LCD or projection screen, along with printed text panels, enhanced by video and ambient sound.

Site Lines

Perimeters and cartographic grids constitute a network of overlying lines on the landscape delimiting the margins or intersections of places. The site lines Thematic Programme Area examines the edges of places—often distinct places in themselves—and the interaction of physical place with conceptual lines. The structures that emerge along linear transpositions, such as fences, berms, and signage, are part of this land use language. CLUI's photography project, The Limits of Fun, examined site lines by documenting the perimeters of theme parks and the physical and social structures at their fringes.

Erosive Forces

Landscape change is due largely to erosion. Counteracting erosional decay are the building forces—the forces that pile things up—such as tectonics, and the human agents of landscape such as architecture, drainage control, landscaping, and paving. The interaction of human changes to the landscape and erosion is the subject of this special CLUI programme theme.

Two CLUI exhibitions, Formations of Erasure: Earthworks and Entropy and Ground-Up: Photographs of the Ground in the Margins of Los Angeles focused on the theme of erosive forces. Formations of Erasure: Earthworks and Entropy consisted of contemporary photographs of earthworks across America, focusing on those that do not have extensive maintenance programmes, and thus have been altered by time and the elements, such as Robert Smithson's *Spiral Jetty* and Michael Heizer's *Double Negative*. Most of the depicted pieces were constructed in the 1970s and, over time, these structures have receded from the pure, intentional form of the artist's idea, into dynamic forms that represent the collaboration between humans and the non-human world.

Ground-Up: Photographs of the Ground in the Margins of Los Angeles, used soil maps of the county of LA as a tool for re-examining regional physio-geographic phenomena, as such maps provide a unique and compelling view of the landscape, and the human interventions within it. The exhibit featured several large format photographs of these selected ground locations. The fine grain of the photographs matched the grain of the depicted ground, and the authority and weight that large, finely crafted images convey contrasted implicitly with the non-places that filled the frame of each exposure.

Isolate Zones

Some places are intentionally cut-off from the continuum of the landscape, becoming discrete, inward looking worlds in themselves. Radioactive sites, for example, have to be disconnected from their surroundings for obvious reasons, and can remain that way for millennia. Military training areas too can function as self-contained cities or stylised enemy nations. This Thematic Programme Area examines the sites, land forms, and architectures of such isolate zones.

The CLUI exhibit, The Nellis Range Complex: Landscape of Conjecture, explored the isolate zone theme and was installed inside a customised mobile exhibition unit. The exhibit contained images, text, maps and supporting documents that describe this mysterious landscape in southern Nevada, the nation's largest restricted area, and a veritable nation unto itself. 2,000 miles of roads and an extensive fiber-optic and microwave communication network connect target areas, maintenance facilities, tracking stations, testing grounds and a few full scale bases. An interactive and evolving simulated enemy landscape, with command and control bunkers, radar and missile sites, convoys, railways, industrial areas, and hundreds more individual targets, prepares pilots for confrontations in Middle Eastern, Asian, Soviet and other potential theatres of war. On the undisturbed mountains within the range there is a landscape frozen in time. Closed to public access in 1940, it is an area where bighorn sheep and wild horses roam among petroglyphs of by American Indians, and where miners' cabins remain unvandalised.

Residence Programme

In addition to developing internally produced programmes CLUI assists other organisations with a residence programme that supports the development of new interpretive methodologies and ideas. The programme is open to artists, researchers, theorists, or anyone who works with land and land use issues in an innovative and engaging manner. Residents primarily work out of CLUI facilities at Wendover, Utah, and explore and interpret the landscape of that remarkable desert region. During the course of the residency, participants are asked to produce work that explores themes related to the area; work which will then be exhibited.

Wendover is a small town on the edge of the mountains and the salt flats and sits directly on the Utah/Nevada border on Interstate 80. It is located at the point where the Nevada Basin and Range spill into the Great Salt Lake Desert of Utah. It resembles the Arctic: a remote place of barren rock and snow-white alkali. Wendover was established because it was out of the way, a place where people wouldn't want to live. Though there was a small community to service the railroad established early on, the first major modern settlement was an airbase, built at the beginning of the Second World War to train bomber crews (including the crew of the Enola Gay). Through the 1940s and 50s, the land around Wendover was bombed, strafed, and dusted with chemical and biological agents.

Today the region is intensely industrialised. Military operations continue in the surrounding acres of restricted access lands. Large scale industries remove salt, and process minerals from the flats, and copper and gold are extracted from giant pits in the mountains. Hazardous waste facilities and obsolete chemical weapons have found refuge in the remote, nearly uninhabitable landscape. The Interstate makes Wendover itself a pit stop for travellers, from San Francisco to New York City, and points in between. The town is bisected into two distinct halves: the boom town of West Wendover,

Nevada, adjoins the stagnated Utah half, which is dominated by the remains of the Airbase, abandoned in 1977. It is at this former airbase where CLUI has established the Wendover Residence Programme and a segment of the American Land Museum. The sites used by CLUI in Wendover and its environs comprise the CLUI Wendover Complex.

In addition to exhibition, R&D, storage, and other facilities, CLUI leases a portion of the former military airfield known as South Base, one mile into the flats from the airport flight line. These structures are left over from the munitions storage and atomic bomb programme at Wendover, with some recent additions, including the control tower, built by the Walt Disney Company (for a film called *Conair*). Military and law enforcement personnel conduct SWAT team-style training in some of the buildings, including those leased by CLUI.

The so-called "Remote Location" is a 40 acre piece of land 40 miles north of Wendover, available for projects addressing issues of isolation, accessible most of the year by high-clearance vehicles only. The parcel has a varied topography, extending from a dry lakebed surface, up a slope to a level plateau, offering views of the Silver Island Mountains to the east and south. It was the first Utah property purchased by Robert Smithson and Nancy Holt.

The American Land Museum

CLUI is the lead agency in the establishment of the American Land Museum. The purpose of the museum is to create a dynamic contemporary portrait of the nation, a portrait composed of the national landscape itself. To establish this far flung museum, the country has been divided into separate zones called Interpretive Units. Each unit is to have a museum location to represent it, providing regional programming for the area it corresponds to. Interpretive Units were created out of the continuous national fabric through an accumulation of criteria, and finally actualised through the process of combining 'districts' and 'regions'.

Regions are general topographic and land use areas with gradual or transitional boundaries. They broadly follow physio-geographic features (such as mountain ranges, and drainage systems), as well as cultural, economic, and historical development patterns (which are often delimited by physiography). Regions could be described as being defined from within, rather than from without, as the edges of these regions are often indistinct, overlapping and dissolving into one another. Unambiguous boundaries were then drawn around these regions, following the existing political boundaries that separate states and the cluster of states define the district that makes up each Interpretive Unit.

The physical form of the individual museum locations will differ according to site considerations and available development resources. The primary 'exhibit' at each location is, naturally, the immediate landscape of the location. As other interpretive exhibits are prepared for the location, they will be installed in structures that reflect the architectural styles of the region, and usually occupying existing structures. Collectively the individual exhibit sites comprise the Museum; a museum both situated in and made up of the landscapes of America.

Emptiness and Imagination
• Marie-Paule Macdonald

This text is a reflection on emptiness and imagination—that is—on emptiness as a condition of imagination and the spatial consequences of that notion. The subject of *l'informe* or 'formless' could be associated with an idea of randomness. One precedent might come from the Japanese tradition: for example, a text written in the fourteenth century, translated as *Essays in Idleness: The Tsurezuregusa of Kenkô* by an author known as Kenkô; a Buddhist priest.[1] The writing ranges from one-sentence remarks to longer meditations. The themes address beauty and cultural sensibility, favouring impermanence, imperfection, simplicity, understatement, restraint, incompleteness, asymmetry and irregularity, interspersed with some obscure references to ancient rituals. They narrate casual incidents or appreciations of the seasons, and are either subtly linked or arranged in a seemingly random order, what is described as brushstroke-style; there is not necessarily an apparent continuity from paragraph to paragraph:

> A man with no business will never intrude into an occupied house simply because he so pleases. If the house is vacant, on the other hand, travellers journeying along the road will enter with impunity, and even creatures like foxes and owls, undisturbed by human presence, will take up their abodes, acting as if the place belonged to them. Tree spirits and other apparitions will also manifest themselves.
>
> It is the same with mirrors: being without colour or shape of their own, they reflect all manner of forms. If mirrors had colour or shape of their own, they would probably not reflect other things.
>
> Emptiness accommodates everything. I wonder if thoughts of all kinds intrude themselves at will on our minds because what we call our minds are vacant? If our minds were occupied, surely so many things would not enter them.[2]

The appeal of the text is its informality—it is both philosophic and ordinary. The theme of *l'informe* refers here to Georges Bataille's definition of the term. In *Documents*, he parodied an authoritarian position by impersonation: with the academic gesture of defining selected words such as *l'informe*—translated as 'formless'—and 'architecture'. His definition indicated:

> Formless is not only an adjective with a given meaning but a term which de-classifies, generally requiring that each thing take on a form…. To declare, on the contrary, that the universe is not like anything, and is simply formless, is the same as saying the universe is something like a spider or spittle.[3]

The universe—in Bataille's definition, shaped like spit—is the ultimate *l'informe* or formless infinite space. It contains within it infinite irregular/regular shapes, including geometries.

In parallel with this text I made a video recording of the opening day of Perimeter Institute, a formally composed building whose programme is devoted to twin mandates of scientific research and educational outreach in the field of theoretical physics. The building accomodates researchers and students who consider space, time, matter and information; from the genesis and the form or formlessness of the universe, to black holes and a universal 'theory of everything'. On this day, like other public events, the building was accessible to the public. It drew a large crowd, numbering nearly ten thousand; all curious about the theories relating to the areas discussed above and eager to populate a sophisticated modern space occupied by international scientists. This institute was made possible by a large personal donation from the founder of a technology company as well as public investments. It was designed by Montréal architects Saucier + Perrotte, who also were selected to represent Canada in the 2004 Venice Biennale.

Marie-Paule Macdonald
Rockspaces, underground music hall (model), 1999
Lexan, mixed media,
Image courtesy of the artist.
Photograph by Peter MacCallum.

Opposite left
Marie-Paule Macdonald
View of the Atrium,
Perimeter Institute,
on opening day,
2 October 2004.

Opposite right
Marie-Paule Macdonald
Mobile Inhabitable
Cell, 1996
Mixed media
Image courtesy
of the artist.

Lately the paradoxical phenomenon of the fascination with 'formlessness' in relation to the quest for relevant architectural and urban form has become a dominant issue for designers. Buildings have been built which look like blobs, angular spaceships, or simple planes on which arbitrary patterns of windows are scattered, in this quest for new and interesting, if not necessarily meaningful, contemporary building. A blurb from an LA architecture curriculum, described in a student blog, gives a sense of the current preoccupation: "Using double curve relationships, we propose to engage the dialogue of skin and structure to mutate the boundaries between inside and outside, opening and closure, liquid and solid systems." Referring to the drawing software, the student comments enthusiastically, "be fully prepared for Maya, Rhino, and NURBS".[4]

One of Bataille's more incendiary remarks on architecture describes built form as the 'official face' of society. Bataille suggests that architects are not among society's heroes:

> Architecture is the expression of the true nature of
> societies, as physiognomy is the expression of the nature
> of individuals. However, this comparison is applicable to the
> physiognomy of officials.... Only society's ideal nature—that
> of authoritative command and prohibition—expresses itself
> in actual architectural constructions. Thus great monuments
> rise up like dams....[5]

Bataille may have meant this assertion as radical at the time: a radically negative identification of the authoritarian nature of architecture. This attitude—recognising exclusively what is known as 'major' architecture—has become obsolete, or at least has been tempered in contemporary thinking about 'minor' architecture. Research and publications, starting perhaps with the early twentieth century Italian urbanist, Gustavo Giovannoni, as identified by present day architectural theorists—in particular, Françoise

Choay—acknowledge the significance both of 'major' and 'minor' architecture, and the importance for the city of the relationship between monumental and ordinary building. This was a concern of an influential Italian architect, Aldo Rossi, who explicitly incorporated forms from ordinary vernacular building into official commissions. In some ways the line between 'major' and 'minor' has become blurred over the course of the twentieth century. The categories persist, but it is no longer clear what should belong—a "de-classifying" to use Bataille's definition, has taken place. One reason may be a sense of the loss of legitimacy of the expert or professional, and the way 'signature' architects blatantly market their ordinary, often derivative but 'branded' product to public and private institutions in Europe, North America and Asia. Another may be the predominance of a generic architecture assembled from mass produced components using software programs for drawing. Another is the interest shown by designers and artists in the appearance of the informal or formless: the work of sculptors Mike Kelley or Thomas Hirschhorn, for example, could be seen as aggressively anti-formal. In that sense, one could see all twenty-first century architecture as becoming somehow 'de-formed', distorted. This issue appears more urgent as Bataille emphasised the significance of architecture, with the somewhat absurd taunt that the 'human' is a mere stage in civilisation; architecture being its ultimate development:

> It is clear that mathematical order imposed on stone is really
> the culmination of the evolution of earthly forms, whose
> direction is indicated within the biological order by the
> passage from the simian to the human form.... Man would
> seem to represent merely an intermediary stage within the
> morphological development between monkey and building.[6]

A philosopher whose work collapses the boundaries between 'major' and 'minor' in subject matter, cross referencing the most exalted

philosophical reference and banal popular experience of visual form in his writing, is Slavoj Žižek. I attended a series of seminars by Žižek where his discourse was in itself an exercise in a formless, but stimulating, series of random associations and digressions. One of the themes that returned in the lectures was the significance of fantasy and the unexpected places where fantasy resides (for example, in reality, in daily life, in ideology).[7] Writing in a chapter on ideology, he focused on an idea of form that is analogous to an industrially-produced candy that has a sphere of substance, usually chocolate, enclosing an empty air pocket, inside of which rattles a kernel: a plastic toy; the Kinder Egg:

> … a commodity is a mysterious entity full of theological caprices, a particular object satisfying a particular need, but at the same time a promise of something more, of an unfathomable enjoyment whose true location is fantasy…. The plastic toy is the result of a risky strategy actually to materialise, render visible, this mysterious excess….[8]

Žižek goes on to locate the notion of the sugary void in the tradition of spaces for dining—in the specific rooms for eating desserts, and the role of empty confections in the rituals of hospitality—ending dinner by moving to an informal lounging space, or the anticipatory quality of awaiting dessert. Roland Barthes placed great emphasis on the Japanese notion of voids in cuisine. In a text on 'the interstice', he remarked on dishes which are "reduced to a tiny clump of emptiness, a collection of perforations, here the foodstuff joins the dream of a paradox: that of a purely interstitial object all the more provocative in that this emptiness is produced in order to provide nourishment (occasionally the foodstuff is constructed in a ball, like a wad of air)".[9]

One could expand this notion from the dining hall to the scale of architecture, even to an entire city. Barthes recognised the remarkable case of the city of Tokyo, a metropolis with an effectively empty centre:

> [Tokyo] presents this precious paradox: the city possesses a centre, but this centre is empty. The city revolves around a place at once forbidden and indifferent, a residence masked by greenery, protected by moats, inhabited by an emperor who is never seen in public, so to speak, by an unseen unknown. Daily, their nimble, energetic trajectories as expeditious as the arc of an arrow, taxis avoid this circle, whose low parapet, visible form of invisibility, hides the sacred 'nothingness'. One of the two most powerful cities of modernity is thus built around an opaque ring of walls, of water, of roofs and trees, whose centre itself is nothing more than an evaporated idea, existing there not in order to radiate power, but to lend to all urban movement the force of its central void, requiring the traffic to perpetually detour. In this way, so to speak, the imaginary is deployed in a circular fashion, by detours and returns along an empty subject.[10]

In the empty centre is a site of the subject of a collective fantasy, a laminate of nation, history, capital. Perhaps not all cities, but some others, could be considered as parallel examples. In addition to Tokyo, Barthes might have seen the fortified citadel, on a hilltop in the centre of Halifax, or the forested park Mont Royal in Montréal, as quasi-empty centres, places not forbidden but only occupied temporarily, subject to appropriation by collective dreaming.

A key notion for modern architecture is this Japanese-influenced idea of a built form as a slim, brittle exterior layer enclosing the void of space conceived as a positive. This introduces modern architecture. The notion of the building as a solid block belonged to Classicism and its traditions of domes, symmetry, carved columns

Marie-Paule Macdonald
Freelab Move-ible, 2000
Wood, plywood
Image courtesy of
the artist.

and friezes. Obsolescent, the classical *défilé* of rooms was replaced at the beginning of the twentieth century by ideas of the Modern Movement, where walls were crusts and casings attached together of assembled components, and the design began with an emphasis of the character of space as a void. The hypermodern or supermodern architecture of today pushes the antimonies a step further, separating form into a recipe of the hollow and the shell, the surface or skin.

John Summerson suggested that, at the core of the modern idea of architecture was an abstraction, a social fantasy of ideal daily roles: a contemporary programme that described the vocation and activity to go on in the building.[11] The building programme is not something fixed, it must be defined, element by element, as identified in British architect Tony Fretton's remark: "The process of design is a speculative investigation into the social life of the building."[12] Thus the genesis of an architectural design project is emptiness, potential. This emptiness, the kinder toy, the meaningful kernel, is mutable, but locates a site for a fantasy—on an ideological plane for an ideal society, or for minor architecture, perhaps more personal dreams and speculations.

A project that fascinated architects in the 1970s was the cemetery at Modena by Rossi. In this case, it was the drawings that elicited the fascination, since the project was constructed in a casual, even indifferent, manner. The built form was a simple cubic husk, a storage structure marked by the plain regular grid of openings of ordinary vernacular architecture. In its lack of architectural development from the compelling architectural drawings it seemed like an inflated miniature. Yet the notion of architecture as an empty gridded shell may provide the key to fascination exerted by the Rossi cemetery. Architectural writers have commented on the emotions it aroused, identifying the "melancholy and nostalgic" nature of Rossi's interest in an 'autonomous' architecture. While his Classicist tendencies have since been rejected, much contemporary architecture could be seen as following on this enigmatic cemetery: a consistent, undifferentiated

skin enclosing a hollow, emptied volume. While there may be floors and an architectural programme, there is a fundamental sense of disconnection between the architectural crust and its conception, and the architecture's interior concepts. The melancholic's cemetery may be seen as a despondent rejoinder to Adolf Loos' famous classification of architecture as exclusively the tomb and the monument.

At the scale of a building, not only is the concept of the primary substance of architecture as a void a fundamental principal; the location and position of openings to the void give crucial character to built form. One of the celebrated architectural works of the 1990s is a public bath built in the mountains of Switzerland, in the small town of Vals. In this building, the valley itself is of such significance that it constitutes the first void, at the scale of the landscape. The principal elevation of the bath perches on a steep slope, facing out to the velvety grassed slopes of the mountain across the void. The placement of deliberate openings in the principal elevation by the architect, Peter Zumthor, attests to an exquisite consideration of the fundamentals of the site. In contrast, here opacity and the powerful density and severe detailing of local stone has demonstrated powerfully the relevance of the 'solid' at the small, intimate scale of the body, in the cosseted design. The meditated quality of the openings and their position facing across the void of valley to the wall of mountain, dramatically frame the facing grassed, velvety hillside, dotted by small, beautiful examples of traditional vernacular wood architecture,

A recent, pleasing and disturbing work of architecture, La Ferriera in Locarno by Ticino architect, Livio Vacchini, expresses the building as a cubic shell encased in a steel grid. An ordinary office building takes on a mysterious character due to the dark crisp surface of steel set off from and masking the glass curtain wall. The elevation appears to be a metaphysical conceit, transforming the impression of the building from the commonplace to the ineffable. It is a structural exoskeleton, a trilith that is, a wall opened to allow light to enter. Vacchini traces the black metal structural reference to the underside of the steel canopy of the National Gallery in Berlin, one of the great architectural achievements of Mies van der Rohe. While Vacchini makes no reference to Rossi's melancholy cube at Modena, one cannot but view *La Ferriera* as a secular iteration of the theme, revved up to the sophisticated level of design and construction that distinguishes Swiss and Ticinese building. Something in its suave iconic presence discloses and mocks the contemporary fascination with the autonomous building skin. Vacchini has great ambitions for his architectural propositions, and sees the architectural space as synthetic, asserting: "In fact, much architecture still separates the skin from the structure, rejecting the fundamental relationship that connects structure, space and light."[13]

Vacchini made one of his most plain and engaging public works some 15 years ago: an outdoor projector booth for the Locarno Film Festival. It was made of commercial pools bolted together—an inexpensive, easily assembled and dismantled weatherproof container, for the projector, the machine projecting collective dreams to a crowd in the open public square. This witticism, an indulgent, modestly spectacular urban device is still in use.

I have used the statements of Brazilian architect, Lina Bo Bardi, and the insights of Vacchini as a guide for research into relevant areas of contemporary design, and as guidelines for teaching subjects. My projects tend to the conditional and provisional. They would take their place in the discussion of "spaces that are hypothetical, contingent, or fictional".

In the early 1990s I proposed a portable bubble, a bit of froth in transparent plastic, as a temporary residence for a refugee, the mobile inhabitable cell. Another more immobile, subterranean project that addressed the notion of an empty centre was the underground music venue, the major space in the Rockspaces Project. It was proposed as the excavation of a vernacular building; its below grade space hollowed out and replaced by a glass structure for the performance of popular music, a multi-storey void, a great glass hall.[14] Another project that consisted primarily of an architectural enclosure, with only a narrow corridor as an interior, was the 'movible', a temporary pavilion built with a team of students on the lawn of the School of Architecture at Dalhousie University in 2000.[15] Lastly, I mention a studio I designed for a sound artist who wanted a place to paint, built in collaboration with Steve Topping, in a laneway of Montréal. While under construction it was, for a time, nothing but a dream-like pair of swinging doors.

To return to the theme of emptiness and openness: if formlessness de-classifies, will it despectacularise? Architectural goods are promoted as if they were as liquid as cash: can architecture ever be classed a commodity? Architecture was about the distribution of a society's resources: building ties up resources for a very long time. It is expensive and often immovable. Even portable architecture is very expensive to design—the human labour that attaches a building to a site cannot be easily dispensed with, demolished, or erased. In the search for the hospitable spaces that inhabit the voids of contemporary architecture, it is the social relations, the human connections, which matter most. *L'informe* describes the current 'relaxed' social conditions of a paradoxically tense hypermodernity. It is perhaps not so much the form-full, or formless, that permit dreams and fantasy to seep or percolate through into the membrane of daily life, as these available empty pockets, that we must purloin and appropriate.

Wir Meinen: die selbstrasierer sind die helden alle zeiten und lander
• Knowles Eddy Knowles

Wir Meinen: die selbstrasierer sind die helden alle zeiten und lander is the title of a performative action by Knowles Eddy Knowles (KEK), which took place in Kronberg im Taunus—a town in the Hochtaunuskreis district, Hesse, Germany—in October 2006. The phrase itself is appropriated from an informational brochure produced by the Braun Museum situated in Kronberg. In English it reads: "In our opinion those who shaved themselves are the heroes of history and all countries of the earth." KEK lived and worked on the edge of a mountain in Kronberg, staking out the premises of

Dieter Rams, celebrated industrial designer for the Braun company. This photographic series registers the constellation of objects, actions, real sites, plans, dwellings and imagined abodes that were developed over the course of the stake out process. KEK drew on the differences between necessity and luxury, and usefulness and excess, in a performed dwelling activity that attempted to conjure an altogether different account of the buddy film genre. Such work resulted in a time-based film work as well as an interview between KEK and Dieter Rams.

Opposite left
Rams' house, which is located in a cluster of developments for Braun employees and clients.

Opposite right
A Japanesque tree expands beyond the fence of Rams' home, an expression of his design conceits.

Left
A cabin on the edge of the Taunus (a dwelling in which to live, spy and work), a few hundred metres from Rams' house.

Right
A model for a camouflage dwelling in the Taunus.
All images courtesy of Knowles Eddy Knowles, 2006.

Bungalow Blitz: On Art, Architecture and Curating
• Aoife Mac Namara

Cultural confinement takes place when a curator imposes his own limits on an art exhibition, rather than asking an artist to set his limits…. Once the work of art is totally neutralised, ineffective, abstracted, safe, and politically lobotomised, it is ready to be consumed by society. All is reduced to visual fodder and transportable merchandise. Innovations are allowed only if they support this kind of confinement.[1]

—Robert Smithson

The art of exhibiting is a branch of architecture and should be practised as such.[2]

—Philip Johnson

In 2001, the Whitney Museum of American Art and the Museum of Modern Art (MoMA) in New York City commissioned a two-site exhibition of the work of Mies van der Rohe. The first chronicled the architect's work in America, the second focused on his pre-war work in Germany. In January 2003, an abridged version of the MoMA exhibition, Mies in Berlin, opened to much acclaim at the Whitechapel Gallery in London's East End as Mies van der Rohe 1905–1938.[3] Curated by Terence Riley of MoMA and Barry Bergdoll of Columbia University, the exhibition was promoted as the definitive retrospective of his career in Europe and the first in Britain. It brought together documentation of 38 of his most decisive projects dating from 1905, to his departure for America in 1938, a film about his life and work, some three-dimensional computer animated walks through his domestic buildings and l.m.v.d.r.—a series of newly commissioned photographic prints of photographs taken by Thomas Ruff of Mies' work from this period.[4]

Fortuitously enough, Mies van der Rohe 1905–1938 opened at the Whitechapel Gallery just as those of us working on the Bungalow Blitz project were tying to make sense of what our project might be about. Three years and two exhibitions into the project, this questioning might seem a little behind schedule (especially when so many of us are expected to work within the pseudo-scientific research models favoured by funding councils worldwide). And, while we certainly began with an idea of what the project was concerned with, part of the pleasure was finding ourselves redirected by that which we produced and encountered along the way: photographs, paintings, exhibitions, installations, conversations, books and so on. This exhibition was one such moment. Ostensibly, the project was concerned with how art and photographic practices might be able to lend hitherto elusive insight into the controversy that had erupted in Ireland when, in the 1970s, the popularity of Jack Fitzsimons' book of house plans, Bungalow Bliss, sparked a proliferation of one-off suburban-style houses. Such proliferation spread along the roads and hillsides of Ireland, and particularly the west of Ireland with its much-vaunted untamed landscapes (there is nothing quite like the ubiquitous suburban-style lawn for rendering ordinary even the most exceptional environment). In reality, once our first exhibition had been held at the Museum for Domestic Design and Architecture (MoDA) we soon became as concerned with issues of epistemology and historiography as we were with the specifics of the bungalow debate.[5] Accordingly, Jack Fitzsimons' bungalows began to shift from being the focus of research to acting as an organising structure around which questions about how practice-based research in art, photography, video, curating or installation might open up knowledge about architecture and the built environment; the foundations, scope and validity of which might lie outside (and perhaps challenge) those produced out of conventional architectural or art historical discourses and their attendant methodologies.[6]

In the context of an exhibition about the architecture of a period of radically disruptive practices of display and presentation, Mies van der Rohe 1905–1938 was, for many of us, a disappointing but nonetheless significant show.[7] The exhibition was drawn from

Mies van der Rohe 1905–1938 exhibition at
the Whitechapel Gallery, London, in 2003
Image courtesy of the Whitechapel Gallery.

numerous studies of individual architectural projects, from the Riehl House in Potsdam-Neubabelsberg, 1907, to the Resor House in Jackson Hole, Wyoming, 1937–1938, and included the traditional range of models, architects' drawings, objects, archival photographs as well as digital animation movies, a biographical film and *l.m.v.d.r.*.[8]

Arranged over two floors with a screening room in between, the exhibition charts the development of Mies' career from designer of bourgeois suburbs to architect of modern America. For the purposes of the exhibition, the downstairs galleries were divided into three interconnected rooms. These spaces were used by the curators and designer to display two distinct bodies of material. The first was a collection of archival models, objects and drawings produced by and for the architect over the course of his work on these; his earliest commissions. The second displayed digital animations and photographs of these commissions by contemporary artists and designers responding to the work nearly 80 years after its conception.[9] These are strikingly different strategies of display: the first explicatory, the second prospective and, as such, they engender different sets of responses in their audiences. The displays produced out of the Mies' archive suggest that his earliest work was comprised by unexceptional suburban houses built for affluent middle class clientele while the contemporary computer animations and photographic work invites consideration of the productivity of these spaces; directing the viewer more toward questions of experience than of intention. The large and sumptuous chromatographic photographic prints produced by Ruff of these projects not only confer an aura of exceptionality on Mies' early, respectable, (but also orthodox and bourgeois) villas. They, crucially, forge a striking connection between these "lesser" works and those other rather more prestigious buildings more often associated with Mies and part of the continuous interwoven story of architectural development organised by the exhibition: a story that begins in Weimer Germany, develops under the Third Reich and blossoms in America.[10]

Ruff's photographs of these largely overlooked domestic villas, sandwiched between images of more acclaimed public projects, share with Andrew Kearney's photographs of the figureless bungalows in southwest Donegal an understanding that in making photographs—even those of inanimate objects and buildings—one is always as involved in the process of making meaning as one is with the literal subject of the image.[11] In an interview about her work in graduate school at UCLA, the artist Uta Barth spoke about how this curiosity with photographic epistemology developed in her approach: "I was very interested in the analysis of how images make meaning in the world, particularly how images make meaning in relation to each other, in context."[12] Both Ruff and Kearney seem to share this fascination. Both artists use extended exposure times, a mildly synthetic colour pallet, artificial light and laboured anti-naturalistic print surfaces to confer on their (arguably unremarkable) subjects a measure of the formal power, glamour and authority ordinarily reserved for photographic representations of the outstanding—whether buildings, objects or people. Both artists employ a calm, cool and rigorous pictorial style that tends to privilege the building over and above its immediate, symbolically loaded, environment.[13] In this way, their respective images arguably prompt the viewer to re-examine the architectural clichés associated with, on the one hand a great architect such as Mies, and, on the other, the much-maligned Jack Fitzsimons.

The Ruff display spread to the end of the first floor where a flight of stairs took the visitor to the displays on the second floor by way of a heavily curtained screening room, in which a short film about the life and work of Mies was running on a continuous loop. The upper galleries were devoted to displays produced out of the archives of his later and more highly regarded work, including Perls House in Berlin, the Barcelona Pavilion, 1926–1928, and the Tugendhat House in Brno, 1928–1930. Here, in the context of his already acclaimed and highly regarded work, the exhibition has reverted to type. Gone was everything the provenance of which could not be traced to the architect's studio. In its place, a display comprised by (often exquisite) tabletop models, drawings and photographs, all of which were drawn from established Mies archives and collections. While the large scale charcoal drawings included here gave some idea of the impact that these projects must have generated at the time, the greater part of these displays relied on objects and images which—unlike Ruff's *l.m.v.d.r.*—were, in and of themselves, incapable of eliciting in their viewers the kind of responses normally associated with 'overwhelmed' consumers of 'great' architecture. Rather, I would argue, the power of these displays rested in their evocation of already established ideas and beliefs about Mies and his architecture: Mies 'myths'.[14] So, the deployment of conventional architectural archives as objects of display effectively served to reproduce an already established claim for architectural greatness. However, this same range of material—architects' drawings, models, examples of furniture—will probably struggle to establish a fresh case for architectural greatness, whether for Mies' pleasant and bespoke bungalows or for Jack Fitzsimons' more 'rough and ready' self-build bungalows.

The exhibition seemed premised on such an argument: making the case for Mies' architectural greatness. Following this, the curators' decision to commission a series of photographs by Ruff seems to have been a wise one, even if they did not quite have the confidence to let these photographs stand alone. They did not have to stand in opposition to, or in contrast with, much earlier photographs of these same houses, looking as they did when they were actually lived in by the men and women who had commissioned them.[15]

A number of issues came out of our encounters with this exhibition: concerns that helped to restructure our collective work on the Bungalow Blitz project. First, the productiveness of the Ruff photographs in the context of otherwise illustrative exhibition practice encouraged renewed confidence in the value of contemporary practices of representation as opportunities for prospective inquiry into architecture and the built environment.[16] Second, from a brief clip in the film screened at the Whitechapel show, we were introduced to Mies' own curatorial work: the 1947 retrospective he designed with the support of MoMA curator Philip Johnson, who wrote the catalogue for the exhibition.[17]

According to the film script, three years after he had been granted American citizenship, MoMA invited Mies to present a retrospective of his work at the museum; an autoretrospective, if you like. There was nothing exceptional about this invitation; it was policy for MoMA to develop retrospective exhibitions in and around the work of those living, or mid-career artists, architects and designers seen to have profoundly impacted on their fields and disciplines.[18] What was exceptional was that it extended to offering Mies—and not the museum's curator—control over the design, content and display of the entire exhibition and the graphic and interpretive materials that accompanied it. Johnson limited his work to the production of the accompanying catalogue.[19] The images of this exhibition—Mies' autoretrospective—included in the film, stood in startling contrast to the design of the exhibition which surrounded the screening room.[20] Whereas (perhaps borrowing from the structure of the original Johnson catalogue), Mies van der Rohe 1905–1938 was designed more or less as a chronological survey drawn from archival materials, the 1947 exhibition appeared to pay little attention to chronology. It relied not on archival material for its displays, but on objects, images and displays constructed specifically for the exhibition.

In his essay, "Making History: Mies van der Rohe and the Museum of Modern Art", Riley describes the 1947 exhibition as "a visual demonstration of a style rather than a chronology—even an edited chronology—of development" and suggests that the "large, in some cases huge, photographs of the Barcelona Pavilion, the Tugendhat House and the glass skyscraper projects were juxtaposed in ways that took less account of dates than of visual effect".[21]

Thomas Ruff
l.m.v.d.r, 2002
© DACS, London 2008.

The distinctive, almost minimalist, character of the 1947 exhibition documented in the photographs of Herbert Matter and Charles Eames is perhaps most strikingly characterised by the oversized floor-to-ceiling photomurals fitted directly onto the gallery walls, often buttressed into its corners. Such a design strategy was to directly inform the installation of Bungalow Blitz at the Walter Phillips Gallery. Drawn from copy prints, negatives and studio photographs of models and drawings, the scale of these new photographic prints and montages not only recalled the large charcoal drawings he produced of Berlin skyscrapers in the 1920s but, in conjunction with their situation in the gallery, gave what curatorial assistant Ada Louise Huxtable described as "the effect of actual buildings".[22] According to Riley:

> Within the existing gallery space, an area roughly 21 metres square, Mies designed a configuration of four freestanding partitions arranged in a pinwheel fashion. To one side of each of these partitions he attached a large photomural, edge-to-edge and floor-to-ceiling, so it appeared to float in space.... Mies also used groupings of the furniture he had designed for the Barcelona Pavilion, 1928–1929, and the Tugendhat House, Brno, 1928–1930, to further delineate the space, much as he had in the projects on display.[23]

If, today, it is generally accepted that contemporary art practice precipitates transformations in the environment and its perceptions, in 1947, it was exhibition practices like this one that gave credibility to the argument that art, architecture and installation can make a positive contribution to how the significance of the built environment may be interrogated, researched and, of course, mythologised. Unlike subsequent exhibitions on Mies and other architectural work at MoMA, the 1947 exhibition made minimal use of conventional wall texts, detailed labels and other interpretive devices. Instead, the exhibition was presented—or appears to have been presented—as a single work: an installation that was as much a work of architecture and design itself as were any of the built and unbuilt projects represented in it.[24] The status of this exhibition as an original architectural design was reiterated during the retrospective by a text panel that read: "This exhibition, the first comprehensive retrospective showing of the work of Mies van der Rohe, is also the architect's latest design. He is responsible for the nature of the display, its plan, and the appearance of the room in which you stand."[25]

While Mies' privileging of visual experience over conventional historical 'accuracy' may have been most clearly asserted in his refusal of chronological narrative in the design of the retrospective, Riley is among a number of commentators who have suggested that this disruption of conventional curatorial practice was further reinforced by his use of new (as opposed to archival) photographic prints throughout the exhibition: "The effective newness of all the material in the exhibition is evident in the installation photographs; no wear and tear distinguished the older prints from the newest."[26] In this way it is clear that, for Mies at least, the exhibition was less an historical overview of his work to date and more a project in its own right: a scheme of research with its own objectives, questions and outcomes. For those of us working on Bungalow Blitz, our encounter with Mies' curatorial work was a productive one, prompting as it did a fundamental reconsideration of the role of the exhibition itself—not simply its constituent parts—in the overall research scheme.

The same could not be said of the overall exhibition schemes in MoDA, Limerick or Letterkenny.[27] Informed by an understanding of site-specificity and installation practice in fine art, the design of the first exhibition at MoDA was developed in response to the challenging spaces of the museum.[28] However, no matter how attentive and responsive the installation at MoDA might have been to its immediate physical environment it was, in retrospect, ignorant of its broader discursive context within the histories of architectural exhibitions and curating. Furthermore it was only superficially engaged with the histories of exhibition practice in the fields of photography and fine art. The archives and images generated in and around Mies' 1947 exhibition pointed to some of these possibilities within exhibition practice. The photographs, plans and interviews included in the archive recall a model of prospective curatorial work; both material and intellectual. In so doing, they propose the production of exhibitions as a speculative practice where 'artistic' outcomes might promote reflection on the historical and material evidence from which they were generated, while at the same time opening up epistemological questions about how, and in what ways, knowledge is constituted in the field. In this case, questions surround the disciplines of architectural and spatial culture and their concurrent exhibition and curating practices.[29]

While the earlier versions of the Bungalow Blitz exhibitions had included—even relied upon—newly commissioned work by artists and photographers as both subject and object of display, the potential of the exhibition itself as an original text was underestimated. Such an oversight was partially accounted for by the challenges to authorship that this strategy generates for projects such as this that draw on work by a number of artists. A consequence of this oversight was that while much thought was given to how Paul Antick and Andrew Kearney's photographs, Jim Grant's installation and painting and my own video work might operate as texts in their own right (as well as in relation to previous texts of this kind) the relationship between these outcomes and the physical and discursive spaces of the gallery was largely unexplored. In other words, while Antick, Kearney and Grant's individual work was not literally 'about' painting, installation or photography, it did—on a metaphoric level—explore these discourses as conceptual models for the representation of representation itself. Thus refocused, the work on Bungalow Blitz became absorbed with trying to place our interdisciplinary art, curatorial and installation practices at the centre of a project that was also interested in understanding something of the animosity generated when areas of outstanding natural beauty are turned into private property by the building of houses. Therefore, while the first three exhibitions gave priority to the exploration of the cultural significance of a particular house for a specific group of people at a given time, our work now attempted to understand and articulate some of the ways in which practice-led research methods might generate a new set of knowledge or, in relation to the bungalow debate in Ireland, an alternative set of myths. In short, the project's post-Mies concerns shifted from historical and cultural to historiographic and epistemological.

In keeping with this new dual research focus, a two-fold approach to methodology was needed: one that allowed for the opening up of the archive in a number of different registers; empirical, experimental, experiential, theoretical, reflective and analytic; and one that would enable the practice-led outcomes—the photographs, sound work, installations, paintings and exhibitions—to promote reflection on the historical and material evidence out of which the archive was constituted.[30] Approached in this way, the research methods were—from photograph to exhibition, from review to installation and from exhibition to book—calculated to allow practice-led findings to be tracked against those generated by more conventional academic research and enquiry and visa versa. Consequently, while projects such as this—those that begin as research into the social and cultural history of building types—might conventionally find their home in the field of historical or spatial studies, this project was involved in the production of its own archive of primary source material.

Thus, one set of methods succeeded in opening up the collection of Bungalow Bliss documents produced by Jack Fitzsimons between 1971–1989 (and those histories of architecture and the built environment concerned with the development of domestic architecture in general and rural buildings in particular).

The other set of methods focused on the production of new resources: texts produced in and through the practice of research in photography, video, sound, installation and painting.

If the work by Antick and Kearney included in Bungalow Blitz can be characterised by its close scrutiny of an eclectic range of photographic genres—architecture, newspaper images, portraiture, fashion and advertising—and Grant's by its dialogue with contemporary sculpture, installation and painting practices, then the exhibitions developed for the Walter Phillips Gallery can be summarised by their concern with exhibition practice as it has developed in the context of architecture and spatial culture. However, just as Mies' exhibition in 1947 was concerned more with the production of a new, speculative design than with illustrating or explaining any preceding work, these exhibitions do not set out to provide a summary or overview of either the history of bungalows in Ireland or that of exhibition and curating practices in architecture. Rather, they were conceived as opportunities for the production of new and critical texts. Each borrows from Mies' 1947 exhibition, both formal and conceptual devices that enable them to scrutinise not only their ostensible subjects (the bungalows) but also the very devices and strategies they have themselves deployed. Bungalow Blitz became, in other words, as much an exhibition about exhibitions as anything else.

The floor plans developed by Mies for the 1947 retrospective show a large, roughly square, gallery space broken up by two pairs of partitions arranged in what Riley calls "pinwheel" fashion, and resembling, in many ways, the drawings of Piet Mondrian.[31] Each freestanding wall was allocated to a different project and designed to act as ground and structure for the floor-to-ceiling photomurals and montages Mies had produced from his records of projects both built and unbuilt. The smaller walls are dedicated to skyscraper projects, while the larger ones are assigned to important examples of exhibition and monument work: the Barcelona Pavillion, 1928–1929 and the

monument to the November Revolution, 1926. Parallel to these walls and perpendicular to the skyscrapers, sections of the existing gallery walls were allocated to the Illinois Institute of Technology and the —as yet unbuilt—Mountain House in the Tyrol region of Germany.[32] Equidistant from the space allocated to the Mountain House, and on opposite corners of the room, Mies installed two additional oversized panels abutted into the corners of the existing space: murals depicting exterior images of the Concrete Office Building, 1923, and a living-room view of the Tugendhat House, 1928–1930. The space produced out of the intersection of the Circular Skyscraper installation and the work on the Illinois Institute of Technology, was allocated to "full sized corner detail" of what he referred to simply as the "administration building".[33] Finally, the design was completed by clusters of furniture designed for the buildings, minimal wall texts, labelling and a series of tabletop models. Together, the different elements of the design promised an exhibition that, in fusing the technological and the artistic means of its age, produced a text that was as disruptive of architectural history and the idea of the retrospective exhibition as it was productive of it. As Johnson wrote in the exhibition catalogue:

> Mies' exhibition work at MoMA challenged expectations of curatorial and exhibition design work in ways that forced stakeholders to reconsider the status of exhibition design. For, with this exhibition, it was clear that far from the production of representations of the architecture of another place or space... Mies' installation was a 'branch of architecture' in its own right.[34]

Written nearly 50 years apart, essays by Johnson and Riley both agree that Mies' decision to deploy the large photomurals, montages and full-sized installations that became the signature motifs of this exhibition was born, in the first instance, out of necessity: most of his original models and drawings had been left behind in Germany.[35]

Jim Grant
Plan No. 8, 2004
Live Installation
From the exhibition Bungalow
Blitz, Walter Phillips Gallery.
Photograph by Tara Nicholson,
courtesy of The Banff Centre

Whatever the beginning of this process, it was one that shifted—in significant ways—not only the look of architectural exhibitions, but more significantly, its purpose. In so doing, it acknowledged, albeit in covert ways, some of the intellectual and political radicalism of earlier European avant-garde interventions in curating and exhibition design.[36] So, while the 1947 exhibition was my first encounter with such critical exhibition practice, it was not Mies'.

In the late 1910s and 20s (some 25 years before the MoMA retrospective), Mies's association with Berlin Dada introduced him to concepts of art, architecture and design—including exhibition design—formed not as speculative refuges from reality in the way that their Expressionist counterparts might have been, but as practices designed to force artists and their audiences into direct and immediate engagement with the here and now.[37] The internalisation of contradiction, chaos, flux and chance, central to Dadaist practice could also be read as the organising principal around which Mies' apparently rational and formalist exhibition scheme was organised. In this context, there is a significant argument that the 1947 exhibition was (like Mies' earlier forays into exhibition work) as ambitious a statement as any initiated by the individual works therein.[38] It was, in other words, an intervention not only in the world of architecture, but in the cultural politics of exhibition design. From this point of view, the very idea of a retrospective must, for Mies, have posed some serious conceptual challenges.

If a retrospective is generally designed to present, as a coherent whole, work produced by a single artist or architect at different periods of their life (their *oeuvre*) it also—necessarily—privileges the artist as author not only of their life, but of the continuous interwoven story of their creative and stylistic progression from provisional and speculative to enduring and distinct. The retrospective is—almost by definition—backward-looking, traditional and nostalgic: the antithesis of the avant-gardist principals around which Mies had constructed his practice.[39]

Moreover, if the necessary premise of the retrospective is the inimitability of the artist and their work then it is no surprise that, in its traditional form, the retrospective pays little attention to the social, technological, cultural or historical conditions that underwrote their passage from obscurity to centre stage. There can be nothing common, ordinary or familiar about the subject of a retrospective. Instead, its conventions—its interpretive texts and panels, the chronology and so on—work together to produce and sustain an idea of the artist and her work as an exception to the ordinariness of the everyday. Understood in this way, the concept of the retrospective, as a form of practice, seems unsympathetic to Mies' work in either architecture or exhibition design: work situated very much within an avant-gardist context, one dedicated to innovation, immediacy, modernisation and revolution, not continuity or tradition.

In his essay, "Montage and Architecture", Sergei Eisenstein wrote about the politics of this aesthetic intervention: "The long path from material through function to creative work has only a single goal: to create order out of the desperate confusion of our times."[40] Mies's apparent rejection of the form and practices associated with conventional exhibition display is, in this context, unsurprising and it may be seen to represent something of a renewed engagement with certain strategic practices championed by earlier innovators in the field, including Herbert Bayer's innovative and influential design for the 1935 Building Workers' Union Exhibition.[41]

In film, the term 'montage'—as opposed to 'collage'—is generally used, after Eisenstein, to refer to the transition from one shot or one sequence to the next one.[42] An approach to editing developed by the Soviet filmmakers of the 1920s such as Pudovkin, Vertov and Eisenstein, montage emphasises dynamic, often discontinuous, relationships between shots and the juxtaposition of images to create ideas not present in either shot by itself. The second image may continue the theme of the first by a kind of visual metaphor

Opposite left
Andrew Kearney
Plan No. 12, 2004
Digital photographic
print on tarpaulin
35.6 x 43.2 cm

Opposite right
Andrew Kearney
Plan No. 18, 2004
Digital photographic
print on tarpaulin
35.6 x 43.2 cm

(for example, a couple kissing to train entering tunnel) or ironic juxtaposition.[43] In art history, the term "photomontage" is associated with techniques that combine, on a single surface, the outcomes of a range of signifying practices from film and photographic negatives, to printed or handwritten text to—in Mies's case—drawings. By sandwiching multiple negatives or layers under the enlarger's light, and projecting from them a single photographic image—onto a photosensitive surface—the photomontage merges many images into one. The resulting image will thus include more than one point-of-view and perspectives and will reference many different modes of representation, not all of which will be lens-based. In this way, photomontage can be understood as the production of composite images where disparate elements inhabit a unified space. Together, these aesthetic strategies produce texts that are, albeit in different ways, epistemologically and aesthetically self-conscious. Montage and photomontage, as forms of spatial and temporal assemblage, draw attention to their own fabrication and, in so doing, ask a series of questions of their audiences: questions such as where the objects are located in relation to each other; to perspectival space; to us, (the viewers) and why (and how) the objects are put together in one frame or sequence.

I suggest that Mies' 1947 exhibition did for the retrospective what montage did for continuity editing: calling attention to the dynamic relationships between the different elements of text by juxtaposing images, objects and spaces in ways that both shattered the idea of any chronological continuity between his work and created a text constituted of ideas not present in any of the original material.[44] Eisenstein wrote:

[In cinema] the word 'path' is not used by chance. Nowadays it means the imaginary path followed by the eye and the varying perceptions of an object that depend on how it appears to the eye. Nowadays it may also mean the path

followed by the mind across a multiplicity of phenomena, far apart in time and space, gathered in a certain sequence into a single meaningful concept; diverse impressions passing in front of an immobile spectator.[45]

Here, Eisenstein contrasts the position of the spectator within this scheme with those assumed by spectators in the pre-cinematic era. "In the past, however, the opposite was the case: the spectator moved through a series of carefully disposed phenomena which he observed in order with his visual sense." In this passage, Eisenstein suggests that the practice of understanding our environment in and through mobile encounters (with its colours, movements, forms, rhythms, spaces and sensations) is best understood through a consideration of children's drawings where "not only has the movement of the eye been given back to the action of the child himself moving in space, but the picture itself appears as the path along which a number of aspects of the subject are revealed sequentially". Using the free-standing partitions and the floor-to-ceiling photographic murals in conjunction with models, life-size installations and objects, it could be argued that Mies' design functions in a similar way. Where the cinematographer might use the camera to track a protagonist through real and imaginary space and an editor will cut and arrange the sounds and images from which the film is constructed, Mies chose instead to use architecture to move the spectator through and around the image.

In *The Practice of Everyday Life* Michel de Certeau argues that space is composed of "intersections of mobile elements" that are "actuated by the ensemble of movements deployed within it".[46] For de Certeau space, as opposed to place, is a concept without stability. It has no proper place. It is, "in a sense actuated by the ensemble of movements deployed within it.... It occurs as the effect produced by the operations that orient it, situate it, temporalise it and make it function in a polyvalent unity of

conflictual programmes or contractual proximities."[47] In this way, montage, whether in film, photography or exhibition, can be understood as a form of spatial practice.

In film, techniques such as the long take, jump-cut, establishing and tracking shots, camera-tilt, zoom, continuity editing, cross-cutting, voice-over and eyeline match are used to open up the text to a range of interpretative and representational strategies. In exhibition design and curating, such work is undertaken by spatial and visual interventions; partitions, oversized photographs, text panels. The division of space by partitions set at specific angles to the existing architecture enables the construction of a range of different 'shots' of the gallery and its contents. The passage of the viewer in and around, across and through these images and space is constantly disrupted by walls, partitions and other architectural structures that serve to obscure, exaggerate and distract as much as they unite, display or represent. Thus, removed from any traditional chronological sequence, it could be argued that these 'montage installations' enable the production of a set of other knowledges and ideas that would remain inaccessible to those of us encountering these objects in other, more conventional exhibition environments. From carefully composed 'establishing' views at each entrance to the confusion created by the juxtaposition of table-top models with blow-ups of architectural detail, this carefully considered scenario not only "links montage technique with architecture; [it] vividly underlines the even closer, more immediate link within montage between *mise-en-cadre* and *mise-en-scene*. This is one of the corner-stones without which... there [would] be no understanding of either sphere."[48]

Thus, this montaged exhibition scheme deliberately unfixed the quoted architectural work from any predetermined interpretation or historicised context. By this logic, the entire exhibition—and not just the elements within it—can be understood as a spatial and temporal montage: a text composed by the viewer as their movement through space causes the different materials, images and objects presented to assemble and overlap in such a way as to allow for the production of new meaning not conveyed by the constitutive parts.[49] Moreover, in its manipulation of scale, categorisation and display such a scheme abolishes the usual operative distinctions between inside representation and outside experience that characterise exhibitions of architecture, particularly the architectural retrospective. In place of the authoritative retrospective, Mies' exhibition (or certainly the archival records of it) produces architecture as a dynamic, contradictory and often confused practice: a field of activity in as much flux as the world out of which it has developed. The buildings, plans and designs included in this exhibition are articulated not as definitive statements of a particular period or practice but, more modestly, as another distinct series of creative interventions.[50]

In the early 1960s, the American conceptual artist Dan Graham used a snap-shot camera to photograph the suburban homes and diners that characterised his native New Jersey.[51] Unlike the bespoke and montaged prints used by Mies in his 1947 exhibition, Graham's images were printed without adjustment and developed not with an exhibition in mind, but for publication in glossy or mass-circulation magazines. According to Graham, these photographs were intended as a critique of a particular mode of photojournalism and of the architectural elitism that surrounded discussions of the tract housing that had fast become the dominant form of architecture in the working class communities of America's eastern towns and cities.

In those days, *Esquire* was publishing sociological investigations like David Riesman's *The Lonely Crowd*, using photographs in the Walker Evans mode, photographs showing lower-middle class, suburban clapboard houses, but usually from a negative, humanist standpoint. I wanted to take all of the same components of meaning and empty them of their pejorative, Expressionist connotations.[52]

The subsequent project, *Homes for America*, 1966, included a combination of photographs and text in the style of a 'magazine layout' which described those buildings that could—like other mass consumables—be ordered directly from a catalogue. Like Mies' work on the 1947 retrospective, Graham's *Homes for America* served as a critical assessment both of the conventions of a particular genre (photo journalism for Graham, retrospective exhibition for Mies) and the ideas about art, architecture and design enabled by them. However, while Mies's images focused on his work as an auteur architect, Graham—like Antick and Kearney—directed attention to the more anonymous buildings in which most of us live.

For those of us working on Bungalow Blitz, both approaches were important, particularly because those strategies already deployed in the representation of Fitzsimons' bungalows produced little more than one-line, value-laden assertions of worth. If the significance of these houses was to be opened up to more productive argument, it was clear that more attention needed to be directed at the nature of those photographic, art and exhibition practices used in the structuring of the inquiry.

Obviously, there was nothing particularly unique in Mies, Ruff, Graham and the photographers working on Bungalow Blitz taking photographs of buildings. For many decades, photographs have been used for the presentation and representation of both amateur and auteur architecture, a realtionship as old as the medium itself:

> … since the earliest days of photography, architecture has been the artists' most willing accomplice. The physical characteristics of building—unmoving yet animated by a daily wash of nature's light—made them far more reliable as subjects than the human figure. Nonetheless, the early photographers' attraction to architecture seems to have cooled when technical means allowed them to pursue more animate subjects.[53]

What is interesting about the work in photography discussed here is the use made of the medium to construct these images and of exhibition work to install them and present them for consumption. Working with buildings—whether the high-cultural examples photographed by Mies and Ruff or the mass-cultural forms favoured by Antick, Graham and Kearney—means, almost inevitably, to try to stimulate one's audience to look at the architecture represented from a new perspective or, at least, to pay fresh attention to it.

My decision to work with Antick, Grant and Kearney was based on a sustained interest in their work over (in the case of Kearney and Grant) a period of more than 15 years. My proposal to them was that they should deal with some of the bungalows built in reference to the first edition of Jack Fitzsimons' *Bungalow Bliss*, 1971. Together, after a series of research trips, we settled on those bungalows built in and around the parishes of Kilcar and Glencolmcille in County Donegal. In the beginning, the outcome was open. None of us had any clear idea as to where, exactly, the research might lead. After the third trip to Ireland, the houses had already largely been selected and the place where the exhibition was to be first produced had already been decided: MoDA. Beyond this, what was expected of the artists was left open. It was entirely up to them how closely they would attach their work to the proposed topic (the controversy surrounding the popularity of Fitzsimons' bungalow designs in the west of Ireland). They were free to think of the book and its attendant controversy simply as a starting point, as a premise, or just as a background. The photographers already knew the houses; they were familiar with them from personal experience, as well as from the numerous images reproduced in the 11 editions of the book and the criticisms of it.

As the overall research director on the project, one of the first things I did was to survey the existing images, to discover if there were any that might stimulate the artists' interest in the subject matter. For unlike me, none of them were especially interested in the house designs themselves or the debates spurred by their construction. For the photographers, and the oral history researcher working with them, the next phase took place on site, in Donegal. Here their low expectations of the buildings' potential as photographic subjects quickly proved unfounded, as they explored unexpected perspectives, exposures, situations and details. The result of their research trips was the production of a large, relatively manageable, body of raw material; transparencies, notes, diagrams and interview transcriptions. Material which, together with the 11 editions of *Bungalow Bliss*, the archival photographs of Mies's 1947 exhibition and my historical and archival research material now constituted the much expanded project archive.[54]

The next steps were taken back in London in the studio, darkroom and on the desktop. There, together and individually, we sorted, sifted and otherwise worked our way through dozens of letters and articles, four hundred or so photographic transparencies, nearly 28 hours of video tape and over 36 hours of audio recording generated by our research.[55] What, we wondered, was this material about? What questions emerge from it and how might they be addressed? It was at this stage that we committed to the development of a book and exhibition, both of which aimed to engage this archive and these questions at a number of—often conflicting—registers, including empirical, experimental, experiential, theoretical, speculative and analytic programmes of inquiry.[56] We determined that exhibition and book should use the archive as both material for and context of their respective inquiries. Our plan followed Mies' 1947 exhibition and Graham's engagement with the magazine layout, in that the asymmetrical spatial arrangement "articulated by freestanding planes and columns… enhanced the sense of movement within the interior and, implicitly, acknowledged inhabitants or viewers moving within and through a structure".[57]

Gallery floor plans and quick-time movies in hand, we had to make decisions about which photographs and what material would constitute the exhibition and, in what relation to the architecture of the gallery. Borrowing, quite literally, from the treatment of photographic material in Mies's 1947 show, we settled on producing wall-sized photographic prints—photomurals—rather than the 'painting-sized' framed photographic prints included in the first three exhibition projects.[58] While eventually agreed to by all, this decision was not easy to reach. In using unifying aesthetic strategies (same scale, ground and surface) to collectively render what were individually authored images, we were blurring any distinction between them. Having settled on the form of the photographic material, we then shifted our attention to the subject and positioning of these prints. Which images would we use and where would they be installed? We knew that Grant was planning to install a life-size sculpture—developed in response to the first edition of *Bungalow Bliss*—in the centre of the main gallery space. So, our decisions about which images to print and where to put them needed to be informed by the ways in which we imagined these images would be encountered by the viewer, specifically in relation to those architectural features within which they would be situated.

One of the widespread criticisms of the bungalows proposed by Fitzsimons has been the insensitivity of their placement in relation to the areas of outstanding natural beauty in which they are frequently located. The houses have routinely been accused of forming "a bungalow blizzard", which is rapidly obliterating the landscape, spoiling the view and otherwise contributing to the "ruination of the Irish landscape".[59] Grant responded to our plan to have wall-sized photographs of the exterior of the bungalows and portraits of their occupants on the walls surrounding the gallery floor. As this was where he was planning to build his installation, he developed a proposal for a life-size bungalow sculpture—titled *Plan Number 8*—that would begin as a single course of building blocks that would, over the course of the exhibition, rise upward to 3.7 metres and, in so doing, partially obscure the photographs on the surrounding walls.[60] Toward the end of the exhibition period, Antick's portraits and Kearney's landscapes would be visible only as fragments seen through window openings, over half-built walls and from the uncomfortable angles produced by the asymmetrical relationship between *Plan Number 8* and the gallery walls. In this way the ongoing construction of the bungalow acted metaphorically both for the history of the building of these houses by migrants over the course of many summers and the criticisms of these houses in relation to the landscape mentioned earlier. While the steady development of the full-size bungalow sculpture from footprint to fully fledged structure, was the centrepiece of Grant's installation, the work also included the installation of a couch in conjunction with the 'establishing' sequence of the exhibition and a vitrine display including the first edition of *Bungalow Bliss* and details from the text from it "Plan Number 8".[61] Together, the photomurals, furniture, vitrine and *Plan Number 8* quoted from and extended the techniques deployed by Mies in his 1947 scheme. By juxtaposing the exhibition design of such a renowned auteur architect with images and objects from *Bungalow Bliss*, the exhibition called into question the distinctions between amateur and auteur. An outcome of Grant's installation strategy was Antick's decision to move away from the exhibition of group portraits, electing instead to install three larger-than-life portraits of individual men and an enormously enlarged detail from the interior of one of the bungalows.[62]

In the *Architecture Without Shadow*, Gloria Moure borrows from Barthes' "The Rhetoric of the Image", to explore some of the challenges facing artists using photography as a practice through which to engage their audience in questions of architecture:

> The artists, meanwhile, in spite of starting out from a subject matter that is extremely dense in terms of the sign (given that architecture—and especially creative, *auteur* architecture—is a pristine material and formal residuum

of the linguistic codes), do not transfer this with strict and formal neutrality. Rather, its configuration oscillates to a greater or lesser degree, but always deliberately, between a cold and elementary documentalism and the creation of a composition of images rich in inflections and new relationships. In other words they develop a poetics and a critique of the image by way of the image.[63]

While clearly working outside the realm of auteur architecture, Antick, like Nan Goldin and Tina Barney, directly engages his audience with the previously distinct conventions governing both candid and tableau portraiture in the domestic sphere. Moreover, the compelling combination of characters, style and print formally adopted by Antick for this series makes our position as spectators socially and culturally ambiguous. On the one hand, we are transformed into "voyeurs peeping through the camera's keyhole into another world", where we experience the slightly guilty pleasure of social trespass. On the other hand, we are being placed in the uncomfortable position of having to judge that which we have vicariously seen—all of which is happening in and through the site lines opened up, crossed into and merged by the changing structure of Grant's *Plan Number 8*.[64] Following Antick, Kearney chose to attend to the impact of *Plan Number 8* on available site lines. The position of *Plan Number 8* within the available space radically altered the sightlines produced by the original architecture (in its provision of uninterrupted space and long running walls, clear sightlines allowing for entire walls to be seen as a series of long, panning and establishing shots visible, without the distraction of architectural detail). Once *Plan Number 8* was under way, it became impossible to see any of the walls (or whatever may have been hung on them) without first negotiating those paths that had been opened up, closed off or blocked by the sculpture's walls, openings and shuttering. Working in floor-to-ceiling heights, Kearney combined three separate landscape images on a single wall-sized and highly glossy tarpaulin print, grommeted directly onto the walls. In this way, *Plan Number 8* did for Bungalow Blitz what Mies' pinwheel arrangement of freestanding walls did for the 1947 exhibition: it activated the constitutive elements of the exhibition as something other than representations of things that exist elsewhere. By disrupting the conventions of display that generally underwrite the production of exhibitions of this type, the overall installation drew attention to the conventionalised, and often constraining, language of exhibition form.[65]

Subordinating individual work to the formal and conceptual unity of the exhibition, those of us working on the Walter Phillips Gallery exhibition became more concerned with weaving the photographs, sculptures and found objects we were working with into the structures and spaces of the gallery than we were with telling—or attempting to tell—any truth about their meaning in Ireland. This is not to say that we had lost sight of Donegal, Ireland, and the bungalow debates, but rather that we had come to think that, working as we were in the space of that particular gallery at that specific moment in time, we could no longer afford to ignore its physical, architectural and contextual specificity. Organised along the design of Mies' 1947 retrospective, the exhibition was now able to open the project up to many of the questions absent from our earlier work: questions about the representation of a debate; the retelling of an old story; and the re-invention of the Irish bungalow. In this way, the exhibition became a self-conscious acknowledgement of the way in which the architectural exhibition space can be used to represent not only that which exists prior to the act of representation itself (as in the conventional retrospective or thematic exhibition), but also how it can play a critical role in constituting the meaning of the object of representation. Thought about in this way, exhibition practice shifts its focus from summation to speculation: a practice designed to effect change in the kind of conversation that is to be had about the subject of representation: in this case, the much maligned Irish bungalow. The fact that this is always arguably the case is something that Bungalow Blitz and its audience is bound to take into account.

This project was generously supported by The Arts Council of England, The Irish Arts Council, Culture Ireland, Middlesex University and by the generosity of the many families and individuals in Donegal who allowed us access to their homes and shared with us the architectural histories of their communities. I am particularly indebted to the Gillespie, Byrne, Doogan, Doherty, Mooney, Murray, Cahill, Gallagher and McDevitt families in southwest Donegal and to Charlie Byrne of Galway, a chance meeting with whom in Stansted Airport resulted in the surprise receipt, by post, of my much sought after edition of first edition of *Bungalow Bliss*.

Research Photographs
• Kim Adams

Termination of View

• Bernie Miller

Termination of View is an urban design concept formalised in the Beaux Arts Movement but is probably a much older practice for which there was no agreed upon term. It may still have some currency in present day architectural and urban design practice. In formalised practice, the idea posits that in a 'view corridor', a prospect, or a particular approach there should be located a focal point such as an obelisk, a fountain, some statuary or, more often, an important civic building or a church. (The latter had also the practical problem of needing a longer approach so that the entirety of the structure, including a tower or a spire, could be taken in from a single vantage point.) Some city layouts lend themselves particularly well to termination of view situations. Winnipeg, a river town, is one such.

To start with the deep structure of the plan of Winnipeg, and its earliest history, I recall learning in elementary school how, in the nineteenth century, the people of Winnipeg took these issues of urban structure very seriously. The killing of an English surveyor (I don't know if the story is apocryphal or not) was the culmination of conflict between the French-based land subdivision system (and essentially French cultural influence) and the arrival of the English settlers. The closeness of this time to the present day should not be forgotten. There are several 'Urban Fields' which relate to Winnipeg:

1. The urban structure perpendicular to the Red River, the French River lot system.
2. The structure perpendicular to the Assiniboine River.
3. The field north of Notre Dame.

Urban spaces and streets created within the urban fabric form the background for places offering axes and focused views and may be seen as a language of field and axis. The spaces between the grid fragments offer unlimited potential for interpretation.

In the twentieth century city structures show up as what Colin Rowe referred to as "popcorn in an open field": individual building

with space around them. Older portions of some towns, by contrast, are marked more by figural voids, with spaces seemingly carved out of the solid fabric of the city. Here we often see placed 'set pieces', city squares and monuments forming focal points within the plan. The sequence of spaces, of urban rooms, focus upon a civic or ceremonial piece. A second organising system can be seen as the axis, a linear organiser.

The movement through these places takes place literally as one's path of travel; and may be see as a visual route, or as a conceptual axis that links moments or events. In the creation of a city on the characteristically North American grid, we can see that each owner has the right to develop their own building. (This contrasts greatly with many European cities, for example Paris, where each owner coordinates their piece of the urban wall with already exsisting structures, paying close attention to facades.) Such urban density creates spaces that appear as 'rooms' often containing a focal point.[1]

Where urban fields or grid fragments collide, the effect produces 'termination of view' situations or opportunities. When one becomes aware of such urban situations and opportunities, one also becomes aware that quite a few termination of view opportunities have also caught the attention of and been taken advantage of by commercial interests. Where one would expect a meaningful 'civic or ceremonial' structure one is just as likely to be confronted by a billboard or video display screen. What seems to be of particular interest to advertisers here is the length of approach, (which, historically, was utilised as device to take in a taller building in a single view). With billboards and the like, such an approach translates into 'eye-time'.

In 2003 Alan Tregebov and I initiated a series of proposals for specific locations which present termination of view situations or opportunities in downtown Winnipeg. The works in the series are fictional or imagined in the sense that they are proposals for physical works for real civic sites but current circumstances assure that they will never be actualised. They are nonetheless very

Bernie Miller and
Alan Tregebov
*Termination of View
Series, Notre Dame
Avenue*, Winnipeg
(panel 2), 2003
Inkjet print on
photographic paper
mounted on gatorboard
67.5 x 101.5 cm

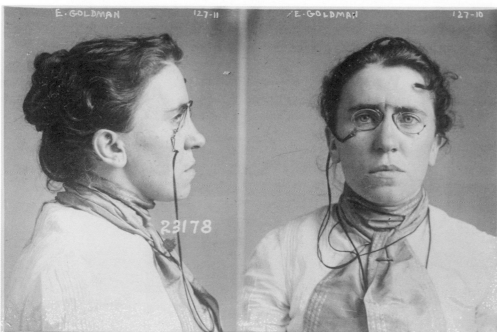

much a consideration of the existing built environment as well as a consideration of how that environment informs the realisation of personal and collective history.

The series, predictably enough called *Termination of View,* is an open ended, ongoing work as additions are continually being made to the series as appropriate sites come to our attention. The series is comprised by impossible proposals for works in the public realm (particularly the urban streetscape). It is reassuring to me that these proposed works fall into a short, but compelling, tradition of the proposal-as-commentary (I am reminded here of Jonathan Swift's "Modest Proposal" and, in architectural history, of the 'protest proposals' associated with the *Chicago Tribune* design competition).

In the *Termination of View* series, there is a persistent format of two presentation panels. A left panel presents a particular urban situation, while the right is an intervention into that situation. We propose in each, a standardised structure, a tower on a traffic island with some cantilevered signage in the form of an image panel or a free standing shape or character. The tower in each case is a 10.2 centimetre structural aluminium I-beam fastened with aluminium aircraft riveting. Included on each of the right hand presentation panels is a site map showing the location of the tower as well as some dimensioned elevations.

Termination of View proposes to deliver interference into the view corridors taken up by commercial interests, to adjust the noise to signal ratio. There is a sense that such corridors have become sites for communication rather than offering a prospect or view for a reverent approach to an important site.

Rather than simply evolving as a response to our contemporary environment, the series traces a lineage back to concepts and issues relating to freedom of speech which have long been prevalent in our work. In 1997 Alan Tregebov and I proposed that a monument to Emma Goldman would be a suitable addition to a small park in mid-town Toronto. Goldman was a storied anarchist known as

'Red Emma', quite active in the early twentieth century. She had been exiled from America by J Edgar Hoover for a trumped up connection to the Mckinley assassination (the assassin had once attended one of her lectures). She was then deported to the USSR but exiled shortly after for reporting (to Western newspapers) of the oppressive conditions there. After short stopovers in France and England she settled in Toronto where she lived out her days.

Goldman spent those last years of her life only a few houses down from the same small park. The monument intended for the triangular-shaped area was to be a landmark piece sited at the corner of Bloor Street West and Spadina Avenue. The competition brief called for a work that summed up the history of the street, so we chose to celebrate its politically active roots, spanning over 100 years. We wanted to focus on an emblematic figure to encapsulate this era; 'Red Emma' was the obvious choice. The following is taken directly from the text we submitted with the model and two visual display panels:

Artwork Description: the tower is meant to be a focal point to be seen in approach especially from the south. It is 9.8 metres tall and constructed of riveted aluminium beams, channels and angles. Located at the top of the tower, on the south face, is a solid red rectangle of enamelled steel. This tilted piece of abstraction, could be representative of many things: The red of 'Red Emma', a representation of modernist idealism, and progress that Emma Goldman was part of [red, as we know, was used a great deal in early modernist and revolutionary artworks], or it could be a kind of oversized traffic sign that signals a veer to the left ['Veer' in fact was the title of the proposed memorial]. It could also be a cancellation of the advertising billboard that is aligned immediately behind it on Bloor Street.

The tower structure supports the speaker's podium which itself is quite minimal. It is a simple raised platform, accessed through the tower with a small lectern or tablet at one end. The idea of the podium component as memorial creates a facilitating gesture, embodied within it the promise to carry on the good works of the remembered person by facilitating the activity of public speaking.

Emma Goldman's idealistic struggles engaged many fronts. We wish to pay special honour though, to her fierce attachment, above all else, to the ideal of 'freedom of speech'. She insisted that freedom of speech must be coupled to intellectual understanding and unrestricted access to education.[2]

The connection of this older proposal to our most recent work derives directly from the language of the proposal description: "Could also be a cancellation of the advertising billboard that is aligned immediately behind it on Bloor Street."[3]

The Termination of View exhibition in Winnipeg, which evolved out of the Emma Goldman proposal, was comprised by seven proposals altogether, four of which were for sites in Winnipeg, three for Toronto. The structures in each take for their main purpose the interference or cancelling out of the view and content of billboard messages located in a given urban design configuration. (Alternate names for such configurations are: vistas, prospects, outlooks, focal points, focal accents, visual accents, visible marker but the preference was for termination of view for its metaphorical and ambivalent potential.) There is some irony associated with the fact that the proposals are for monuments that interfere with, and censor advertising, in the name of a great historical figure who was known foremost for her struggle for freedom of speech. While thinking about this issue of freedom of speech there was a persistent return to two ideas: the democratic ideal of freedom of speech and the more obscure idea of rhetoric. Rhetoric has suffered from a bad reputation for the last 200 years. Along with its interchangeability with bombast or propaganda, it had come to mean the dressing up of truth with various ornaments of language to impart a persuasive edge.

In most understanding rhetoric has been often reduced to a simple taxonomy of ornaments or figures of language. There are two types of rhetoric: secondary (metaphor or alliteration) and, for our purpose, primary (a de-emphasis of the taxonomy of figures and a re-emphasis of persuasive language or elocution which relate to the persuasive effectiveness of language).

To discover present day relatives of ancient rhetoric, we need not invoke specialised research on 'speech acts' or the 'pragmatics of communication', which are both attentive to the active and operant value of language. It suffices to refer to modern techniques of mass communication, whether advertising or political propaganda. Our 'mediatised' societies, however different from Sicilian or Athenian democracies are, nonetheless, similarly regulated by a rhetorical politics centred on the persuasive power of the probable and of popular opinion.... Given the phenomenon of the mass media, how can we doubt that rhetoric is alive and well in the heart of our societies? Our very lives, both public and private, tend to turn (or return) to rhetoric.[4]

Alan and I had also looked to a few other cities for termination of view situations. In Barcelona and Rotterdam we were unable to find any instances of commercial-type terminations in the centre core of the city and took this to mean that there was some sort of regulation in effect. Regulation in the physical environment, for media-as-signage, is feasible without invoking censorship or freedom of speech legislation. (The reason being that the physical nature of supports for this particular media may be regulated through zoning and bylaws directed at the structure proper.)

There is one additional observation that occurred to us while engaged with the *Termination of View*: that the physical siting of billboards (and similar environmental media) is highly reminiscent of the 'panopticon' — but in reverse — as sightlines are directed from multiple points back to a centralised point of emanation rather than out from a single point.

The focus on billboard advertising should not be construed as our principle aim. We mean our action to be on the order of an emblematic gesture aimed globally at commercial 'culture'. With commercial culture the entanglement with what we think of as 'culture' proper, is approaching the point of no return. The underwriting of all media by commercial interests has very few exceptions. Content is no longer simply wrapped in commercial messages. The connection between the message and the messenger is becoming more tenuous. Witness the 'advertorial', product placement, PSA sponsorship and the dictates of major supporters of cultural programming.

Regulation through standard freedom of speech legislation is at best, difficult; at worst, impossible, due to the unique print and speech bias of the legislation being brought to bear against what is quickly becoming an entirely visual phenomena. When confronted with regulation advertisers retreat behind protective freedom of speech legalities which, through an accident of history, have been extended to include corporate entities. There are a number of compelling texts we came across while working on the project, chief among these is *The Death of Discourse* by Ronald KL Collins and David M Skover:

- Each day of our lives, 12 billion display ads, 2.5 million radio commercials, and over 300,000 television commercials are dumped into the collective consciousness.

- Advertising consumes almost 60 per cent of newspaper space, 23 per cent of network television prime time, 18 per cent of radio time and over 50 per cent of magazine space.
- The American Postal Service annually processes 38 billion assorted ads, and 14 billion slick mail order catalogues.
- During a lifetime, most people will devote a full year and one-half to watching commercials.
- Television home-shopping stations already reach some 50 million homes, generating three billion dollars in annual sales.
- Product and service messages are plastered on everything from the painted sides of cows to dyed hot dogs, placed strategically in everything from books to movies, situated on everything from billboards in space (the space Advertising Prohibition Act of 1993 was introduced in Congress to keep the heavens free of commercial advertising: with the failure of the proposed act, its looming First Amendment litigation issues were temporarily suspended) to the bottoms of holes on putting greens, pumped into everything from doctors' reception rooms to grade school classrooms, zapped through everything from phones to fax machines, and launched into the far reaches of 'cyber-space'.
- The *Philip Morris Magazine* — a slick and upscale periodical — boasted a circulation of more than 12 million, making it one of the largest circulation magazines in America.
- Over half of all American journalism and communications students forsake the fourth estate for careers in advertising.
- All this and more are made possible by the some 149 billion dollars dropped into advertising annually.
- And the electronic highways to the future are already being paved with untold commercial possibilities spanning from advertiser-produced interactive computer programming, to interactive home-shopping, to a new computerised generation of infomercials, to online advertising. Inevitably, the once ad-free Internet will be overrun by commercialism.

• By commercially recontextualising images and ideas, mass advertising debases the core values once associated with them. When messages are disseminated largely because of their market value, the ideals of citizen democracy succumb to those of consumer democracy. The commercialisation of communication not only affects our self-identity but also our identity in the citizen polity. That is, talking about and consuming commodities are now among our most significant political acts. (Bush's 'Back to the Mall' or 'the terrorists have won' plea) One of the pillars of (the American) ideal of a republican form of government is an informed and active citizenry. Essential to this paragon of democracy is vigorous participation in the processes of representative government, reasoned decision-making, equal responsibility to the community, competent exercise of the franchise, and, when needed, meaningful dissent. Candidly, this eighteenth century revolutionary notion of democracy ultimately cannot exist with a self-indulgent polity and a highly commercialised political state… Once the self had thus been transformed, it was entirely predictable that corporations would eventually seize First Amendment liberties for their own expression as well.… What is more immediately relevant to our inquiry is the question of how the commercial culture of mass advertising affects the key freedom of speech values identified by the court and commentators.[5]

These two final points provide a convenient entry to our own conclusions. While working on *Termination of View* what has been repeatedly drawn to our attention is the overbearing financial means, not to mention the choice of prime locations within an intensively mediated public realm, which 'commercial culture' has at its disposal. It seems that there exists a profound asymmetry between one side of a properly democratic debate and the other. This asymmetry operates as a *de facto* form of censorship.

One should ask then, who is it that is really effacing or erasing the public space of discussion and debate? How are the citizenry able to achieve a fair and balanced exchange of views when there exists such an asymmetry of persuasive power and an asymmetry of available financial resources? The intent behind the series *Termination of View* takes the form of a blunt interfering gesture, calling attention to an asymmetry of means and effects.

Corner Pieces (Banff)
• Lance Blomgren

Banff Elementary School

At a school similar to this one in Anoka, Minnesota, 682 miles from here, a first grade class was recently terrorised by an eight-point buck that leapt through the window during morning sentence review. A cougar in the hallway of Adams Elementary in Spokane, Washington—only 257 miles from Banff—singled out the smallest boy from the crowd and fatally crushed his throat and few Albertans will forget that nasty business with the black bear in the school yard outside Parkland, where a boy died trying to rescue his sister. It is in times of crisis that we rediscover our families. Walking home from school, I screamed in terror as a crow pecked my face and hands until my brother chased it away. It really makes one think (especially here in Banff, where the animals convene at the edge of the forest, just beyond the playing field). We know herbivores can turn predatory when survival is in question and it is clear we are not doing our children any favours by buttering them up under the guise of vending machine educational revenue. We all know the expression "like babes in the woods". The animals are hungry and irritable and, unless something is changed, the children of this school will certainly become the latest recipients of their protest.

The Banff Springs Hotel

This hotel, like many local employers, offers accommodation for its workers. During the peak seasons, the population of Banff swells by thousands as young people from all over Canada migrate to the area to work in the service industry and indulge the various recreation activities the area provides. A recent study by Planned Parenthood Alberta reports that nearly 35 per cent of the hotel's employees lose their virginity here and that 50 per cent have had more than two sexual partners in the residence complexes. Over the past few decades, a short-term job at the Banff Springs Hotel has become a national rite of passage. But like many people who have missed out on such great, unifying rituals, I carry a strange feeling of separation from those who have lived and worked here and still cringe in envy whenever anyone mentions this hotel.

I learned recently that a man named Laszlo Funtek was responsible for the renovations of the hotel in the 1980s, around the same time the Banff ritual was gaining momentum. His renovations are generally considered tasteless by preservationists and architects, but perhaps suitable in light of what we have been discussing. This hotel is a indeed a funtek. Behind the facade of Victorian propriety, the halls teem with salaciousness and possibility, less than subtle reminders of the weight of regret.

Banff Avenue

It has been almost 60 years since the last person froze to death on this street. Back then, the town was still an outpost where itinerant workers could find work in the booming tourist/building trades. A small homeless population existed, occasionally camping under the Banff Bridge. Sometimes the temperature would dive, catching the unlucky person in a deep chill or snow storm. But the last victim, whose name is not mentioned in the local newspaper report, was neither homeless nor a travelling worker. He was a skier and mountaineer, who lived part-time in a house on Otter Street and was reportedly well-versed in mountain survival techniques: he had once climbed Mount McKinley. According to a neighbour, the man had recently gone door-to-door to ensure everyone on the street was adequately prepared for the brutal cold snap of January 1947. I find these stories disheartening. All forethought, groundwork and practice turn useless so quickly. Even the strongest, most sensible, among us can become pathetic in any number of

unpredictable circumstances or mild lapses of judgment. In minus 48°C, severe hypothermia can develop in half an hour, faster if there is alcohol involved (which was the case with our poor sportsman). Overconfident in his usual fastidious preparation, he drank too much, chose his wardrobe poorly and underestimated the elements. Only two blocks from home, he passed out in a snow bank and was not found for two days.

Behind the Bus Station

Over the years this spot has been a regular meeting place for the teenagers of Banff. In October 1977, it gained special notoriety as the gathering point for what was dubbed The Halloween Riot in the local newspaper. It was right here that two groups of high school students met just before midnight. They reportedly lit fireworks, set fire to an armchair and consumed an abundant amount of hard liquor. Approximately an hour later, the teenagers hatched a plan to take over a bar on Caribou Street. At one o'clock in the morning, they entered the establishment and demanded service. When the bartender refused, the infamous revolt ensued with the youths easily overpowering older patrons and forcing them outside as planned. By the time the police arrived, the teenagers had already barricaded themselves inside and had free reign of the liquor. Empowered with intoxication, they refused to open the door. To avoid a volatile situation, the RCMP wisely decided to let the uprising run its course, which it did by four o'clock the next day, when the group vacated the building in exhaustion. The bar was a wreck, but no charges were filed. This riot is vastly different to the one that happened at Whistler ski resort on New Year's Eve, 2000. Without a gathering place at which to plan, the drunken celebrators were undisciplined and disorganised. Police were quickly able to suppress them and 106 arrests were made.

The Banff Pavilion

This is the infamous site of Frank Lloyd Wright's third and final Canadian building, the Banff Pavilion. It was on this marshy ground, where the tennis courts now sit, that a large indoor recreation hall opened to public outcry and scorn in 1913. Long and airy, and perhaps a little pretentious with three large fireplaces, the Pavilion was quickly declared impractical, uncomfortable and ugly. Admittedly, there is something not right about this area, and it is easy to imagine the water damage and dry rot that quickly overtook the building. You can smell the decay here. There was something cancerous about the Pavilion, as were a number of Wright's projects from the same era. In 1911, when he won the Banff commission, Wright was preoccupied with Taliesin, the protective bastion he was building in Spring Green, Wisconsin, for his lover Mamah Borthwick Cheney. The smell was there too, a sharp odorous rot built into the structure itself, as if somewhere in the architect's mind; a silent battle was being lost and spilling out into his work. Some of us know this fear and recognise its acrid scent, but for Wright and Cheney the smell had floated around them so long it had become undetectable. This wasn't the case for their friends, some of who stopped visiting Taliesin altogether, and certainly not for Julian Carleton, their servant from Barbados. In 1914, just as the Pavilion was showing its first signs of decomposition, the smell drove Carleton crazy. He killed Cheney and two of her children before setting fire to the building. The Banff Pavilion was demolished in the early 1930s. Its last remains sank into the wet earth and finally disappeared for good in late 1964.

Death by Chocolate:
Dan Graham in Conversation
with Anthony Kiendl

Dan Graham: I first got into the skateboard pavilion when I went to the Hayward Gallery in London. There were skateboarders all over the curved and concrete structure. So I thought, why not put together art and skateboarding?

Thurston Moore of Sonic Youth turned me onto a magazine called *Thrasher* that featured Minor Threat and Black Flag, and I saw some designs; one was a bowl shape. If I made the skateboard pavilion, I would allow the skateboarders to design the ramps themselves. I would make the top into a cut-away pyramid, two-way mirror glass, a little like a nineteenth century music gazebo.

In the late 1980s, all major cities had buildings with pyramid-shaped roofs. So I thought I would make this scintillating diamond pattern, so that when you are up in the air it's a little like making 1980s neo-Fascist architecture; something that is psychedelic. When you're up in the air, you can see everybody looking from the side; the sky will change, back and forth. I was also coming from the same influence that Gordon Matta-Clark did: Louis Kahn.

It was almost made in Leeds in 2000, however city officials, decided to construct a big water drum instead. Vito Acconci did a skateboard pavilion, of course based on mine, and in Rem Koolhaas' Prada shop in New York there is also a ramp.

Anthony Kiendl: I wanted to ask you about Gordon-Matta Clark and your take on his work, especially the cutting pieces.

DG: Gordon Matta-Clark studied at the school of architecture in Ithaca, and I'm sure he read *Oppositions* (which I read) by Peter Eisenman. I also think he was deeply influenced by Kahn, which nobody mentions. Instead of making monuments, Kahn made anti-monuments; in other words, he cut away at and memorialised something that was about to be destroyed anyway. And of course this cutting originated from Michael Grey's first house, the Benserof house, where he cut away at an existing structure. I think Frank

Gehry also comes from this direction. American president, Jimmy Carter, was also an influence on my work. His mantra was that we shouldn't consume any more, due to limited energy supplies. So the ideas was to cut away, to eliminate. In other words to take Mies van der Rohe's "less is more" more literally.

Matta-Clark was very fascinated by the city plan, certainly in his conical intersect, for Les Halles area in Paris. It was an historical, working class area that was being torn down for the Centre Pompidou. Matta-Clark, however, wanted to cut away; to reveal, rather than to build in this instance.

AK: You describe his work as anti-monumental. Do you see your own work as anti-monumental?

DG: The people I used to be compared to by Benjamin Buchloch—Michael Asher, John Knight—perceive my work as monumental. They are very against the DIA Foundation (piece); they think I should deconstruct, not construct. I think my work is humanistic. It is never that large.

My work derives from Russian Constructivism. It was half functional and quasi-utopian symbolic. Things that are functional, interest me because they are somewhere between art and architecture, or minor architecture. I was very influenced by Flavin and Sol Lewitt. Unlike Flavin—but more like Lewitt—my work is concerned with the city plan and city grids. I think Matta-Clark was very aware of such things.

AK: I am interested in your early performance work. In the same manner as these video pieces, the pavilions show the reflection of the viewers in relation to one another.

DG: When I was 14, I read parts of *Being and Nothingness* by Sartre, which led me to Lacan's concept of the mirror stage. This influenced

Dan Graham
Death by Chocolate:
West Edmonton
Shopping Mall, 2005
Production stills

the first pavilion I made, which was a philosophical model with two two-way mirror cubes that faced one another. The way I used the glass is very different from corporate use which is always a one-way mirror. Inside its dark, and you can see outside without being seen. From the outside you just see a mirror reflection. I wanted to make that into a heterotopia, being both transparent and reflective.

The relationship of spectators to one another became very important to me. This is something you find in normal architecture in the city. Even though I had not read Walter Benjamin, this notion has a lot to do with his Arcades Project.

AK: When you talk about the shopping mall, I am reminded of the West Edmonton Mall. You've talked about how it is read in relation to youth culture. What do you think of it architecturally?

DG: West Edmonton Mall has to do with the onslaught of entertainment; everything is amusement park oriented now. I think the biggest problem for modern architecture, and modern cities, even art, is the omnipresence of Disneyland; in other words, theme parks. West Edmonton Mall is a consumer paradise that's themed. It goes one step further than the arcades of the nineteenth century and corporate atriums and shopping centres. It is more international in scope than Disneyland.

Shooting at the West Edmonton Mall fed into my later interest in corporate atriums. When we shot it was a very business orientated period. The 1990s became more narcissistic, which the mirrors in the Mall communicated to some extent.

AK: To go back a bit, you quoted Mies' "less is more"….

DG: In the late 1970s, because of the oil crisis in America, Jimmy Carter wanted to get rid of nuclear power. He had been a nuclear engineer, but turned around and said we should not produce or

consume any more. In response, architects and artists eliminated rather than built structures. The idea was to make a cut, and that would be the artwork; to construct by taking away. In this sense such an action contradicts Mies.

Venturi reacted against Mies, equating the architect with corporate power (he reduced everything to corporate power). Matta-Clark was definitely a Marxist; he wanted to subvert the system.

AK: Did he live in your neighbourhood?

DG: He lived on Forsyth Street very close to me. I went to a party that he gave once where everyone was rolling around on beds and sofas. He and his friends were heavily into drugs, and I thought this is not for me. This was in the 1960s/1970s. I don't think I really saw much of his work at the time, we just came to the same conclusions reading *Oppositions,* and from having a similar interest in Kahn. I'm sure he began with Kahn as an antidote. All his work is about sunlight or moonlight coming through cuts.

I have a theory about Kahn that no one else has mentioned. Kahn was very involved in Egyptian and Sumerian architecture and I think he was worshipping the sun. People say he is a Medievalist, but I think he was responding to these kinds of primitive forms.

Although his primary influence was Grey's Benseroff house, Matta-Clark anarchically reacted against Kahn's monumentalism by cutting away. With work by architects such as Frank Gehry, we now perceive the action of cutting away as simply a stylistic trick. Gehry, however, began work as a social critic. He was political in a kind of cynical way. I think this is the same with a lot of artists' work, it starts as political and then changes.

AK: Do you think it loses its meaning?

DG: I think you have different sponsors. With Matta-Clark, we don't know what his work might have become. Essentially he was competing with his father, who was also an architect, but he also shared his interest in Surrealism.

AK: When you talk about Jimmy Carter, is this how you felt at the time, or something that you reflected on later?

DG: No, I was definitely influenced by him at the time. The whole country was influenced. I don't think he was a great president but, in the late 1970s, one of the most radical issues was ecology and this was something he addressed. America was the first country to be involved in ecology, and now it is the biggest abuser of the environment. I am still inspired by this period. There is an architect who I love from that era, Emilio Ambaz, who makes things underground; he was a huge influence on my Children's Pavilion project.

AK: How does the destruction of the World Trade Center impact American society?

DG: In Mexico City they asked me what I thought about 9/11. I said I had always hated it. The World Trade Center was for me a symbol of what was wrong with the Reagan period in the 1980s. It is a badly designed building. It was erected too quickly, so doesn't have many safety features, and was basically under-rented for a long time. It is symbolic of what happened in every major city — the last being Berlin — of people speculating on the downtown area and making huge high rises where people work during the day, and desert at night. Trevor Boddy's notion that it was destroyed for symbolising capitalist architecture made sense to me. I think he over-stated what he was meant, but the intuition was correct.

AK: But there is something iconic about the World Trade Center.

DG: I think it is a phenomenon of the 1980s. This was a period where everything was geometrical. We used pyramids on rooftops (which IM Pei did at the Louvre). Corporations dominated; it was a move of corporate power. In the 1990s, however, all corporate building became elliptical — very Baroque — making them more pleasurable and without the rigidity that such buildings used to have.

This is particularly prevalent in the city in London and was the impetus for making the elliptical pavilion for Waterloo Sunset. In a sense I was competing with and criticising Herzog and de Meuron's Tate Modern.

AK: You seem very optimistic about new buildings, that they are pleasurable to be in.

DG: Well they are Baroque. When I made the DIA Foundation piece, I used anamorphic distortions, the idea was to really break away from minimal art. (I have learned a lot from minimal art, but of course I'm also resisting it.)

AK: Do you say that now, upon reflection, or have you always felt as such?

DG: Minimal art is less concerned with subjectivity and also denies many things. For instance, Donald Judd's work has a lot to do with female imagery but he's a very macho guy, so I think he was looking to make a void. In some ways his work is also more expressionistic than some people realise, because minimal writers only talk about formalism. Flavin was also overtly expressionistic, coming from such influences as Caspar David Friedrich and German Expressionism, even American Abstract Expressionism. Barnett

Newman too. So I think the subjectivity of minimal art was denied and, as a consequence, I focused on the relationship between subject and object (for, in philosophy, phenomenology and Sartre, there is always a relationship between subject and object). When I use materials in my work, they are real materials appropriated from the city, thus reflecting and relating to real spaces within it.

Benjamin Buchloch, who hates minimal art, thought my interest was in reducing minimal art to a kind of sociological critique. However, it's a state of ambiguity that I create in materials. For example, with the Venice Biennale piece, if you were there alone, you would interacting with a big minimal work of art. When a crowd culminates, however, it transforms into something psychological and social.

AK: The one that's there now?

DG: No, the *Two Audiences* public space from 1976.

AK: You said before Flavin was destroying other art. Can you expand further?

DG: Well, with garish lights it made the art irrelevant. I think artists first start making work, particularly men, the results are both destructive but also homages to other art. Flavin's work is an homage to Barnett Newman in many ways, who actually befriended him. There is also an aspect of Pop in Flavin. One of his first pieces was a flower pot. Inside he installed a light bulb with a rose inside, which was illuminated. He called it Barbara Roses; the same name as the leading critic at the time. He really had a nasty sense of humour!

AK: We talked about anti-monumentalism. Would you say you're anti-modernist?

DG: In architecture, late modernism was mostly comprised by people who copied Mies van der Rohe, or awful work such as the Walker or the Carnegie by Andrew Laraby Barnes. I don't go so far as Jeff Wall who denies all of modernism, by harking back to the nineteenth century and early representationalism. I think my work is mimetic of contemporary city architecture, its all about the city, and also about Benjamin who was a student of the city and early media culture. I discovered him indirectly first, through Marshall McLuhan and then via *Illuminations* by Hannah Arendt. I feel a great affinity to Benjamin. (Of course, his hero Baudelaire has almost the same birthday as me, although I never read Baudelaire.)

I am not into Adorno, because he hated American culture. He was a bit old-fashioned European. Buchloch, John Knight, Michael Asher, however, all those people worshipped him. I had a problem reading him because I love popular culture.

AK: And he said, "how can we have poetry after the Holocaust…"

DG: The worst architecture I have seen recently is the Holocaust Museum by Liebeskind. It hits you over the head and makes you feel guilty. The great thing about the Holocaust is that both Jews and Germans feel guilty together; they can relate. Jewish guilt is very important to Jewish culture, it has a lot to do with humour.

AK: Liebeskind has also been involved with the reconstruction of the World Trade Center site.

DG: Yes, but it is becoming diluted. I don't like deconstructivism in architecture. It was a false period.

AK: Have you seen the drawings for the new World Trade Center site?

DG: No, not in person, only bits and pieces on television.

AK: What did you think of them?

DG: I think it looks good on paper.

AK: The last thing I want to ask you about is architectural models, particularly your Scotch tape models. What are your thoughts about models as opposed to actual architecture or pavilions?

DG: They are very useful pragmatically. I used to make them early in the morning, and would take them to a site so the client can see what they might actually look like. Also, I cannot work with computer renderings because they don't show the optics or materiality. The Scotch tape models are perfect for this. The first models I did were actually vernacular models and they were much more interesting than the Scotch tape models.

AK: What kind of vernacular models?

DG: Alterations of a suburban house, the TV projector outside the house. There was a model for Clinic. They were very small and vernacular… and became normal for artists to do.

AK: Overall, your interest in children…

DG: Kids like my work. I think most artists' work relates to their earliest childhood memories. I am slightly schizophrenic, and Matta-Clark's piece *Splitting* (the idea of splitting the ego) has some interest for me. It is also the influence of Jean Paul Sartre. The other influence when I was young was Margaret Mead. I read her books as a child because I was interested in sexuality and she was very strongly for the matriarchy. I also read Shiumeth Firestone, a Canadian from Ottawa, who wrote about feminism. Benjamin Buchloch says my work is sociological. It's not really, its 'fake'

sociology, it's more about anthropology. I'm very interested in the family structure.

CONSUMPTION/
RUIN

Post-Peasant Architecture: The House Bunică Built, a Case Study
• Donald Goodes

An old farmhouse sits decaying on the Canadian Prairies not far from the grid of gravel roads near the Manitoba/Saskatchewan border. It is close enough to the Riding Mountain National Park so that black bears regularly make their way into the community and packs of coyotes can be heard howling at night. Eventually the house will be unceremoniously demolished, like so many before it.

According to Winnipeg landscape painter, Leo McVarish, pictures of decrepit farm buildings were in great demand in the 1970s and found their way into many suburban houses. However, if we go deeper, farmhouses reveal themselves to still contain meaning. They reach deep into the Canadian postcolonial subconscious and surfaces as a symbol of a troubled, and still unresolved, part of many people's identities. With one foot in peasant traditions and the other in consumer culture, the farmhouse embodies the excitement and the trauma of integration; of making decisions to leave behind 'what one was' and become something new. Like so many transitional living spaces of immigrants who come to 'better' their lives in Canada, it reveals the drama of resistance to the dominant culture; of trading in one's culture, language, economy, beliefs and values, for class mobility, wealth and a future.

On the opposing page are two homes that were built in Winnipeg just before Bunică's house was constructed.[1] Both stand as evidence of the industrialised consumer economy and culture that had taken form in the city not far from her own community. While regular street cars rolled down Winnipeg streets, huge Victorian homes went up in its better neighbourhoods. Bunică's community remained far from the waves of modernisation. Up to the 1920s, and during the Great Depression in the 1930s, they were principally practicing subsistence farming in the peasant tradition.

The century-old critiques and the counter arguments of modern capitalism are in their own way a cliché. However, the contested value of Bunică's house suggests the ongoing relevance of the neglected place subsistence cultures hold in Canadian identity—despite having been categorically dismissed by the dominant industrial paradigm long ago. I would propose that there are two dialectics at work here, both of which are deeply rooted in Canadian culture: one is that of the dominant consumer economy and culture, the other is that of latent subsistence economies and cultures. Consumer culture argues that resources are infinite (or at least infinitely recyclable) and that it is our right to consume because this consumption leads to economic prosperity as well as to our fulfillment as citizens. Subsistence cultures—such as those of Canada's Aboriginal people or of its peasant immigrants from eastern and western Europe at the turn of the last century and later from Africa, Asia and South and Central America—argue that resources are limited and we must be frugal in order to survive (and thus maintain a connection with ancestral traditions).

Subsistence and consumer cultures obviously have opposing world views. The history of the modern industrial colonisation of Canada holds many examples of the drastic measures taken to discourage and eliminate the continuation of subsistence economies: from genocide to social evolutionism and the positivism used to explain and justify the devaluation of the non-Western 'other'.[2]

It is important to remember that Eastern and Southern European immigrants to North America (including Romanians, all Slavs, Italians and Greeks), most of who came from the peasant class, did not fall under the privileged banner of 'whiteness' until well into the twentieth century.[3] They were the non-Western 'other' until they proved their willingness to assimilate. There were many who felt that peasant immigrants should not be let into Canada:

To Hugh John MacDonald, son of Canada's first Prime Minister, the Galitians were 'a mongrel race'. In Manitoba, Premier Rodmond Roblin referred to the Eastern European immigrants as 'foreign trash'. The *Brandon Independent*

Previous pages
Lida Abdul
White House (Kabul), 2005
16mm film transfered to DVD, 4'58"
Image courtesy of the artist and Giorgio
Persano Gallery.

Above
Cameron House, Winnipeg, circa 1910
Image courtesy of Archives of Manitoba.

Below
Hayward House, Winnipeg, circa 1905
Image courtesy of Archives of Manitoba.

classified them as 'human vermin' and *The Edmonton Bulletin* described them as 'a servile shiftless people... the scum of other lands... not a people who are wanted in this country at any price'.[4]

Eastern European peasant immigrants also had their champions; otherwise they would never have come to Canada. The most famous of these was the Minister of the Interior, Clifford Sifton, who, at the turn of the nineteenth century, worked with officials in the Austro-Hungarian Empire to engineer a mass exodus of Ukrainian and Romanian peasants from Bucovina and Galicia to colonise the Prairies. The argument was that they had great potential: first to overcome the laborious task of clearing the land in west Canada for farming; second, that they would provide much needed food for the urban industrialised colonial economy; and third, that they had a weak character that lent itself to assimilation.

In the end, they proved Sifton right on all accounts. They were industrious and willing to adopt the ways of their host culture: language, beliefs and economy. While they kept some folkloric traditions alive, they did everything they could to disassociate themselves from being subsistence peasants. Those who were accepted into 'white' circles became something that resembled nobility. In less than three generations, Eastern European peasants became 'ordinary' Canadians, engendering more ordinary Canadians, who now cultivate our own 'nativist' complaints about immigrants.

It would seem then that the battle is long over, and that consumer culture succeeded in squashing its adversary. However, masters of marketing have long known that the latent effects of Bunică's subsistence culture must continually be addressed. Spike Jones' television advertisement for the ubiquitous retail giant Ikea from 2002 is an obvious example. In it a woman is shown carrying an old goose-neck desk lamp to the roadside for waste collection. She stands outside what looks to be a lower Manhattan apartment. We see slow dolly shots of the neglected lamp at night in the rain while sentimental music plays. The discarded lamp looks downtrodden, still intact, but bent over, personified. At the end a man suddenly walks into the frame and says: "Many of you feel bad for this lamp. That is because you're crazy. It has no feelings. And the new one is much better." (At which point the logo appears with the slogan "unböring" under it.)

Jones' advertisement evokes our latent subsistence desires to save things, to make them live as long as possible, to limit our impact on our environment.[5] It cleverly locates these desires in the realm of sentiment. The narrator then embarrasses us by diminishing such sentiments to a case of mistaken personification. He decisively reveals how our desires contradict the realities of the prevailing consumer culture, and declares them irrelevant.

Ikea's 2007–2008 Canada slogan is "Love your home". What is implied here is that one must buy new things for it to express this love. Bunică loved her home, but had little need to buy much for it.

Bunică's house is an excellent example of post-peasant vernacular on the Canadian Prairies. It is a subtle transitional dwelling, a hybrid embodying both her inherited subsistence culture and the new consumer culture of capitalism that dominated the world around her. It speaks of how she set limits on how far she was willing to assimilate, and ultimately is a proposition of how a subsistence culture can co-exist with consumer culture on its own terms.

Bunică's farmhouse has occupied a significant place in my imagination since I can remember. The way she lived was so different from the norm I experienced in the brand new suburban subdivisions in Winnipeg and Ottawa in the 1960s and 70s. The prevailing wisdom of that era was that one's ethnic and class histories were irrelevant once you were reborn into the middle class, even if by only one generation. In other words: a suburban Canadian consumer is a suburban Canadian consumer, end of story. In Bunică's case, however, I secretly knew that this wasn't true.

Arriving at her house was a journey back in time and into another world. What was surprising was that she lived a life of what many would consider to be poverty. Yet she clearly was not suffering, but rather seemed powerful and content. In fact, her home was a kind of cultural refuge, in whichever room told a story.

Given the central place of food in subsistence cultures, it is not surprising that the kitchen was the most important room in Bunică's house. This is where the food that was grown on the farm was eaten and endlessly talked about. Preparing and eating meals was the backdrop for long visits. Whatever the food—perogies, beet rolls, meat and sauerkraut, or radishes and onions from the garden—eating was a celebration.

Bunică's house was built in stages. The first part was a provisional shelter that would later become the kitchen. In the spring of 1916, during the First World War, Bunică's future husband, Alexander Gudz (later Goodes or 'Mosu', as we called him), was granted full rights to the quarter section Northeast 6–24–27 in the Rural Municipality of Shellmouth-Boulton, Manitoba. Under the Dominion Land Act of 1872 a 160 acre land grant was available for a ten dollar registration fee, as long as the homesteader improved the land, grew crops and lived on it for three years.[6] This represented about a month's wages and would probably have come from Mosu's labour work for established local Anglo-farmers or ranchers, cutting logs for the saw mill, or doing road work and other labour for the municipality. The division of homestead into 160 acre squares ensured that families would not normally live closer than half a mile apart, effectively undermining Eastern European peasants' old-world settlement patterns of living close together in agricultural villages and going out to the fields to work the land.

The first Romanians had come from Bunică and Mosu's community, from the village of Voloca, 17 years earlier. When Mosu obtained his homestead Romanians and Ukrainians were well-established in the district. Voloca is near Romania's northern border in the contested province of Bucovina, which takes in the northern slopes of the northeastern Carpathian Mountains and the adjoining plains, and is half situated in Romania and half in the Ukraine.

Like most other Carpathian and Bucovinian peasant settlers across the Prairies, Mosu chose to build a *bordei* as the first dwelling on his homestead. A *bordei* is a rectangular structure wider than it is deep with a slanted roof running from a high wall at the front of the structure to a low one at the back. It was made using horizontally layered sold-timber technique called blockwork or log cabin, which was widespread in the vernacular architecture of Carpathian peasants at the time both in Canada and the old country. This technique relied on placing timbers horizontally in successive layers and jointing them at the corners to form load-bearing walls.[7]

Mosu cut the logs directly on his land. These were sawed into lengths and stacked to make the walls. At the corners, the ends of the logs were jointed using a 'saddle-notch' joint so that they nested one-in-another. Because the trunk of a single poplar or aspen tree from this area of Manitoba parkland (ie. the transition zone between prairie and boreal forest) would not have been long enough to run the six metres of the long walls, two logs of similar diameter would be jointed together using diagonal joints hewn with an axe. A hole was drilled through the two overlapping logs and they were fastened together with a dowel made from a branch. These dowels were also used to increase the structural integrity of the log walls. Once the four walls were raised, the spaces in between the logs were first filled with clay and straw or dry grass to insulate from the cold.

Mosu and other local immigrants would go to work in the saw mills on a casual basis, making them familiar with its products and providing them with wages to purchase commodities. The local men would travel there on horse-pulled sleigh trains during the winter (there were few roads at the time and it was easiest to pull heavy loads over the snow-covered ground), they would cut spruce trees in the forest reserve and then had the logs cut into boards at the mill.

The lumber was brought home on the sleighs. Since the trees were green, the lumber would be piled in a special way to dry during the summer, and would be ready to use in a year's time.

To construct the floor and slanted roof of his *bordei*, Mosu used rough lumber and cedar shingles, purchased from local merchants. This is a departure from the techniques used by the earliest Bucovinian settlers who, with fewer resources, made their roofs from branches covered with tightly packed sod (or in some cases thatched roofs) and their floors in the traditional way with packed dirt "smoothed over with clay and water and regularly washed over with a mixture of cow or sheep dung and water. This imparted a shiny appearance to the floor and kept dust down."[8]

Mosu cut two small window wells in the heavy logs of the short north-facing wall and another in the end wall facing east. The door to the *bordei* was hand built and installed in the high south-facing wall, which was the tradition for all peasant vernacular houses. This is the door that would later connect the kitchen and the living room. The house would have been furnished with a bed, benches and a table all made of rough lumber. The whole process, minus the year for drying the wood, would have probably taken less than a week.

In 1917, Mosu and Bunică married and she joined him at the *bordei*. Over the next year or so, they would prepare the wood and build the rest of their house; their first daughter was already born when it was completed. In the years of bringing up their family the kitchen changed little. A large wood stove and stove pipes were purchased and a smaller heating stove would have been moved to the adjoining living room.

Over the years, Mosu and Bunică would purchase very few large manufactured consumer items. Goods like the kitchen stove and horse-drawn farm equipment would always be acquired second-hand at local auction sales in Russell. In essence this represented the surplus of a blossoming consumer culture. Western-European and Anglo-farmers who had been established in the area for much longer than the Eastern European immigrants—desiring newer and 'better' amenities and equipment or leaving farming all together to live in the city—would sell off what they no longer needed or wanted. The post-peasants would take advantage of this economy for many years to come.

Smaller items, such as pots and pans and fabric, were bought new from the Eaton's catalogue—deliveries were made through the well-established Canada Post system. Mosu and Bunică made money by selling cream from their ten milking cows, as well as butchered ducks and turkeys, and the 1,000 bushels of grain that came from their land. Their annual income would have peaked at 2,000 dollars, but there was not much to buy.

Wood to fuel the stove was cut from the bush on or around the farm. Splitting and managing this wood was a constant task. Bunică cooked the meals with help from the children. They were served three times a day at a handmade kitchen table large enough to accommodate everyone. Meal times revolved around chores (feeding animals and milking cows), school and other farm work. All their food—meat, dairy, eggs, grains and vegetables—were grown on the farm. Only well-established food commodities from the international colonial economy, such as sugar and tea, were purchased from local merchants. Scraps and water used for cooking would go into a slop pail, the contents of which were fed to the pigs or chickens. Meat scraps would go in a separate pail for the dog.

The kitchen was also the place where washing took place. Bunică and Mosu built a wash stand out of scrap lumber. There was a reservoir in the stove that warmed up the rain water collecting in a barrel under the eaves of the roof. Baths took place once a week. A tub was placed in the middle of the kitchen and the children would take turns, from the youngest to oldest. Everyone honoured each other's privacy and all used the same water. The wooden floors of the kitchen were scrubbed with a stiff brush every Saturday by the girls; over the years the rough floorboards became quite smooth.

Later in the 1940s—a period of unprecedented economic growth in Canada that filtered down to rural communities—linoleum and wallpaper were purchased to decorate the kitchen and make it easier to keep clean.

When we went to visit Bunică recently not much had changed in her kitchen. There were many more layers of linoleum and wallpaper, the ceiling was painted, and there were a few appliances that her children had purchased for her, such as a hot plate and toaster. Yes, there were marshmallow cookies and store-bought butter, and fewer animals in the yard but, for the most part, she still grew her own food (with supplements from her daughters' farms) and managed her kitchen in much the same way as when she was young.

For a period from about 1903–1914, across Canada, Ukrainians and Romanian peasant settlers from Bucovina built homes that used a vernacular domestic architecture whose design was taken directly from the Bucovinian Carpathian Mountain region. The materials necessary to build in the Canadian parkland were no different than in the old country, and the expertise to build them was carried in the collective memory. It was a natural impulse to reproduce the familiar. Symbolically, these homes also suggested the optimistic hope that they could continue their cultural traditions in this new land, in the same way the ruling Anglo-culture was doing. They turned out to be wrong.

John C Lehr, geography professor at the University of Manitoba, has researched and written extensively on Ukrainian and Romanian vernacular architecture on the Canadian Prairies. He notes:

During the period of 1914–1925, agricultural markets were good and prices high, and the material prosperity of the Ukrainian farmer increased dramatically. His newly-found wealth often brought about the building of a new house; larger and more Canadianised than the earlier folk house. For

the first time the vernacular tradition was not strictly adhered to, though neither was it completely abandoned. The result was an architectural ethnic hybrid.[9]

Bunică and Mosu were part of this trend. They were familiar with the traditional Carpathian homes in their community. However, when they went to build what would become the living room and bedrooms of their home, they chose a layout that was mid-way between a traditional peasant house and a bourgeois Anglo-Canadian home.

They constructed a two-storey house with a gable roof. The design recalls typical Western-European and American prairie homes, and was probably taken from models that Mosu and Bunică saw when they visited towns like Inglis or Russell. With windows on three walls of both floors, including a dormer protruding from the south side of the roof, they had a much brighter interior than in traditional houses. Furthermore, although the new addition to their house was much smaller than Anglo-Canadian equivalents, measuring only nine by six metres, it represents a re-organisation of room function. Traditional houses were divided into two main rooms: a kitchen and an entertaining room (traditionally called "the great room" or *casa ce mare*), both of which doubled as sleeping areas. Now, with a separate kitchen and living room area, sleeping had its own space in the second-storey room—though for the years Bunică lived alone in her house, she always slept on the living room sofa.

The construction techniques used for the new part of the house were a combination of new and old-world. The walls were built with the familiar saddle-notch, load-bearing, log-wall construction. There seems, however, to have been an effort to make the walls with smaller logs than in the *bordei*, which gave the look of the frame houses in town. The disadvantage of a frame house was that they were difficult and costly to insulate. With their thin log walls, made with materials available on site, Bunică and Mosu had the best of both worlds: modern walls that were, nonetheless, well-insulated.

The interior walls were further insulated using the traditional method; pitching the spaces between logs with clay and straw and whitewashing them with lime (acting as both a protective coat as well as making the rooms brighter). This surface was maintained for many years but, eventually, the walls were covered with wallpaper, which Bunică liked because of the colours and patterns, and which she changed regularly over the years.

When Mosu built the kitchen *bordei*, he also whitewashed the exterior walls of the dwelling, which is the tradition in Carpathian vernacular. With the new part of the house, however, he chose to cover the entire exterior with clapboard siding. For the ceilings in the living room and kitchen, Bunică and Mosu had a large quantity of tongue-and-groove boards made. Covering the exterior of their house with wood instead of clay was more costly—in addition to the wood, nails had to be purchased—however it had the symbolic advantage of appearing less like the home of immigrants.

In later years, Bunică painted the front wall of her house. Painting a house, by this time, was a matter of course for normal Canadian homes. However, her choice of bright colours, with a particular taste for lavender trim, was anything but conventional. In the end, ease of maintenance became the most important concern, and the painted wall was covered with *faux* stone wall, tarred paper.

The house, once complete, was finished with a mixture of purchased and homemade elements. The roof was covered with cedar shingles. Glass for the windows was purchased but the frames were built on site. The house's two doors were handmade. Door hinges would have been bought, but other metal elements, such as hooks (as well as the closures and hinges for farm buildings) would have been made by Mosu (who enjoyed blacksmithing using the steel that he scavenged from old farm equipment).

A dirt root cellar was dug under the living room, and was accessed through a trapdoor in the floor under the stairs. This is where potatoes and other root vegetables, as well as homemade sauerkraut and preserves, were kept over winter for the life of the house. There were narrow stairs leading up to the second floor. They were built according to peasant vernacular standards rather than those of Anglo-Canadian homes. They rose at such a steep angle that they required some skill and care in ascending and descending, but this ensured that the opening in the floor upstairs took up little space. These too were never altered.

Originally, the upper floor was open plan with slanted ceilings. In peasant cultures it was not the norm for everyone to have separate sleeping quarters. Mosu slept in the northeast corner, the smaller children in the southeast corner all in one bed (sometimes when cousins or other children were staying over they slept crossways, so they could all fit in it). Bunică and the oldest girls slept in the southwest corner at the head of the stairs. By the 1950s, Mosu had passed away and all but one child had left home. Over the years, little had been acquired but there was enough stuff in the house to require a place to store it. Bunică had three small closets for storage of clothing, bedding and her children's school things built. At the same time, the upstairs was divided into two small rooms, acknowledging the trend towards individual sleeping spaces. When I visited Bunică as a child, we would sleep upstairs. Even with the walls the space seemed unusually intimate.

From the beginning, Bunică and Mosu purchased manufactured metal bed frames, springs and mattresses at auction. Beddings were purchased from the Eaton's catalogue, but quilts and pillows were made by hand using wool and feathers from farm animals and fabric purchased locally. Up to 1950, Bunică and the children would normally go to bed at sundown because the only light they had came from oil lamps. When electricity was installed in the house it was easier to stay up late, and Bunică often did.

During the period when the children were growing up, the downstairs area functioned as a traditional *casa ce mare*. It was sparsely furnished with a storage cupboard that Bunică and Mosu made out of leftover tongue-and-groove boards, and a large table and benches made from rough lumber. The room was only used for social events or when the traditional travelling *Irod* pageant came at Christmas. Today it may seem strange, that with the limited amount of space available in Bunică's house, one out of three rooms would only be used occasionally. One explanation might be that because of their subsistence lifestyle, Bunică and Mosu's family spent relatively little time indoors. The house was for eating, sleeping and entertaining; all that was needed was a room for each.

It was in the late 1930s that the *casa ce mare* became more of a living room. The first addition was a dark green velour chair in which Mosu would often stay up late at night reading religious philosophical books in Romanian or the farm papers in English by oil lamp. Bunică liked to sleep in it. At the same time they purchased a battery operated radio. After lunch, the children would sit around listening to a pioneering CBC variety show called the *Happy Gang*. By the time Bunică was living on her own, the room had filled up with more furniture: a sofa and a round dining room table and chairs, which was covered with knick-knacks, decorated Easter eggs and Bunică's medications, but seldom used for eating. When guests came they would socialise in the room, but meals would always be taken at the table in the kitchen.

As Bunică's children become more independent, they would influence the house in new ways. In 1955, they bought her a fridge, which remained her trusty companion for 40 years. It was installed in the living room in front of the southward facing door, condemning this traditionally all-important entrance in a symbolic gesture of change. From then on, only the west facing door in the kitchen was used. In the early 1960s, she also had a freezer and black and white television from the children.

Bunică's house—from its construction, through the years of raising a family, then alone—adopted changes incrementally, at a rate that is found in many other traditional subsistence cultures no matter what the era or nation they existed within. She never embraced the dominant capitalist system, but her parallel post-peasant lifestyle was dependant on her monthly government pension check, low taxes and the financial favours of her children, all of who were part of the dominant system. Nevertheless, Bunică insisted on maintaining her subsistence livelihood. Despite her meagre income her expenses where so low that she always had enough money to give her grandchildren pocket money when they visited. She didn't have running water or a toilet in her house. She wanted to grow and eat her own food. She cooked on her wood stove. She wanted to live in her old house. As we have seen, she embraced communications technologies or amenities that facilitated the management of food, but she never became a consumer. She would still rather fix a hole in an enamel pot using a bolt and a piece of fabric, than buy a new one. According to IKEA, Bunică would be 'boring'.

Historically, all changes, even the most desirable and clearly beneficial, bring losses with their gains. For the millions of post-peasants around the world, this exchange was more often than not engaged under duress. I realise that my father's generation could be seduced away from their peasant culture with the promise of wealth, comforts and the trappings of nobility, because they grew up close to the suffering and other problems of a subsistence peasant culture. However, later generations are now, in turn, aware of the suffering engendered in their system. We feel the latent trauma of turning our backs on our ancestors, our language, our cultures and our economy: the baby was thrown out with the bath water, and it's time to deepen our knowledge of this history.

itourist? Notes on the Affective Economies of Holocaust Tourism
• Paul Antick

For many people, electing to visit places like Auschwitz represents, in part, not only a desire to suspend the present by immersing oneself in the physical residues of the past, but also a perverse wish to be moved or affected by the specific events to which such uncanny environments refer. To experience, in other words, what Ulrich Baer calls a "traumatic flashback"; something that may well "hark back to its temporal frame in the past" but which also, paradoxically, resonates with meanings that derive their potency from events that are firmly situated in the present.[1]

Baer's use of the term 'trauma' is interesting. If the "flashback" he refers to is the articulation of a symptom of some prior event (the Holocaust), the memory of which has long since been repressed, then it follows—for Freud at least—that one can only manifest such a symptom if one has in fact actually experienced the event that gave rise to it. Clearly, for most visitors this is unlikely to be the case. (I should add that, in this essay, I will not be referring to those with first-hand experience of the camps—a quite different category of visitor about whose experiences I neither have the wish nor the knowledge to remark upon). So perhaps what Baer is actually referring to is a metaphorical or pseudo-symptom—a postmodern symptom of sorts—something that realises itself through a sudden, yet meticulously planned and much anticipated, jolt; an emotional and physical manifestation of a pseudo-trauma, triggered not by a repressed incident in one's own personal life history, but the position one consciously assumes in relation to the various forms, rites and rituals of Holocaust 'remembrance'.

The masochistic desire for "traumatic flashback" which must, to varying degrees, be the motor that propels many visitors toward such places is both cultivated and precipitated—although probably never satisfied—by the various techniques used to represent the savage events that occurred 60 years ago at places like Auschwitz, Chelmno, Belzec, Sobibor, Treblinka and Majdanek.[2] One can, for example, wander unaccompanied round the formal and informal spaces and architectures of mass extermination that remain. One can run one's fingers along the rough stone walls of the women's barracks at Auschwitz, stand alone in what was once a gas chamber at Majdanek, traipse around the empty field that is all that remains of the death camp at Chelmno, as if they had really been there (which in one sense, of course, they were). However, where they really are is at the representational epicentre of what is now no longer present—incarceration, humiliation, slaughter, genocide—and what one is party to, as James Young puts it, is an act of administration (which is to say the administration of memory). But how might we begin to conceptualise the relationship between memory, affect and the commodification and consumption of those sites and spaces associated with the Holocaust?

Unlike the genocide itself, which was relatively exclusive, 'Holocaust tourism' is an experience that potentially remains as freely available to Germans as it is Poles and as affecting for non-Jews as it is Jews. However, the democratisation of the Holocaust, if one can call it that, of which Holocaust tourism is an index, has recently given rise to a number of anxieties that are as pertinent to the representation of the Holocaust's affective economies: who now feels and how; who then suffered, how, to what extent and why.

In particular, I want to focus on the affective economies of Holocaust tourism and the ways in which constructing an understanding of such economies—specifically in art historian, Griselda Pollock's exemplary text, "Holocaust Tourism: Being There, Looking Back and the Ethics of Spatial Memory"—can often serve to foreclose the possibility of not only acknowledging the experiential and ontological complexities of the subject of mass tourism but also the contemporary Jewish subject (something which to my mind does an injustice to the actually existing, often highly nuanced nature of Jewish subjectivity in general).[3]

Specifically, the figure of the 'Jew' in Pollock's essay, which I think may be understood as symptomatic of a deeply reactionary

Certainly from a conservative Jewish perspective it is precisely that yearning for a 'golden age' of unmediated subjectivity that transcends the vicissitudes of history that appears to characterise such utterances. In other words, the figure of the 'impure' or assimilated Jew has come to resemble, for commentators like Bertram Gold (former head of the American Jewish Committee), as great a threat to Jewish identity as the tourist is to the sanctity of places like Auschwitz.[14]

The relationship between assimilation and subjectivity can perhaps be conceived of in two ways: the assimilated subject as totally occupied by the culture of the 'other', something that leads to a loss of one's 'authentic' sense of self. This, it is often assumed, takes the form of a defensive and highly stylised mimetic gesture that functions, in the first instance, to reassure the host culture that the more intolerable aspects of racial and cultural difference have been erased or, at least, suspended. More productively, perhaps, we might conceive of cultural assimilation as a process where the Jewish self adapts itself to the host culture in such a way that innovative, hybrid, albeit often problematic, forms of identity arise which are neither purely 'Jewish' nor entirely assimilated.[15] Either way, the kinds of anxieties that cultural assimilation can give rise to are invariably premised on a perceived sense of loss, or lack of, cultural authenticity. (Ironically, this often characterises the attitude of the host culture towards those who assimilate as much as it does the latter's attitudes toward the act of assimilation itself.) Either way, the notion of ethnic purity often remains synonymous with the idea of authenticity and it is precisely the spectre of the impure, assimilated Jew—whose absence haunts Pollock's text—that is effectively displaced onto the figure of the tourist. Moreover, it is the figure of the modern, assimilated Jew—which, from a conservative point of view, remains an incoherent, irrational and deeply fragmented figure that threatens to extinguish the basis of an authentic Jewish identity—that motivates the ways in which some conservative Jewish institutions

have framed the contemporary significance of the Holocaust and, in so doing, implicitly specifies precisely what constitutes an appropriate form of engagement with it.

It may be true that many Jewish visitors do not go to Auschwitz "to be informed", as Pollock suggests. It may also be true that, for many Jewish visitors, the Holocaust itself is 'over-known'. This is not to say, however, that visits undertaken by the ideal-type Jewish pilgrim purported by Pollock take place in a social, cultural and ideological vacuum or that contemporary needs—political and ideological—do not serve to partially determine the ways in which the Holocaust, as both spectacle and memorial, might be engaged with.

In *The Holocaust in American Life* Peter Novick examines the ways in which "present concerns determine what of the past we remember and how we remember it".[16] In so doing, Novick points to the fact that the collective American memory of the Holocaust—both Jewish and non-Jewish—is, to a large extent, an effect of the various politically and ideologically motivated ways in which the Holocaust has been deployed in American life. It is by adopting this approach that Novick refuses the kind of essentialist preoccupations with notions of race and subjectivity that implicitly motivate the concerns of conservative writers like Pollock; embracing instead an approach that foregrounds the relationship between ideology, history and experience.

For Novick a raft of issues—including Jewish assimilation and the ideological uses (and abuses) of the Holocaust itself—have all contributed to the various ways in which some representatives of the Jewish community in America have deployed the Holocaust and Israel to precipitate a series of shifts in the ways in which it has sought to represent itself both to itself and culture at large.[17] As Novick asserts, since the mid-1970s, the "American Jewish leadership, in response to a perception that needs had changed, has chosen to centre the Holocaust—to combat what they saw as a 'new anti-semitism'—in support of an embattled Israel; as the basis of revived ethnic consciousness".[18] In this way Novick persuades us that responses to the Holocaust by the Jewish establishment—and, arguably therefore, many so called 'Holocaust pilgrims'—are historically contingent and, as such, motivated by concerns over the degenerative effects of assimilation: what Sheldon Engelmayer provocatively refers to as a "bloodless" or "spiritual Holocaust". In this context, the figure of the Jew—the authentic Jew—is primarily a redemptive character. Fuelled by the memory of the Holocaust, his/her mission is to propel the latter day Children of Israel back to Zion (both actually and metaphorically); to the mythic and spatial cradle of an authentic Jewish civilisation, to a space that invariably includes the contested areas of so-called Samaria and Judea: the occupied West Bank.

In a similar vein Jack Kugelmass argues that, far from entering into an unmediated encounter with the Holocaust itself, the Holocaust pilgrim is endeavouring to "make past time present". Kugelmass suggests that "in so doing they are symbolically reversing reality: they are transposing themselves from what they are currently perceived as—in America as highly privileged, and in Israel as oppressive—[and] presenting themselves as the diametric opposite [to] what they in fact were".

If Theodor Adorno and Max Horkheimer's critique of mass culture was intended to explain how it impacted upon the Germans' ability to resist the onset of Nazism during the 1930s, what it also implies is their need to turn away from the confusion and complexities of the social, economic and cultural upheavals in Weimar Germany after the First World War, to the neatly packaged world of mass popular culture; with its easily digested narratives, unambiguous cast of 'goodies' and 'baddies' and predictably happy endings.[19] Such a world presented a repetitive series of reassuring fictions that did not threaten the political and cultural *status quo* but instead represented a sublimated longing for stability, predictability and 'good cheer' on the part of the German consumer. To paraphrase Kugelmass, mass culture—for many Germans—represented a

journey to a much simpler present in the same way that the Holocaust pilgrimage, for many Jews today, represents a journey to a much simpler past.[20]

If commentators such as Novick are correct in arguing that "the Holocaust's attraction is its very lack of ambiguity", in order to assess precisely how such ideologically driven 'clarities' might specifically manifest themselves, we need to return to Auschwitz and consider the relationship between ideology, affect and what Carol Zemel calls "the Holocaust sublime".[21]

The Holocaust sublime is the "acts of witness intended to transport us to the brink of human existence, to a space between life and death… edging us into barely imaginable terrors".[22] It is the experience—a cumulative effect of the visitor's encounter with various objects; suitcases, shoes, photographs, barracks, cells, gas chambers, memorials, tour guide information, as well as the actual and symbolic enormity of the sites themselves—that denotes, for both pilgrim and tourist, a point of entry into the very 'essence' of the Holocaust. An essence that is, paradoxically (as Novick and Pollock suggest), historically and culturally and/or ethnically contingent.[23] Which is to say that for Pollock, it remains an integral part of the pilgrim's "visit of memory", whereas for Novick and Kugelmass it is the definitive affective feature of the instrumentalisation of the Holocaust. In short, it is not Auschwitz that necessarily makes the impact of the sublime meaningful, but the reciprocal relation that exists between Auschwitz the site, those stories about Auschwitz that are disseminated at Auschwitz, and that body of discourse within which the pilgrim is already enmeshed prior to his or her actual visit.

Together, the site, those stories and that discourse render the sublime intelligible and lend it some measure of cultural value. This, for many pilgrims, remains inextricably tied to an essentialist, one-dimensional and often masochistic notion of Jewish identity that, in turn, is compelled by the redemptive 'primacy' of the State of Israel.

itourist? billboard 4
(Auschwitz-Birkenau, 2004),
London, 2006
© Paul Antick.

For the tourist, the Holocaust sublime—while no doubt equally affecting—is imagined, by critics like Pollock, to be on a par with any other popular cultural experience whose primary aim is a purely sensual form of sadomasochistic gratification. Sadistic because one effectively finds oneself at Auschwitz in a position of mastery (the Holocaust is, apparently, ethically and morally speaking, a perfectly unambiguous event) and masochistic because one is always invited to identify with its victims, never its perpetrators. Thus, in the same way that the sadomasochistic pleasures available in viewing a Hollywood suspense movie, for example, represent the kernel or locus of the viewers' desire so, it is implicitly suggested, the Holocaust becomes subsumed by a quest for the 'base', 'quasi-pornographic' characteristics of mass culture. Of course, for the actual tourist—for whom the Holocaust is no more or less ideological than it is for the Jewish visitor—the Holocaust sublime might serve to simultaneously locate them on the cusp of several affective economies; economies of guilt, pleasure, contemplation, awe, even alienation. Conceivably, however, the same might be said of many Jewish visitors, which, if this were the case, would suggest a very different kind of sensibility than either Novick or Pollock describe.

According to Göran Therborn, "interpellation can never really be effective, as ideologies have an inherently dialectical character, while complex social processes mean that ideologies overlap, compete and clash, drown or reinforce each other".[24] Therborn's remarks are especially pertinent to the subject of assimilation. For it is the assimilated self who finds themselves subject to a deafening chorus of invitations, or demands, from one subject or another.[25] Such pleas enjoin him or her to identify with one or many—often contradictory—subject positions: Jew as pilgrim, Jew as Zionist, Jew as anti-Zionist, Jew as American citizen or simply as the undifferentiated subject of mass consumption; and thus, in this respect, more or less indistinguishable from any other Western subject.

The fact that one's assumed position as a member of one or other ethnic, cultural or religious grouping may inflect the mode in which one consumes with some feature peculiar to that group means that, in order to understand the nuanced, messy nature of subjectivity we cannot afford to think of these different registers of identification as mutually exclusive but, rather, as overlapping and often contradictory. Thus, out of the chaos of subjectivity emerges the spectre of the dialectic; a raft of internal contradictions which, for both the reflexive and non-reflexive subject alike, often produces a kind of crisis of subjectivity. A symptom of which are those feelings of shame and guilt that are often attendant on ones effectively being designated a 'non-person' (which is arguably the case for the Jewish visitor who—like myself—for whatever reason, is unable to seamlessly identify with the dominant or available versions of Jewishness implicitly mapped out in Pollock's essay).

In taking issue with Louis Althusser's 'monistic' theory of interpellation, Peter Dews argues that, "the cry with which the subject greets us must always be interpreted; and there is no guarantee that we will do this in the proper fashion".[26] This is not to say, however, that being presented with a perfectly unified image of the ideal-type Jewish response at Auschwitz—and finding oneself not only unable to identify with it entirely but, moreover, identifying with certain 'impure' features of the tourist experience—will not in any way be experienced as troubling. Indeed in the absence of any alternative, 'alter-ideological' images of Jewishness (images that, in the first instance, serve to confirm the basis of one's own uncertainties and thus enable one to transform uncertainty into 'certainty' through a reciprocal process of identification and self-legitimation) this is bound to be the case. For it is precisely in limiting the possibilities available to the subject—providing him or her with images they are unable to empathise with—that they are cast beyond the symbolic order altogether and into the realm of psychosis or 'non-identity'.[27] In other words, in order to constitute oneself as a subject (however ideological this might be) it seems that one needs to find a likely position, or image, with which to identify.

In this way the messy, often inconsistent and contradictory nature of identity—as pertinent to tourists as it is Jews—is characteristically written out of Pollock's and other similar stories. What we have here instead is a deceptively homogenous, deeply romantic notion of Jewishness (not to mention an epistemologically crude image of the tourist) that refuses to engage with the myriad possibilities, difficulties and—often uncomfortable—consequences of assimilation.

Ironically it is precisely the refusal to acknowledge the existence of profoundly complex internal cultural differences—Jews as working class, poorly educated consumers of mass culture, as opposed to the archetypically quirky, learned modern bourgeois— that marks a point of similarity between the kinds of philosemitic images of Jewishness disseminated by writers like Griselda Pollock and artists such as Rachel Whiteread and the rabidly anti-semitic images promulgated by the Nazis.[28] When Adolf Hitler wrote in *Mein Kampf* that "the Jew has no culture", he was referring to all Jews.[29] He did not attempt to distinguish Jewish society or culture in terms of its various social, spatial or political orientations; there was no need. Identifying a causal link between a negative set of specifically Jewish characteristics—materialistic, uncultured, and so on—and the notion of race effectively guaranteed the production of a perfectly unified, homogenous idea of 'Jewishness'. Establishing a crude, causal link between the idea of race or ethnicity, collective memory and the specificities of consumption does, in its own rather more benign way, precisely the same thing.

Today there appears to be an acute, sometimes painful, split between the spaces within which Jewish experience is visually and linguistically represented and thus legitimated and—for want of a better expression—the 'real world'. (That complicated space where actual Jewish identities find themselves being played out, reproduced, contested and altered in often fraught and complex ways.) The manner in which identity is negotiated, the way in which we 'come to terms' with it is contingent—to varying degrees—on the relationship that exists between the 'real' and the 'symbolic'. One of the problems at present—specifically where Jewish identity is concerned—is the fact that the possibilities for re-imagining it at the level of representation simply do not square with the increasingly fluid ways in which contemporary Jewish identity might potentially realise itself in concrete environments like Auschwitz. Thus if identity, or at least the authentication by some external agency of one's sense of self, is constituted through an engagement with the field of representation then it would seem that too many images—those in Pollock's essay for example—are simply not up to the task. Indeed, although usefully addressing certain features of Holocaust tourism, Pollock's authoritarian image of the ideal-type Holocaust encounter ultimately serves to exclude or de-legitimate many others. As I have argued, in the vein of Novick, there are good ideological reasons for this. In certain quarters, as we have seen, it is clearly important to designate certain experiences 'non-experiences' and certain identities, 'non-identities'. However, from the point of view of one who effectively finds himself trapped, once again, in this 'non-place' I find myself attempting to absent myself from Pollock's panoptic gaze in order to do a little gazing of my own. Whether or not it is an 'authentically Jewish' gaze, I have no idea.

Evacuations: De-colonising Architecture
• Eyal Weizman

On the morning of 12 September 2005, Israeli forces completed their withdrawal from the Gaza Strip. The gate through which the last Israeli—Brigadier General, Aviv Kochavi, commander of the Gaza Division—left was immediately covered with sand piled up by military bulldozers after his exit. Kochavi, who would order his forces to re-enter Gaza nine months later, convened a small press conference at which he hastily announced: "Our mission has been completed.... Israel's 38 year presence [in Gaza] has come to an end."

Behind it, the military left the bulldozed rubble of more than 3,000 buildings; mainly single-family homes, but also public buildings, schools, military installations, and industrial and agricultural facilities built for the benefit of the 21 settlements and the scores of military bases that protected them (incidentally, around the same number as that of Palestinian homes destroyed by the Israeli military in Gaza since the start of the second Intifada in 2000).[1] An Israeli journalist who visited the Gaza settlements a few days before the evacuation described "mounds of building rubble piled at the centre of what used to be private gardens… the disturbing stench of food remains… pools of water and sewage… endless swarms of flies… and miles upon miles of nylon packing rolls".[2] The only structures remaining afloat on the swamp of debris and liquid waste were the 19 synagogues of Gaza, whose destruction was halted by an Israeli High Court of Justice ruling and a last-minute government vote. One of the synagogues—designed as a three-dimensional extrusion of a Star of David and built of reinforced concrete (in order that, as its architect Gershon Shevah stated, "Jews [can] rid themselves of their diasporic complex")—best embodied the aesthetic immediacy and inevitable fate of the art of Israeli occupation.[3] A day after the withdrawal, Palestinian youth completed what the High Court of Justice had left undone, and torched the synagogue buildings. Thousands of Palestinian flags, of all organisations, and banners displaying images of many Palestinian leaders and 'martyrs', were raised over the settlement rubble. The

Palestinian Authority organised guided tours and renamed some of the ruined settlements after dead militants and leaders. The ruins of Neve Dekalim became Yasser Arafat City, and those of Kfar Darom, Sheikh Ahmed Yassin City. After the celebrations were over most of the destroyed settlements were occupied by militant organisations. Those close to the border were used as launching sites for Qassam rockets against Israeli towns and villages adjacent to Gaza. Israeli Air Force bombing and the constant pounding of Israeli artillery routinely shuffled the remaining mounds of rubble, reinforcing what the Israeli military called an "aerially enforced closure" meant to make the evacuated areas 'off limit' to all Palestinians.

Prior to the withdrawal, and ignorant of the impending destruction of the settlements, a number of local and international interested parties speculated upon several alternative scenarios for the possible re-use of buildings in the settlements. The impending evacuation opened up a unique arena of speculation, in which, between April 2004, when the plans for evacuations were firmed up, and August 2005, when they were carried out, some of the world's most powerful international players grappled with questions that normally belong to the domain of architecture and planning. Although the evacuation was conceived and undertaken as a unilateral Israeli operation, the fate of settlement buildings was debated by America, Europe, the UN, the World Bank, the International Monetary Fund (IMF), some of the wealthiest Arab property developers, a variety of NGOs and security and policy think tanks. In addition, the different political parties within Palestine and Israel also had differing opinions, ideas and proposals. In the political rhetoric that surrounded the period immediately prior to evacuation, homes have alternately been referred to as physical entities embodying power relations, as symbols to a set of ideologies, as sentient (even haunted) active agents, as military weapons or ammunitions, bargaining chips, economic resources, accumulation of toxic waste or instruments of crime.

Gaza Evacuation,
August 2005
Photographs by
Miki Kratsman.

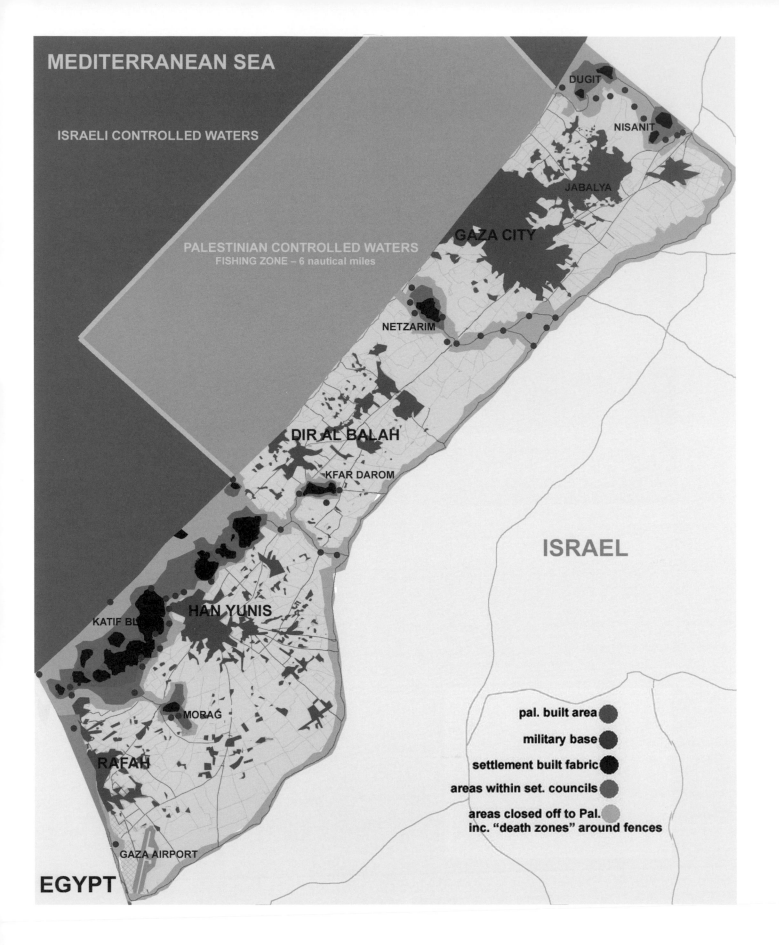

MEDITERRANEAN SEA

ISRAELI CONTROLLED WATERS

PALESTINIAN CONTROLLED WATERS
FISHING ZONE – 6 nautical miles

DUGIT

NISANIT

JABALYA

GAZA CITY

NETZARIM

DIR AL BALAH

KFAR DAROM

ISRAEL

HAN YUNIS

KATIF BL

MORAG

RAFAH

GAZA AIRPORT

EGYPT

pal. built area

military base

settlement built fabric

areas within set. councils

areas closed off to Pal.
inc. "death zones" around fences

Although all aspirations to re-use the settlement architecture were later flattened into the debris of their destruction, these visions are nevertheless valuable in contemplating the potential re-use of Israel's architecture of occupation; if and when the rest of the occupied territories are reclaimed by Palestinians. Furthermore, these plans present us with a rare opportunity to examine more general problems associated with the re-use of the architecture of exclusion, violence, and control, at the moment when such architecture is unplugged from the socio-political-military power that created and sustained it. The ritual destruction, re-use, *redivivus*, or *détournement* of the single-family house may even suggest a possible repertoire of actions for its possible transformations at large.

State of Architectural Emergency

The economy of the Gaza settlements had been based mostly on agriculture—in particular hothouse crops for European export—and was sustained by low-paid workers from China and Thailand who gradually replaced Palestinian workers since the Oslo process began. 17 of the settlements were concentrated within the large enclave of Gush Katif on the southwestern beachfront of Gaza, the rest were strategically positioned as isolated strongholds near Palestinian cities and refugee camps, or as traffic valves on the main routes connecting them. The more 'isolated' settlements also acted as bridgeheads for military operations in Palestinian urban areas. After the start of the second Intifada in September 2000, some of the settlements were surrounded by eight to 12 metre high concrete walls constructed of the same modular components used to build the wall in the West Bank. Hundreds of Palestinian homes and numerous acres of Palestinian orchards surrounding the settlement walls were destroyed in what the Israeli Defence Forces

(IDF) called "landscape exposure operations" aiming to remove cover for putative Palestinian attacks. Seen from the air, the settlements appeared as pleasant, green islands, resting in the middle of a series of concrete cylinders (the surrounding walls) and woven together by a thick web of infrastructure (roads for the exclusive use of settlers).

In the weeks leading up to the August 2005 evacuation, the architects and planners of the Palestinian Ministry of Planning operated under 'state of emergency' regulations: all holidays and weekend vacations were postponed and routine work suspended. The fact that architecture and planning were seen as services essential enough to be included in a state of emergency demonstrates the prominent status of the built environment and its transformations in this context. The Ministry became the centre of intense meetings between Palestinians and a variety of NGOs, different UN agencies, the World Bank, foreign governments and international investors, who all outlined their proposed use for the evacuated settlements. The building itself appeared like a fortified beehive too small to contain all of these delegations, especially since the number of people making up each doubled when foreigners were obliged to maintain personal bodyguards.

Israeli discussions about the fate of the settlement buildings focused on the potential symbolic effect of Israeli architecture under Palestinian control. Representing the attitudes of the right wing faction of the Likud party, Benjamin Netanyahu—who later resigned his office of Finance Minister in protest at the evacuation—demanded that all settlement homes be destroyed. This was purportedly in order to avoid the broadcast of what he felt were ideologically destructive images: Arabs living in the homes of Jews and synagogues turning into mosques. The Palestinians "will dance on our rooftops", Netanyahu warned, referring to broadcasts aired on Israeli television during the 1991 Gulf War, which showed Palestinians standing on rooftops in Ramallah cheering Iraqi Scud missiles aimed at Israeli cities—overlooking the fact that the roofs of most settlement homes are in fact pitched and tiled. His rhetoric conjured up images of a murderous Palestinian mob storming the gates of settlements, looting and re-occupying the homes of 'decent' settlers. This "apocalyptic scenario", he feared, would become the image for a reversal—and thus imply the reversibility—of a Zionist project previously characterised by the seizure, destruction and, in some cases, re-occupation of Palestinian dwellings that became highly prized real estate among an 'orientalised' Israeli bourgeoisie. Images, broadcast internationally, of the evacuated settlements taken over by Palestinians may have as well triggered barely-repressed middle class anxieties at the root of the suburban project itself: the internally ordered, well-serviced outposts of a 'First World' collapsing in the face of a 'barbaric' surge of the 'Third World' irrupting on it from the outside. Together with a vision of technological superiority, it may have been this fear that prompted a high ranking Israeli military officer, inspired by newly developed techniques for building relocation, to seriously propose rolling settlement homes across the border on steel tracks.

The American administration was opposed to the destruction of the settlements. Handing over homes, public buildings, agricultural and industrial assets was seen by President Bush and Condoleezza Rice as more than a mere economic stimuli.[4] What could better befit the American agenda of civilising the Middle East into a liberal society with broad middle class values than having Palestinians live in American-style single-family homes? In response to American demands, the Israeli government announced that it would reconsider its decision to demolish settlement homes. Deputy Prime Minister, Shimon Peres, sought to sell them to the Palestinians or to give them 'on account' of any claims Palestinians might make for the homes they were forced to leave behind in 1948 in areas now under Israeli control.[5] Mohamed Alabbar, the flamboyant Arab businessman, arrived in Israel six months prior to the evacuation, met with Shimon Peres and briefly with Sharon, and offered to buy all the homes and other real estate assets in the settlements of Gush Katif for 56 million dollars. Alabbar is the chairman of Emaar Properties, a gigantic real estate company registered in the United Arab Emirates that has been a central player in the frantic development of Dubai, specialising in rapid construction of themed onshore tourist and residential projects. He imagined Gush Katif to become a possible tourist enclave.[6] This resulted in bizarre and grotesque plans for Dubai-style, large high-rise hotel complexes, and settler homes becoming a part of a set of tourist villages, on what was now dubbed 'the best beach resort of the Mediterranean'. If they had come to fruition, such complexes would no doubt have become extra-territorial enclaves set against the deep poverty that surrounded them. These fantasies would have robbed Palestinians of the evacuated land to which they are entitled to, and desperately need, as a public.

It was therefore no wonder that, when Palestinians were asked to pay for the structures by which the occupation of their lands was excercised that they responded angrily. Palestinian minister, Saeb Erekat, stated that the Palestinians were not interested in purchasing the infrastructure and told Israel simply to "dismantle the houses and take them away".[7] Jihad Al-wazir, permanent secretary of the Palestinian Ministry of Planning, claimed that "the settlements are an alien body that was forced on the Palestinians", and that if it were up to him, he would "have a big bonfire [of the settlements]... where every Palestinian should come with a hammer and bang on a building".[8] In Israel, these and other similar Palestinian pronouncements were interpreted as bluffs, rather than as sincere rejection, in the context of haggling over the price of the homes. Accordingly, Israel continued 'playing pocker' over prices up to the final weeks before the evacuation.

In November 2004, I attended a discussion regarding the fate of the Gaza settlements in Shaml, the Palestinian Diaspora and Refugee Centre in Ramallah. There, proposals that Palestinians reside in evacuated settlement homes were met with objection, even aversion: "How could anyone expect us to reside in the same homes, look out of the same windows, use the same rooms, that our oppressors have used?" Architecture was commonly understood as one of the direct instruments of occupation. For one of the speakers the settlements even seemed to be haunted—a settlement site in the West Bank was referred to as Tel A Jnein, "hill of the demons". In Palestine/Israel—where almost every act of settlement is an act of erasure and re-inhabitation—each side considers different locations haunted. Here, no one is ever the 'first' or 'original' occupier; but being a subsequent—either to one's present day enemies or to an imagined or real ancient civilisation—is a condition that turns the inhabitation of old cities, archaeological sites, battlegrounds and destroyed villages into culturally complex acts of co- or trans-habitation.[9] Buildings have themselves acquired an active role in the unfolding political drama. Not only were the settlement houses seen as haunted sites containing 'ghosts', but they themselves also seemed to have acquired a kind of subjectivity in which architectural elements were seen as living organs. To be exorcised, architecture must burn to produce, in Alwazir's view, a "cathartic release".[10]

Other grounds for objection to the re-inhabitation of settlement homes were articulated in the typical language of planning. While settlement homes might suit families of three to six, an extended family in Gaza is more than double this size. Furthermore, the 1,500 homes that were to be evacuated were seen as irrelevant in the face of the urgent housing needs of more than half a million Palestinians.

Plans drawn up by the Palestinian Ministry of Planning anticipated the destruction of most settlements and the reruralisation of the evacuated areas. I was shown the masterplans for the area of the coastal Katif settlement block by Khalil Nijem, Director General of the Ministry of Planning in Ramallah; they were coloured with different shades of solid and hatched green, delineating the nature reserves, recreational areas and beaches that would replace the evacuated settlements. This *tabula rasa* scenario resonated well with an awakened nostalgia for the period before the occupation, when Gazans had access to such sites located among the white sand dunes on the shores of the Mediterranean.[11]

Several months before the evacuation was scheduled to begin, the appointment of James Wolfensohn, formerly president of the World Bank, to the newly created office of Special Envoy for Gaza Disengagement on behalf of America, the UN, Europe, and the Russian Federation testified to the broad international commitment to and engagement with the project. However, it also highlighted the kind of economic approach these countries wanted to adopt. Although Wolfensohn initially attempted to broker a "peaceful handover of all structures", and even gave half a million dollars of his own money to help buy back Israeli greenhouses for the use of Gazan farmers, other economical prospects caused him to change his mind. Working in cooperation with the World Bank under the presidency of the arch neo-conservative, Paul Wolfowitz, and in line with its reflex response of privatisation, Wolfensohn assembled a coalition of wealthy property developers, including Alabbar, who would invest large sums of money in exchange for long leases on the evacuated land for various schemes of private development.[12]

De-camping Refugees

Seeing other prospects for development, Europe's foreign policy coordinator, Javier Solana, wanted the "settlement villas" destroyed and removed in order "to make way for high-rise construction" for the housing of refugees.[13] The Palestinian Ministry of Planning itself examined proposals submitted to it by the Foundation for Middle East Peace, the Washington DC-based think tank that proposed, in the context of similar evacuations in the West Bank, that refugees would be resettled in settlements close to Palestinian cities.[14]

Proposals to house Palestinian refugees in the abandoned settlement homes, or in European-style housing blocks built in their place, treaded a political minefield. Attempts to implement permanent housing for refugees would be perceived by many Palestinians as the undoing of the temporary nature of the refugee camps and, with it, the physical proof for the urgency of the Palestinian claim for return to the places from where they were deported in 1948. For many refugees having an address in the camp maintains the address in the lost city or village. Sometimes building a new house in the camp could be seen as a betrayal of the national cause, and it is primarily the younger generation that rejects plans for reconstruction.[15] A sense of temporariness is often maintained by Palestinians political organisations, in their insistence on keeping the infrastructure in camps to a bare minimum. Sewage often runs over ground, trees are not planted, and other signs of permanence are avoided.[16] The refugee camp is thus kept in an Orwellian "endless present" without past and with no future. This policy became apparent in the 1970s when, under the influence of Marxist ideology (then prevalent within the Palestine Liberation Organisation) domestication was seen as anathema to the Palestinian revolution. The 'permanent revolution' relied on the negation of the home as a sign of bourgeois culture. Maintaining the temporary, harsh conditions in the camps also formed part of the revolutionary guerrilla warfare that is termed in French *la politique du pire*—the politics of making conditions worse—the worse things get, the deeper the crisis, the faster political change would arise.[17]

It is thus not surprising that counter revolutionary approaches often tried to induce domestication. From British-built New Villages in Malasia through to the Portuguese *Aldeamentos* in Angola, and the French *Douars* in Algeria, resettlement projects were carried out as central components of strategies of 'counter insurgency' and pacifications, demonstrating that the default response to the violence of the colonised has always been increased

spatial discipline. These housing projects were seen as part of a general colonial policy variously referred to as 'modernisation', 'urbanisation', 'civilisation', 'hygienisation', 'de-peasantisation' or as in our context, the 'de-camping' of refugees.

In the eyes of the IDF, refugee camps were seen not only as the place in which the resistance is located and organised, but as the socio-physical environment that creates it. Throughout the occupation, periodic attempts by the IDF to upgrade infrastructure and living standards in the very places it believed its enemies are located, attempted to both eradicate what were believed to be the breeding grounds of discontent and enforce a process of 'embourgoisement' that would reduce the motivation of the urban population to support active resistance.

According to a comprehensive study conducted by Palestinian sociologist Norma Masriyeh Hazboun, it is for this very reason that the rehousing of refugees has been a central part of Israeli strategic thinking since the 1967 War, when Israel gained control over Gaza and the West Bank where many refugee camps were located.[18] For Israeli politicians and military officers, turning refugees into city or village dwellers was thought to resolve 'the refugee problem', itself seen as the main precondition of the conflict, and reflected their belief that political problems can be reduced to socio-economic or even urban ones. Indeed, the first proposals for construction in the occupied territories, debated by the Israeli government immediately after the 1967 War, were not only for the building of Israeli settlements, but for the provision of new homes for Palestinian refugees from Gaza.[19] A central component of the Allon Plan sought to "liquidate the refugee problem" by the gradual evacuation of the camps into new, specially conceived towns and villages to be built by Israel with the help of international funding in some particularly arid parts of the West Bank and in northern Sinai.[20] The plan included outlines for the construction of three pilot settlements/ towns on the eastern slopes of the Hebron Desert where the authorities would monitor whether or not Palestinian refugee families could adapt to the area's harsh climate.[21] In 1968 Prime Minister, Levy Eshkol, was hesitant and ambiguous about these resettlement projects but reminisced how when he was in Africa he "saw how to settle primitive nations" and supported "the building of some kind or another of prefabricated houses [in the Occupied Territories]…".[22] These early plans all came to nothing because the government believed that it is the international community that must fund these schemes, but with the objection of the Arab states, found little international help.

Attempts to rehouse the refugees have thus taken a coercive, violent turn. The destruction in Shati, Jebalia and Rafah refugee camps from 1971–1972 by military forces under Ariel Sharon, then Chief of Southern Command, had yet another intention other than widening the internal roadways and creating a controllable urban plan.[23] It was intended to form the necessary first stage—making the refugees homeless and in need of new homes—in pushing the government to implement a refugee resettlement programme. In his autobiography Sharon later explained that the camps "bred the most serious problems…. It would be to our great advantage to eliminate them once and for all… [and] we should take pains to provide decent housing."[24] The destruction of 6,000 homes in the refugee camps of Gaza intended, in the words of Shlomo Gazit, then the coordinator of government activity in the occupied territories, "to evacuate one third of the Strip's refugee population, about 60,000–70,000 people, to new places…".[25] Out of the 160,000 refugees in Gaza in 1971, Sharon suggested the government resettle 70,000 within new neighbourhoods to be built within the towns of Gaza, another 70,000 he wanted to settle in the cities and towns of the West Bank, and 20,000–30,000 more, controversially, within Palestinian towns in Israel.[26] The idea was not accepted by the government but attempts to house refugees were nevertheless implemented with the support of Minister of Defence, Moshe Dayan. Between 1972

and 1979 four new neighbourhoods for refugees were constructed beside the large camps of the strip. They included Israeli-style dense housing schemes, simply replicating existing plans provided by the Israeli Ministry of Housing, constructed by Palestinian developers. The Israeli government took foreign visitors on tours to show the new housing schemes, claiming they demonstrated their enlightened rule and attempts to solve the 'refugee problem' by providing decent housing. But Dayan also explained the behaviouristic logic of this policy when he claimed that "as long as the refugees remain in their camps… their children will say they come from Jaffa or Haifa; if they move out of the camps, the hope is that they will feel an attachment to their new land".[27] In 1974 another approach for the resettlement of refugees was implemented with a programme in which refugees were provided with plots of 250 square metres and with the means to build their own homes. Financial assistance was handed out on condition that refugees physically demolished their older homes in the camps.[28] Methods used by Israeli occupation authorities to convince reluctant refugees included threats and random demolitions within the camps as well as visits by Palestinian collaborators to refugee households. The Palestinian Liberation Organisation (PLO) forbade refugees to accept these Israeli offers and killed some of those who did as well as many of the Palestinian collaborators.[29] The programme received its last momentum from 1981–1982 when Sharon served as Minister of Defence, and died out after he was fired from government at the beginning of 1983 for his role in the Christian Falangist Massacre in the Palestinian refugee camps of Sabra and Shatila in Lebanon. According to United Nations Relief and Works Agency (UNRWA) records throughout the entire duration of the programme, about 10,000 homes for refugees were provided by Israel in total, housing a population that constituted 18 per cent of the total refugee community in the Strip, but amounting annually to little more than the natural demographic growth in the existing camps.[30] Although, some neighbourhoods for

refugees—such as the Sheikh Radwan resettlement scheme north of Gaza City—were successfully constructed and inhabited and even named by the occupation authorities 'Kfar Shalom' (the 'Village of Peace', but referred to mockingly by Palestinians as 'Sharon's Neighbourhood')—the programme failed to subdue Palestinian resistance, and some of the new populated housing areas became themselves centres of resistance.[31]

Re-inhabiting De-colonised Architecture

The Palestinian reluctance to re-inhabit the evacuated Gaza settlements in 2005 was also to resist a strong temptation present throughout the history of de-colonisation. Colonial buildings and infrastructures left behind when their regimes were dismantled were usually recuperated by newly formed postcolonial administrations. Such repossession tended to reproduce some of the colonial power relations in space: colonial villas were inhabited by new financial elites, and palaces by political ones, while the evacuated military installations of colonial armies were often used to prop up new national regimes. Frantz Fanon, pondering the possible corruption of national, postcolonial governments, warned during the Algerian liberation struggle that, if not destroyed, the physical and territorial reorganisation of the colonial world may once again "mark out the lines on which a colonised society will be organised".[32]

In Mandatory Palestine, during the Arab Revolt of 1936–1939, British forces erected a string of military installations near or within Palestinian cities. Most British military infrastructure that remained in Israeli territory after the war of 1948 later served as police stations and military bases. Some of these bases, built within Palestinian areas, were perfectly placed to continue the tactical task of population control for which they were originally built.[33] Some participants in the round table discussion in Shaml in

Ramallah warned that, following these patterns of colonial re-use, postcolonial adaptation of the evacuated Israeli settlements in Gaza might reproduce something of the alienation, hostility and violence of the occupation in turning into 'luxury' Palestinian suburbs.

However, evacuated colonial architecture does not necessarily reproduce its previous use. The evacuated British military infrastructure in the West Bank and Gaza became the nuclei for refugee camps. The Balata refugee camp, at the eastern entrance to the city of Nablus, and the Rafah refugee camp, at the southern edge of the Gaza Strip, are both established within evacuated British military bases. Laid out according to a gridded, military geometry, these camps have now surrendered to the formless topologies of everyday human activity. Unable to expand, they have outgrown their original layout, forming dense maze-like environments.

The subversion of the original use of evacuated colonial settlements was also apparent in the fate of the first Israeli settlements evacuated. The town of Yamit, and the agrarian settlements surrounding it on Sinai's northern Mediterranean coast, were raised to the ground after an evacuation conducted by Sharon, in 1982. Sharon's rational was to avoid an "Egyptian town of one hundred thousand on Israel's border".[34] However, the Israeli settlements of Sinai's Red Sea coast—Neviot (Nuweba), Di Zahav (Dahab) and Ophira (Sharm el Sheik)—were left intact and begot different fates. Around the military and civilian infrastructural nucleus of the former Israeli town of Ophira, Sharm el Sheikh has grown into an international tourist town, hosting more than one million tourists annually. The airport of Sharm el-Sheikh, busy with charter flights carrying European holidaymakers, is an ex-Israeli military airport, (which still carries the name Ophira). Neviot, a small cooperative agricultural settlement of the Moshav type, has become home to Egyptian police personnel and their families. The evacuated Moshav settlement and desert retreat of Di-Zahav provided the infrastructure for the expansion of the tourist village of Dahab.

In the spring and summer of 2005 I took part, together with Palestinian and Norwegian planners of the Palestinian Ministry of Planning, in the architectural formulation of another approach for the re-use of the Gaza settlements. In this scheme, the settlement buildings would be re-used but for a function other than housing. According to this plan, they would be transformed into public institutions: hospitals, clinics, schools, academies and training, educational and cultural centres. If the geography of occupation was to be liberated, we thought, its potential should turn against itself.

In May 2005—four months before the evacuation was scheduled to take place—the Ministry of Planning succeeded in convincing the rest of the Palestinian government to allocate three of the settlements, Morag, Netzarim and Kfar Darom, to public institutions. From the Israeli perspective these smaller colonies, strategically built like frontier outposts outside the main settlement-blocks, were isolated (however, in relation to the Palestinian towns they were built to confront, they were very close and potentially an extension of their fabric). The architectural challenge was to spatialise a set of public institutions into the repetitive domestic shells of evacuated settlement homes. To this end, the settlement of Morag was designated an agricultural education centre, an extension of the University of Gaza. Its single-family homes were to be classrooms, libraries and storage facilities. Some of the small private gardens, surrounding fields and greenhouses were to be devoted to horticultural education. The built infrastructure of Kfar Darom, meanwhile, would be given over to the International Committee of Red Cross for use as a hospital and medical campus. The large agricultural storage facilities of Netzarim settlement were designated to provide facilities for the port of Gaza that was to be built on a nearby stretch of coast. The domestic part of the Netzarim, comprising about 50 small, single-family homes, was to be converted into an education centre. Here, we allocated a place for a growing archive of documents, testimonies, films and photographs, which

were extensively collected by local and international organisations and NGOs throughout the occupation.

Public institutions occupying the mundane fabric of suburban structures, could spawn a new type of institution. They may also help to subvert an entire geography of occupation in the West Bank, with each of the evacuated residential settlements used to a different end than that it was designed and built for.

In the end there was nothing to re-use. Responding to its inner destructive impulses and fearing attempts by settlers to return to their homes, the Israeli government ordered the military to demolish the settlements in their entirety. The World Bank estimated the total amount of rubble generated from this destruction to be in the range of one and a half million tons, between 60 and 80 thousand truckloads. The demolition and the removal of the rubble posed a logistically complex problem as some of the older structures contained large quantities of asbestos. At the end of 2005 Israel and the UN Development Programme (UNDP) signed an agreement regarding this rubble. Israel would pay the UNDP 25 million dollars which would, in turn, pay Palestinian contractors to sort, clear, compact and store the rubble remaining from the destroyed settlement buildings. Without international investments, or the possibility to work in Israel, financing the clear up of the mess it has left behind was presented in a mockingly philanthropic tone as a project "aiming at boosting the economy of the Gaza Strip".[35]

This rubble—composed of the crushed mixture of the homes, public buildings, synagogues, fortifications and military bases that until recently made up Israel's colonial project in Gaza—is now being gradually wheeled into the Mediterranean and deposited there in the form of a large arch; a wave breaker around the site where the port of Gaza is to be built. Standing idle—as the port construction will forever await Israeli security clearance—this giant earthwork jetty may after all demonstrate the best use of the architecture of Israeli occupation.[36]

What Isn't There
• Elle Flanders

Top
What Isn't There (Ayn Karem),
1992–2007
Photo installation
Image courtesy of the artist.

Bottom
What Isn't There (Umm Al-Zinat),
1992–2007
Photo installation
Image courtesy of the artist.

An Informal Architect: Lida Abdul

• Sara Raza

The work of Afghan artist, Lida Abdul, solicits a re-assessment of the local urban space or rather—a more accurate term—the globalised city, which suggests a city or urban space that is both a byproduct of globalisation and the patriarchal power games that are performed in the West and executed in the developing world. In particular, this idea of the city has been a substantial and recognisable influence among the work of Abdul who hails from Kabul; a city with questionable stability (in terms of homeland security) and where portability, both literal and metaphoric, is highly restricted for a variety of reasons—not least war, religion, and poverty resulting from aggressive forms of capitalism.

From her position as a visual-cultural critic, Abdul comments on both real and imaginary urban realities. The visual journey that she carries out implies a unique approach to the poetics of immediacy within the discourse of feminist practices, both actual and assumed, principally defying stereotyped notions of mild and subdued "feminine" or "feminised" approaches concerning gender and ethnicity. The performative works of Abdul employ the use of the body to map out instances of trauma, memory and spatial navigation. In particular, Abdul performs a sense of intellectual remembrance in light of her dislocation from the homeland and also responds to the after effects of war and (male) political games.

Abdul's practice has largely been defined by her personal experiences, which greatly affected her own mobility. Following the Russian invasion of Afghanistan, and the war that followed, Abdul fled Kabul and, as a refugee, travelled from Central Asia to Europe and then to America, settling in LA where she has been based now for almost two decades. The disasters that have fallen upon her country—the Russian invasion, the infiltration of the Taliban regime and the American War on Terror—all inspired Abdul to transfer her experiences of an involuntary (forced) portability into creating highly emotional performances concerning the status of the home and 'homelessness'.

In 2003, Abdul created the *Nomadic House Series*, performances recorded in photographs and video, in which she travels with a wooden, toy house through various deprived urban neighbourhoods in LA. Within these performances, one sees the artist dragging the house across the pavements and roads—sometimes walking, at other times running—resulting in the house colliding with the corner of a wall and smashing to pieces. Her actions mirror the actuality of a broken and fractured home as well as anyone's ability to possess the concept of the home as a pocket sized portable reality. Her choice of location for these performances was an important and premeditated decision; transporting her childhood home from the debris of war-torn Kabul, where millions of American dollars have been spent to maintain an unjust war, to the neglected and poverty stricken innercity areas of LA largely inhabited by black and Latin American citizens, the victims of another war: capitalism. The coupling together of two socially and globally disparate urban environments comments on both familiar and unfamiliar territory. At the same time, by placing herself within another unstable environment, she created a sense of vulnerability concerning the issue of safety as one affecting the ability of all women to perform freely within urban space.

In 2004 Abdul returned to Kabul after almost two decades of separation to create new works that commented on the destruction of the city. Once again the concept of the home was a principle issue for the artist, but in this instance the idea was expanded to include the architecture of the city as a whole, particularly its devastation. By creating a more plural notion of the home Abdul could be said to free the space from any conception of it as a stereotypical feminine domain and instead re-appropriate its meaning to reflect a more unilateral concept about the countless individuals who experience uprootedness, either real or metaphoric. In Kabul the artist produced a new series of works entitled *Painting the Ruins of Kabul*, 2004, in which she was engaged in the act of painting white all visible

remains of the War on Terror, ranging from abandoned army vehicles to the debris of homes, schools and mosques. The act of painting functioned to sanitise the space, freeing it from the constraints of the various ideologies that imposed their power upon the city (and at the same time she marked that which was left unmarked or abandoned as a form of silent witness).

This particular body of work was later expanded in 2005 for new works, like the video *White House*, 2005, that Abdul created especially for the fifty-first Venice Biennale, where she represented Afghanistan. Abdul's *White House* chronicles a journey through the destruction of the city left by both war and men, which can be thought of as inseparable and representative elements of power formations not only in Afghan society, but globally. The title of the piece also echoes and comments on another power house, the actual White House, where world-affecting decisions about the future and policy of developing countries such as Afghanistan are made. Within this piece, Abdul paints a ruined house that exists at the bottom of a hill (another possible parallel with its American counterpart, situated ironically on another hill, Capitol Hill). Within the performance Abdul—after finishing painting the house—diverts her attention to a lone young Afghan man, who has his back turned to the lens of the camera, and proceeds by also painting him white. This deconstructive act is not only a political commentary on the clinical aspect of wiping out—literally bleaching or washing the city of Kabul—it is also a reversal of the celebrated actions in paint of Western modern male artists such as Yves Klein or Jackson Pollock. In Abdul's case, her parodic actions expose the white and masculine vernacular in modern art history, as her canvas here is the city of Kabul. By painting the body of the man, she not only re-appropriates the standardised masculine practice(s) of painting but also highlights the Western or 'white' world's performance of 'bleaching' the Eastern realm and imposing its ideology upon the Afghan people. Therefore it is possible that, by painting the space,

Abdul is also seen to double the negative charge in the work and at the same time signal a potential rebirth of this physical and emotional space.[1]

Opposite, top and bottom
Lida Abdul
White House (Kabul), 2005
16mm film transfered
to DVD, 4'58"
Courtesy of the artist and
Giorgio Persano Gallery.

Overleaf
Lida Abdul
*Clapping with Stones
(Bamiyan)*, 2005
16mm film transfered
to DVD, 4'50"
Courtesy of the artist and
Giorgio Persano Gallery.

Landfills and Lifescapes: The Transformation of New York's Fresh Kills

• Joel McKim

Somewhere buried within the four mounds of refuse that make up the Fresh Kills landfill site on Staten Island lies Gordon Matta-Clark's battered pick-up truck. Herman Meydag, the moniker bestowed on the truck by its owner, failed to survive the confrontation arranged by Matta-Clark in his 1972 film, appropriately entitled *Fresh Kills*. The two bulldozers pitted against the artist's vehicle make quick work of Meydag, the teeth of their steel buckets ripping into the truck's comparatively flimsy red panelling. The truck's pulverised remains are placed ignominiously among the rubbish that forms the stage setting of Matta-Clark's industrial gladiator match. *Fresh Kills* documents a violent but playful act of demolition; a child's compulsion to destroy his matchbox car enacted on an adult scale. Apart from its aggressive, boyish humour, the film is an exploration of a geography that Matta-Clark could hardly have resisted, a resting place for objects one stage further along the cycle of creation and destruction than the abandoned buildings that were the artist's typical targets for intervention.

Before closing in March 2001, Fresh Kills was the world's largest landfill site, infamous for being one of the only man-made constructions visible from space. Between the authorisation of its opening by Robert Moses in 1948 (it was originally intended as a temporary site) and its recent closing, it was the city's busiest rubbish site, receiving 29,000 tons of New Yorkers' household waste daily. The four mounds of landfill that occupy just half of the site's 2,200 acres range in size from 27.4 to 68.6 metres. Despite its menacing name, Fresh Kills in no way indicates the kind of vehicular blood sport organised by Matta-Clark, but instead recalls the days of New Amsterdam, a reference to the Middle Dutch world *kille* meaning riverbed (think Catskills Mountains in the state of New York). The Fresh Kills estuary runs through the centre of the landfill site, bringing water from the Arthur Kill that forms the area's western border to the site's many creeks and wetlands.

A change is now under way at the Fresh Kills site that Matta-Clark could hardly have anticipated. In 2003 the city of New York initiated the process of transforming the landfill site into a public park and wetland conservation area. A design entitled Lifescape (proposed by the Field Operations landscape architecture firm) has been selected by a competition committee and construction is set to begin as early as 2008. The firm describes Lifescape as a gradual process of transition from landfill site to "new nature lifestyle island" through four phases of ecological 'seeding', infrastructure construction, cultural and leisure programming and continual adaptation. The design is an ambitious attempt to respond to the acute challenges presented by Fresh Kills. Through a complex series of diagrams and site plans, the firm accounts for a somewhat dizzying multiplicity of environmental, economic and cultural factors. Field Operations emphasises the seamless integration and interaction of these various concerns:

> Ecological reflection, passive recreation, active sports and exercise, creativity, performance and cultural events, community development, economic enhancement and neighbourhood revitalisation all take their place alongside the micro-macroscopic processes of lifescape. It is fully integrative. Lifescape is not a loose metaphor or representation—it is a functioning reality, an autopoietic agent.[1]

An Architecture of the Living

Lifescape's conjunction of the built and the biological, the cultural and the natural, makes it a remarkable example of what has come to be called "landscape urbanism". The term describes recent architectural discourses and practices in which landscape has usurped the building to become the primary building block of urban design.[2] The movement has partly been propelled by a series of prominent competitions for innovative urban parks that have

Lifescape Overview,
circa 2003
Images courtesy of
James Corner/Field
Operations, New York.

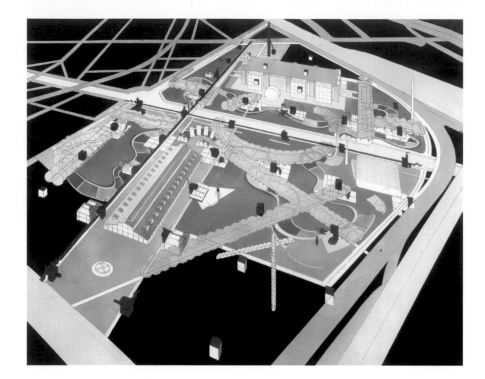

become important reference points for ongoing discussions about the changing nature of architectural design. A certain trajectory can be traced from the Parc de La Villette in Paris (completed by Bernard Tschumi in 1998), to the Downsview Park in Toronto (won by Office for Metropolitan Architects and Bruce Mau in 2001 but stalled by political infighting), to the Fresh Kills site in New York.

Despite the increasing profile of these competitions, landscape urbanism promises to expand its influence well beyond the confines of the city park. The proponents of this emerging discipline suggest that its ability to organise the interaction of multiple systems (biological, social, industrial) with unpredictable yet desirable results, may present a paradigm for architecture's engagement with contemporary urbanism in general. In an age when architecture is attempting to become flexible, malleable and responsive, ecological paradigms are rising to the fore. The time-based processes and soft materiality of landscape urbanism have a particular contemporary appeal (and in many ways exemplify the 'informal architecture' explored by this volume). Landscape in this context refers not simply to the design of greenery and recreation areas, but also suggests a move towards considerations of the infrastructure required to organise and facilitate the movement of people, resources and energy through the urban environment. As the landscape architect Charles Waldheim claims:

> Contemporary landscape urbanism recommends the use of infrastructural systems and the public landscape they engender as the very ordering mechanisms of the urban field itself, capable of shaping and shifting the organisation of urban settlement rather than offering predictable images of pastoral perfection.[3]

The discussion of landscape urbanism engages with a growing body of thought in architecture that takes the creation of difference and mutation—the basis of the natural world—as an ontological starting place for considerations of the built environment. The biologically informed concepts of creative evolution and open systems advocated by philosophers such as Henri Bergson and Gilles Deleuze have been brought into the sphere of architecture by both theorists, such as Sanford Kwinter, Brian Massumi and Manuel DeLanda, and practising architects, such as Reiser + Umemoto, Lars Spuybroek and Greg Lynn. These ideas, with their focus on flexibility and change, are often too easily characterised as a reaction against the monolithic and brutalist structures of modern architecture. The target identified by this emergent architectural discourse is perhaps more often the postmodern and deconstructive architectural theories of the recent past and their emphasis on architecture's relationship to language and meaning. The current, biologically inspired, theories often call for a revival of modernism's large scale engagement with the city on an infrastructural and organisational level. In his book *Architectures of Time*, Kwinter reminds us that there is a line of thought within modernity that orients architecture away from structure and form and towards conceptions of movement and the event. In a provocative series of written interventions RE Somol and Sarah Whiting call for a projective architecture that emphasises the discipline's instrumentality, its ability to produce effects and interactions among multiple economic, social and ecological systems, rather than its ability to represent or signify.[4]

The architect Stan Allen, who is one of the principle architects of the Field Operations design firm, has provided one of the most sustained appeals for architecture's return to the questions of function and implementation that had been sidelined by postmodernism's semiotic turn. Allen claims that, in its attempt to restore history and meaning to an architecture purged of these qualities by modernism's masterplanning and relentless decontextualisation, postmodernism had inadvertently retreated from its role in shaping large scale urban design. An architecture obsessed with self-critique and decorative localism had lost its ability to influence the economic and social infrastructure of the city. Allen calls for an architecture that, once again, seeks to intervene in these processes; an approach that "understands architecture as material practice; as an activity that works in and among the world of things, and not exclusively with meaning and image".[5] Like Somol and Whiting, Allen claims that architecture must own up to its powers of instrumentality that set it apart from other representational media (architecture is importantly not the same as film or literature). Architecture, according to Allen, must once again engage with the question of infrastructure, becoming less concerned with the form and style of individual buildings and more concerned with the fields that dictate what it is possible to construct.

For Allen, this shift also necessarily implies architecture's return to the sphere of politics. This assertion of a renewed political engagement and relevance for architecture is a claim that circulates widely within discussions of landscape urbanism. It is an underlying assumption that can also be found in the writing of James Corner; a landscape architect and the other leading member of Field Operations. Corner writes: "The promise of landscape urbanism is the development of a space-time ecology that treats all forces and agents working in the urban field and considers them as continuous networks of inter-relationships."[6] These comments suggest the political potential of a move away from the publicity and vanity driven system of 'signature buildings' towards an architectural process that acknowledges the multiplicity of voices and stakes involved in the urban environment. This large scale transformation of the city's landscape also holds the promise of re-engaging New Yorkers, long since discouraged with the perpetual delays, political manoeuvring and compromised architecture of the ground zero site. Yet the relationship between politics, nature and the processes of life has been a fraught topic for political and cultural thought. The Fresh Kills redevelopment is an impressive instantiation of landscape urbanism, but it is also one that highlights some of the possible problems of the movement's political claims.

Political Landscapes

It is difficult not to be awestruck by the engineering feat required to make the Fresh Kills site not only inhabitable but also teeming with life. This is truly an evolving topography, as the height of the mounds populating the site may lower as much as 30.5 metres as the waste that constitutes them decomposes. There are two byproducts of this process that require management. One is leachate, a toxic liquid produced by the decomposition, which must be collected and treated. The other is methane gas, which is collected for re-use or burned in a process called 'flaring off'. The flames produced by the methane flares will be the spectacular *finalé* in this magic act of disappearance.

The integration and renewal emphasised by the Lifescape design is not immune to criticism. The project can be challenged precisely on the grounds that it is perhaps too successful in making the cities largest accumulation of waste effectively disappear. As Linda Pollock suggests:

> To the extent that the Fresh Kills landscape is a consequence of our own material desires and consumption, it also reflects a desire to ignore our waste and abject products, to look in a different direction rather than risk being identified with them, to have them go away.[7]

Importantly and incredibly, New York no longer has any active landfill sites within city limits. New Yorkers' waste is now transported by truck to landfills in poorer neighbouring states that are willing to assume the ecological burden. If, as City Councilman Michael E McMahon claims, Staten Islanders were "for 50 years...

the victims of trash injustice", then we must wonder whether that injustice has simply been displaced to less visible locations.[8]

The difficult questions arising from the sealing over of the site's landfill contents takes a more emotional turn when we take into account its temporary re-opening after 9/11 as a containment and processing site for the Word Trade Center debris (an obviously unanticipated need when the Fresh Kills design competition was initiated in the spring of 2001). 1.62 million tons of debris were brought to the landfill and sifted for traces of human remains and forensic evidence. Field Operations has been praised for its subtle incorporation of a 9/11 memorial within the site that avoids the heavy-handed symbolism of the Reflecting Absence memorial at the ground zero site. The planned Fresh Kills memorial consists of a pair of earthworks the length and width of the towers which lie on their sides and point towards ground zero. However, despite this acknowledgment of the site's involvement with 9/11, some of the victim's families are clearly not comfortable with an area that, they claim, still contains unidentified remains being seamlessly incorporated into a leisure-orientated lifescape.[9] These families are also worried that, once the debris mound is covered, their grievance with the city as to where these remains should be located will also be effectively sealed.

These specific issues of contention pertaining to the Fresh Kills site provide an occasion to question some of landscape urbanism's more general political claims. The Lifescape design certainly enacts landscape urbanism's call to re-engage with the urban environment on an infrastructural level and to acknowledge architecture's powers of instrumentality. Yet the political consequences of the convergence of the natural, the built and the social that is taking place on the Fresh Kills site is clearly far from self-evident. Questioning the political implications of landscape urbanism seems particularly necessary in the current period of homeland security, with its many highly problematic attempts to organise life (through processes of

identification, surveillance and detention) and the discussions of the bio-political that have accompanied them. What place the natural world or the sphere of life itself has within the realm of the political is a far more contentious matter than is sometimes communicated within the celebratory discourse of landscape urbanism.

From Hannah Arendt's insistence that distinctions between the sphere of life and the sphere of politics must be maintained to resist totalitarian tendencies, to Michel Foucault's documentation of the repressive modern forces of bio-power and to Giorgio Agamben's more recent investigations into the relationship between sovereign power and the creation of bare life; political philosophy of the past 50 years has offered many cautionary tales regarding a too seamless convergence of the biological and the political. While this is not the place to enter fully into the complexities of these discussions, suffice it to say that the way in which architecture re-engages with questions of infrastructure and the organisation of life processes must be closely examined. All this is not to suggest that landscape urbanism projects are necessarily politically suspect or that architecture should continue to relegate itself to the ornamental expressiveness of postmodernism. Indeed, the bracketing off of the natural world from the public world of politics no longer seems possible or desirable in the ways in which Arendt suggests. We do, however, need methods of evaluating the political configurations produced by landscape urbanism, methods that do not rely solely on a positive appraisal of architecture's return to infrastructural design and incorporation of ecological processes.

Recent considerations of the politics of visibility and invisibility, the writing of Jacques Rancière in particular, provide a possible starting point for approaching these questions. Rancière views politics not as a separate sphere to be bracketed off from the other elements of life, but rather as a process by which the very organisation and division of life within a community is disputed. Here politics is conceived not as a sphere, but as a process by which something or someone that is a part of the community, but has been kept from visibility, struggles to enter the field of vision.[10] Crucial to Rancière's thought is that politics is in constant danger of being consumed by a false consensus encouraged by expert knowledge and the distorted usage of public opinion. Politics, according to Rancière, will therefore never be located exclusively in the seamless integration of infrastructural improvements within a community by the design expertise of an architectural firm, the economic savvy of a building developer, or the secret knowledge of a city official. It will instead be found where members of the community who have a stake in the urban environment come into visibility in order to be counted. Architectural practices need not be consigned to the realm of the non-political or judged as an oppressive force within Rancière's system of thought. Specific architectural practices could be judged on the basis of whether they assist a process by which what has been concealed within the community is allowed to become visible, or whether they hinder this process. Landscape urbanism often succeeds when evaluated on these terms, the plan submitted by Field Operations for the Downsview Park competition, for example, has been praised for its efforts to expose the development process to a public of non-experts that nevertheless have a stake in its design.[11]

There is of course more than a hint of this logic of exposure motivating the work of Gordon Matta-Clark. The artist's pleasure in revealing that which is meant to be concealed, of exposing the inner structures of our built environment, is palpable in so many of his projects. The irreverence of the amateur demolitionist inspires us to take account of urban surroundings that are too often given over to the knowledge of experts. The appeal of Matta-Clark's *Fresh Kills* film is in large measure derived from the artist's success in accessing a location the public is never meant to witness, despite being very much complicit in its creation. By staging the act of destroying his cherished truck, Matta-Clark is actually putting on display a geography to which every inhabitant of New York may have contributed yet never seen. The project to transform the Fresh Kills site has once again brought this same location into public vision. It remains to be seen whether the design process under way will contribute to revealing or concealing the configurations of politics, infrastructure and biological life emanating from the site.

William Pope.L in Conversation with Anthony Kiendl

Anthony Kiendl: Tell me about your installation *Chocolate Fountain*, 2005, and what relation it has to *Historic Building*, made for the Informal Architectures exhibition.

William Pope.L: *Chocolate Fountain* came out of my interest in animating architecture and ritualistic images in horror movies. One important visual conceit for me appears in *The Amityville Horror*. In the film, the home of the central character oozes a black material that eventually takes over the entire building. You have this thing—a building or home—that is taken as very bounded but an event occurs that expands such structures beyond their conventional frame. The same result occurs in *Evil Dead 2*. One of the central characters, from the exterior, is a small cabin. However, upon entering it, the visitor discovers infinite space; room after room after room. It's interesting that, in cinema, you have this planar structure, a two-dimensional screen that, with the addition of projected light, presents a three-dimensional conundrum with architecture.

AK: Has anything moved on in this work from *Chocolate Fountain*?

WPL: Yes, in the sense that I couldn't make this piece in Britain: *Chocolate Fountain* was very site-specific and Britain has a different environmental colour palette. *Chocolate Fountain* was sutured into another work that tied the first floor of the gallery space to the second. In this building there was an atrium, approximately three metres square. On the first floor it was just a hole; on the second it became a glass-enclosed structure. No one knew its function. We built a platform within the atrium with legs extending down to the ground. I did a performance in the space; dressed as an orange yeti and wrote down from memory Wittgenstein's text "Remarks on Colour" interspersed with recollections of a phone conversation with my brother, Frank, concerning his philosophy on power, women and futility. I designed the performance platform to architecturally communicate with the wall of *Chocolate Fountain*—as a backstage area. The idea of what is inside something is always interesting to me.

AK: Can you tell me about the inside of the structure and how it functions?

WPL: Buildings are 'masks', or 'head spaces'. When you are in the presence of a building, you're in the presence of a result of group intelligence. I am interested in the idea of the building as a representation of group mentality and about the way it represents head space. This so-called head space is very 'chunky' and diverse. No matter how sleek and modern a building may seem it is not a single entity but rather a conglomeration of many: ambient, cultural, sculptural and a conflation between the building and its 'mask'.

AK: It's interesting that the work implies that something is happening inside but, as the door is locked, we won't know what.

WPL: Well there's a key in the door. It doesn't work but can be removed (although it won't turn the knob).

AK: I am also interested in the materials: the foam oozing from the edges, the Typar peeling and particularly the choice of the Hudson's Bay blanket. Can you tell me about any of those aspects?

WPL: Again it's a sort of conglomerate/agglomerate or conflation/chunky notion. There are time-honoured notions concerning what buildings can be and what purpose they really serve. Buildings are supposed to be non-sentient, however, there is a long history of suspected sentience in them. They are meant to be reliable, sheltering, a known quantity; but this is simply wish-fulfillment. As such, buildings are sites for negotiating conflict and power. You lock in your logo or stamp on the built environment. In *Historic*

William Pope.L
Historic Building, 2007
Installation
266.7 x 548.6 x 111.8 cm
Images courtesy of The Banff
Centre, the artist, The Project,
and Kenny Schachter ROVE.
Photographs by Tara Nicholson.

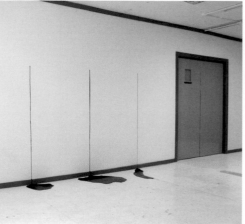
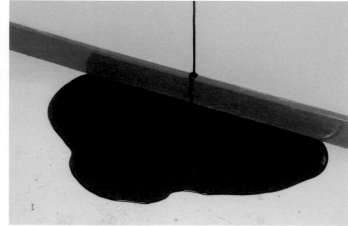

Building you have the residue, the hairy palimpsest of a Hudson's Bay blanket, glued onto the building then carefully peeled off. I did not know that the blanket hails from trade between Europeans and Aboriginal people many years ago. (Often they carried diseases—both intentionally and not—and the latter people had no immunity against them and died.) I wanted to layer this sense of European expansionism—slathered with post and lintel construction—with the prefab time of leisure and associations with death. Its all agglomerate-type thinking; perceiving buildings not only as spaces to house bodies, but also as arenas to let loose ideas, or spirits. I think this is where the agglomerate reflects a structure that is not just what you can see, but what you can feel, think or imagine.

AK: In the way that a plain white wall might represent Western, white modernity, the Hudson's Bay blanket is another kind of reading or portrait of the white impact on Aboriginal cultures. I was thinking of your series of *Skin Set* drawings that are multiple descriptions—this works in a similar way with different identities within this structure; like the chocolate oozing out, impossible to contain. I was curious about the paint on this side because the choice of colour in your other work is very loaded. Does it carry through into this piece as well?

WPL: My colour choices are dictated by conventions of contemporary public landscape and its representation in the media, urban/suburban bio-spheres and contemporary interior decor. Chance also played a role in my colour choices. Before arriving at Banff, I decided I would limit my pallet to whatever paints happened to be in the gallery's storage. I wanted the process of 'working' the building to be composed of a mix of circumstance, convention, planning and history. In any case, to be at Banff is to be in nature, and so the particular landscape I painted on the building has some sketchy stereotypical relation to mountains, hills, trees and animals.

AK: And the audio again plays into that idea of landscape.

WPL: Also the idea of animation: people animate buildings not only with their bodies but with their use of such spaces. In certain African ritual, there are masks that are never used; they are sacred and are not to be worn. So I made this thing that looks like a building, but I allow no one to enter it because I don't want it to function in a typical way.

There are things that fill and fascinate via absence or lack. Perhaps architecture should not be 'said'. Perhaps it should embrace more noise and silence.

AK: I was looking at some of your previous writing and your statement "lack is a value worth having". Is there an element of this in *Historic Building*?

WPL: In almost all of what I do there is a sense of incompleteness that is an important material. Its not that I don't have intentions or think in terms of frameworks. I think the drama or story, if you will, compels my insistence to both achieve something and to reconcile intentions with circumstances or adventures that I don't intend.

When Kristeva talks about this radical incompleteness that humans live, she is saying we will never be able to come to terms with the arbitrariness of things. Instead of treating this whirling absence as alien, why not construct it as an opportunity for positive disasters that instruct a discomfort, a lack that's worth having.

AK: Relating to some of your previous works—specifically their relationship to social space and how to be in the world—I was looking at how it deals with social space and urban space and, hence, architecture. Is *Historic Building* the work that most explicitly refers to architecture?

WPL: My relationship to architecture first came through theatre. Theatre has a very strong tradition of building things for 'the scene'. I was in a theatre troupe for many years and one of the projects we created was a fully standing, working rocking chair live on stage in 30 seconds. It took two years to figure out how to do it. The chair had to be made from seemingly nothing, yet everything. Tools and materials had to be available in plain sight on stage. In performance, once the tools and materials were 'discovered', we cut wood, zipped together boards with screwguns, sat in the chair and recited a complex speech. This was accomplished with little to no transitions. Yes, I've been interested in building for a long time, but not necessarily in terms of 'buildings' or even 'construction'.

AK: I'm interested in the social role of the built environment specifically in your work. I'm also interested in consumption and its role in *Historic Building,* as it clearly exists in your other works such as *Eating the Wall Street Journal.*

WPL: Consumption, at least for me in this project, is more about what comes out the nether end. When people think of consumption, they think of it mostly as something you take in, when it's also what you 'put out'. When I think of a building, I think of it as a sort of sentience that gives off certain effects. Houses are porous and chambered like a creature with air for organs.

In the Robert Heinlein novel, *Stranger in a Strange Land,* the hero Michael Valentine is looking at a house. Standing next to Valentine, looking at the same house, is an alien for whom sense impressions are next to godliness. Valentine asks the alien "What do you see?" The alien responds: "A building with two sides." Valentine is puzzled and says: "What do you mean a building with two sides?" The alien responds: "That is what I see: I see a side, and another side." The alien leaves. A short time later Valentine approaches another character, his lover, and asks her why the alien described the building so strangely. The lover explains that the alien can only express what it can see. Anything else would be a hypothesis.

The front of *Historic Building* should not reveal the back, nor the left or right sides of the structure; these are things you might only be able to infer. The building unmakes itself as you walk around it. The viewer visualises it mentally as they physically interact with it.

I guess I am interested in an analytical consumption. I am interested in culture that speaks to us about how we interact with it. In art we crudely suggest such relations at various times. Most of these instances are proffered as intellectual, not communicative, spiritual or even cultural.

Such an example is Robert Morris' *Box with the Sound of its Own Making.* For me, this piece evokes landscape and issues to do with scale, body-object relationships and what it means to make something. Historically, much has been made of the tautological aspect of the box because it supposedly contains an actual recording of its own making. The conceptual conceit of the work can come off too neat but, for me, it is its scale that provides an added layer of significance. The box is small and suggests the handmade, however, the recording only documents the sound of construction not, for example, the purchase of its constituent materials or the clean up after assembly. The appearance of conceptual elegance was more important to Morris than to me.

I am interested in the social history of plywood, for example; where it comes from, how it's made. I am not afraid to risk visual elegance by making this sort of interest evident in a work. I think we sometimes confuse visual elegance with conceptual rigour. Wittgenstein once said: "What if you make a proof that is so elegant and so precise that it leaves the ground of meaning? What utility can a proof of this sort have?" I was fascinated by Morris' little box because, by turning on itself, it set itself apart as a semi-sentient in a landscape. The box was a performer, it was not about its own making but, rather, its inhabitation.

MONUMENT/
EPHEMERALITY

The Politics of Informal Production
• Andrea Phillips

Politics is the sphere of pure means, that is, of the absolute and complete gesturality of human beings.[1]
—Giorgio Agamben

In contemporary philosophy, art and architecture there is a certain desire to propose, activate and/or describe informal, ephemeral situatedness as a potent political state. On the one hand, many contemporary artists and architects festishise the unfinished, the processual, the gestural and the ephemeral as 'spaces' of radical alterity—spaces in which new political forms of production might emerge out of the morass of monumental or static, privatised production. On the other, inspired by philosophies of 'pure means' but unable to commit formally to this prospect, the same artists and architects search in vain for a staging of ephemeral, gestural and mobile acts that, in its informality, might not be reduced to the reified status of object, building or language. The paradox that is set in motion by this 'to-ing and fro-ing' is evident in many forms. The question is, how can it avow the politicality to which it aspires? The answer (or, at least, the attempt) often comes in the compromised form of the production of an ephemeron: a structurally short-lived, disappearing gesture or act that might stand in for, or stage, the paradox. It goes without saying that in this context the idea of ephemeral (or informal) space is significantly contradictory.

When ephemeral moments and spaces are discussed it is often with the intention of pointing to their ability to exist without recourse to the normal, or regulated, productive capacities of everyday life. Ephemeral spaces seem interesting because they indicate extraordinary ways of living, thinking, being and different ways of occupying time and space. This space and time of difference—mapped out by Derrida and Bergson and articulated by de Certeau—through its aporetic relationship to the 'proper', is echoed and enforced elsewhere by politically and culturally determined tactics, dérive, actions; events that determine to 'make' the ephemeral, to perform

aesthetic and ethical exercises determined by their desire to be fluid, to act out the short-lived. Such proto-discursive ideas must give way to formal brutality, as they are shored up by images and words. Artistic and architectural compromises are found: monuments give way to events, towns give way to tents, blocks begin to move, action replaces stasis. These are the moves that interest many contemporary artists and architects. And yet, artists' and architects' modes, their operations, belie such ways of occupying space: they rarely belong to, and usually cannot access the minimum of gesture that might be expressed in this space, and the notion of a tactical, ephemeral practice is often hobbled by the cultural requirement to produce objects and buildings that subscribe to the conditions of the gallery or the town plan. Given this situation, what is the artist or architect to do to take advantage of the promise of ephemeral space? It is, in effect, a question of strategy: should one attempt to exist below a threshold of representational production (a question enforced on some and sought out by others), or should one strategically adopt a system of representation: passing into radar space, within the field of vision. One relies on the other, and yet is also deflected, paralysed by the other, as even the most radical gesture is co-opted into product. The articulation of an ephemeron—be it an artwork or a building—is full of deficiencies and compromises, and often seems best left unbuilt or unmade (therefore, and importantly in terms of a history of conceptual art and architecture, proposals are perhaps the only ephemeral gestures).

How can we talk about production, how can we incorporate the philosophical-political desires that we articulate through attention to the ephemeron, into an object, a subject that has form? This question—of building and use-value—needs discussion in order to counter the development of political formations that can only attest to 'means without ends'. For the philosophical-political desire expressed in drawing attention to and articulating the ephemeron is one that pushes us, as subjects, towards a space that most of us do

Previous pages
Arni Haraldsson
Corner flat with iron
fence, Thamesmead
South, East London, 2007
Digital print
Image courtesy of the artist.

This page
Francis Alÿs in collaboration
with Rafael Ortega
When Faith Moves Mountains, 2002
16 mm film transferred to DVD
Images courtesy the artist and
David Zwirner, New York.

Francis Alÿs in collaboration
with Rafael Ortega
When Faith Moves Mountains, 2002
16 mm film transferred to DVD
Images courtesy the artist and
David Zwirner, New York.

not usually occupy. For the manifestation of production—artistic, architectural, in the very least, monumental, panoptic, territorial at the easily accessed limit—is what is at stake.

Here, this discussion, this notion of informal architecture and attempt to articulate differences of space ("contingent, hypothetical, temporary, mobile, fictional or weak") is a manifestation of the problem. We want to use this space, this proposition that we might call gestural, but its use drags at, blocks and arrests the ephemeral. What are we to do with the obstructive questions of space; space that we need to be something else, something fluid and flexible, yet that resists such transition as it is mapped cognitively and physically in our daily (artistic and architectural) lives? What are we to do with this point at which art (and artful organisation) both resists and attempts to articulate the ephemeral?

A few years ago Francis Alÿs was asked to make a new work for the 2002 Lima Bienal. Working with collaborators, Rafael Ortega and Cuauhtémoc Medina, Alÿs visited the city and experienced the continuous civil unrest and mounting desperation of people living in poverty during what were the last few months of the dictator Alberto Fujimori's rule. Returning in 2002, the artist proposed a work that would entail the 'moving' of a piece of land by ten centimetres with an act of mass participation. Alÿs and Medina spent time finding an appropriate site to move and eventually came across the giant Ventanilla sand dunes, half an hour outside the city centre, which had become home to the ever-transient and ever-reaching shanty town of some of Lima's impoverished citizens.

Shovels were designed, t-shirts were printed and on 11 April, 500 people assembled at one side of a dune and, moving slowly and fairly rhythmically in a single line, started to climb it, moving a shovelful of dirt at every step. Alÿs gave the work a subtitle that became a manifest slogan, "maximum effort, minimum result".

What kind of space does *When Faith Moves Mountains* occupy? It is, on one level, an ephemeral space: it takes place only once over the course of one day, is performative, leaves no discernible trace, is not repeatable in exact form and accessible only via narratives and images that disperse after the event. It also takes place on makeshift ground: highlighting the temporality of shanty accommodation, the permeable economic structures of survival tactics among Lima's poor. It also raises questions of use and uselessness, it demonstrates the vicissitudes of immaterial labour. It is both banal and radically ineffective as a gesture, and yet it is a high profile and political act. No immediate gain is made (except by the artist, whose Artlink stock rises incrementally). Nothing is lost except energy. Arguably, 'faith' is practised, goodwill is called into effect, teamwork is utilised, temporary community is built and potential, but not explicit, conditions are set for direct collaborative action on housing conditions and economic inequalities, but these things are nominal; side effects. One could argue, like Subcomandante Marcos, that such side effects are of huge importance in the construction of alternative political economies, but no such endeavour was marked by the artist as a stated byproduct of the work. If *When Faith Moves Mountains* occupies ephemeral space it does so conditionally, and in full knowledge of the problems of that space, the ethical inheritance of that space. Who profits? Who does not? Who cares for the gesture that Alÿs, Ortega and Medina have concocted?

Images from the work ricocheted around the art world, appearing on the cover of *Artforum* within weeks. Asked to contribute 1,000 words on the project to the magazine, Alÿs said:

When Faith Moves Mountains attempts to translate social tensions into narratives that in turn intervene in the imaginary landscape of a place. The action is meant to infiltrate the local history and mythology of Peruvian society... to insert rumour into its narratives. If the script meets the expectations and addresses the anxieties of that society at this time and place, it might become a story that survives the event itself. At that moment it has the potential to become a fable or an urban myth. As Medina said while we were in Lima: 'Faith is a means by which one resigns oneself to the present in order to invest in the abstract promise of the future.' The dune moved: this wasn't a literary fiction; it really happened. It doesn't matter how far it moved, and in truth only an infinitesimal displacement occurred, but it would have taken the wind years to move an equivalent amount of sand. So it's a tiny miracle. The story starts there. The interpretations of it needn't be accurate, but must be free to shape themselves along the way.[2]

The artist is, of course, not liable for the work as it passes into historical narrative, whether that narrative is constructed through the stories of people who took part or via the long view of art history and philosophy. Alÿs' work has always slipped along a line of such gestures, in which modest and detailed fruition gives way, suddenly, to wildly excessive acts the nature of which is to broach ethical questions of the surplus and wasteful economies of art (works such as *The Loop*, in which the artist travelled by plane the long way round the globe to cross the American/Mexican border, *Narcotourism*, in which he walked through Copenhagen having taken a different drug each day for seven days, or *The Ambassador*, in which he sent a peacock in his stead to make a work for the 2003 Venice Biennale). Such works are greeted pleasantly by the art world, and Alÿs is treated like a man-child, a type of exotic idiot-savant sent to offer us something poetic but aleatory (this exoticisation is matched by the artist's own counter intuitive trans-national biography, as a Belgian resident of Mexico City; proof as if it were needed of the centre/periphery prevarications of the art world that also rely on an exoticisation of the ephemeral). "Art", says Alÿs, "really exists, so to speak, in transit", as if its transitory status allows it to speak beyond the ethics of waste it proposes. This is a huge claim on the ephemeral. Alÿs says that the faith practised in *When Faith Moves Mountains* is not about the veneration of ideals but "an active interpretative practice performed by the audience, who must give the work its meaning and its social value". The divisive, intriguing and, above all, seductive aspect of Alÿs' work lies in the very fact that *When Faith Moves Mountains* is not simply a social allegory, and neither is it only a story for a specific set of locations and temporal circumstances. It is more canny than that, for it speaks formally (architecturally) as a review of the rules. No doubt it is now a local, and much exaggerated, story, as Alÿs predicted. It also buys into an idea of political agency that is irreducible (and thus, useless in the Marxian sense) to accountable change. Is this what the ephemeral does? What are these quiescent but affronting politics, never enunciated but clearly present?

Agamben makes a claim for a politics of gesture. He locates gesture within a sphere of actions, but sets it apart from both acting and making (in the same way that Alÿs avoids definitive acting and making but calls on others to do both in his production in Lima). He says: "What characterises gesture is that in it nothing is being produced or acted, but rather something is being endured or supported. The gesture, in other words, opens the sphere of ethos as the more proper sphere of that which is human. But in what way is an action endured or supported?"[3] Gesture, he suggests, is useless in and of itself, as it simply implies "pure and endless mediality" (in other words, the constantly deferring mode of producing gestures that might be described as an art, but not an 'acted' one):

The gesture is… communication of a communicability. It has precisely nothing to say because what it shows is the being-in-language of human beings as pure mediality. However, because being-in-language is not something that could be said in sentences, the gesture is essentially always a gesture of not being able to figure something out in language; it is always a gag in the proper meaning of the term, indicating first of all something that could be put in your mouth to hinder speech, as well as in the sense of the actor's improvisation meant to compensate a loss of memory or an inability to speak. From this point derives… the proximity between gesture and philosophy.[4]

In transcribing gestures into faltering speech, Agamben positions them more clearly as something contingent and delimited, existing perhaps—architecturally—as drafts or discarded drawings. In this way, gesture relies on ephemerality as something that fails to occupy space, just as it fails to occupy time, in a concrete sense. The gag, for Agamben, is both a means of not speaking and of speaking differently. This collapsing of things, while in a moment of crisis or extraordinary production, is a political claim similar to that understated one in Alÿs' work. But is it reliable?

Ventanilla is full of the bodies of those left outside of politics, most notably, those peoples refugeed, encamped, returned to the minimum of their being through a sovereign consignment in state space. This space, which Agamben famously calls "bare life" has in his view "a generic mode of potentiality that is not exhausted". The camp lies close to the heart of contemporary life, testifying literality to ephemeral sites outside of the niceties of poetics. The camp is "dislocating localisation that exceeds [the political system] and into which every form of life and every rule can be virtually taken".[5]

But the Ventanilla shanty town has other aspects: it is organised, develops static forms of governance and produces mini-statutes for, and of, sociality. The normalising process of social and spatial production goes on everywhere. Informality also, in this respect, stabilises spatial production.

The fact that the production of *When Faith Moves Mountains* took place as part of an international biennial is not unimportant in the understanding of a politics that utilises the terms of ephemerality to its own end, as it is globalisation that brings objects and bodies together to allow such production, and it is globalisation that produces the idea of potentiality that occurs within such spatially-reproposed, trans-national circumstances.

Globalisation works by eradicating or ignoring physical and conceptual boundaries and borders (thus it is structurally informal and ephemeral by design); it effects a process of technological normalcy across a strata; it works towards the eradication of both distance and difference; and it is based on the circulation of goods, concepts and meanings that not only contradict one another but also work to repeat, replace and compete to supplant each other. Globalisation also makes meaning that is unhinged from the inequalities it produces. It is in this sense ephemeral; reliant on informality and enabling the production of such works as Alÿs' in Lima. Further globalisation co-opts the delicate philosophies of gesture—and its concomitant politics—for its own use. If we, in other words, are happy to promote informal, ephemeral spaces (for the one is reliant on the other) through art and architecture then we will get the politics of such. The bodies and buildings of Ventanilla might appreciate this irony, as their labour is corralled for the sake of global aesthetic gestures. For globalisation's aesthetic in contemporary art makes meaning through the informality of building, through the ephemerality of trans-national artistic production, leaving the subjects of Ventanilla—having shifted a mountain to no effect—to go about their daily business.

Goldfinger Project
• Arni Haraldsson

Ernö Goldfinger's Trellick Tower in Notting Hill, west London, due to its particular layout and gargantuan size, seemingly defies or is beyond photography. This is not strictly due to the physical appearance and complexity of the structure or the technical limitations of the medium, but rather it concerns one's approach to architecture, the thinking about the subject and, consequently, its representation. The question as to where exactly a given architecture begins or ends therefore becomes increasingly complex since it is not only the physical presence of space which is under consideration here but also its placement or location within everyday life, within recent historical memory, cultural practices and other less definable subjectivities.

The Trellick Tower is a 31-storey residential block that, upon completion in 1972, was one of the tallest social housing complexes in Europe. It contains 219 units (or flats) many of which are laid out over two floors. An architectural icon on the west side of the city, from a distance, the Trellick Tower resembles some unrealised futurist drawing come to life. It looms large on the horizon; the lift shaft separated from the residential tower proper, with only connecting walkways on every third floor.

In an attempt to come to terms with the Tower, to regard its perimeters, both physical and conceptual, I tried to photograph it in a manner that might allow for the unfolding of a greater context. Thus, a view from the west incorporates the surrounding neighbourhood near the Grand Union Canal and, in the immediate foreground, the Meanwhile Community Gardens. I thought these four acres of gardens running alongside the canal particularly interesting, as they are used primarily by people undergoing rehabilitation, who have psychiatric problems, various addictions or—for one reason or another—who have been placed 'outside' society. The gardens offer them a way of reconnecting, of reintegrating, back into a social network. A series of views of the Trellick Tower, as seen through the autumnal canopy of trees beside the Canal, reveals the expanse of green space surrounding the building (this space becomes particularly significant, especially when one considers the urban density of the Tower's situation and the urbanity of a capital like London in general).

I was interested in Goldfinger's architecture not simply as a modernist, sculptural entity but also as a social, political, historical marker. Rather than attempting to represent the Trellick Tower didactically (bearing in mind that architecture is always a composite of forces—structural, psychological, social and otherwise—and thus such an endeavour is inherently naive), I nevertheless sought to represent both its affirmative and negative aspects. Such an approach not only alluded to the duality of the photographic medium itself but also allowed for a type of re-authoring of architecture; a process potentially capable of altering and shaping our reception of the underlying meanings inherent to the built environment and beyond.

The views I captured through the trees, therefore, were intended to refer to photographic endeavours of the recent past, to the atmospheric Romanticism of, for example, Alfred Stieglitz or Edward Steichen in their picturesque representations of the Flatiron Building in New York City. A view of the base of the lift shaft, on the other hand—cast in shadow and littered with debris—reveals a forgotten, unconscious corner whose vernacular subject matter conjures a strain of the realist tradition, in the style of Robert Frank or Walker Evans. Another view, straining to look straight up the length of the lift shaft, serves to echo the perspectival dynamism of the 'new vision' of such figures as László Moholy-Nagy or Alexander Rodchenko. Partially visible from this extreme angle is another seven-storey block, known as Block B, designed by Goldfinger and also linked to the Tower by raised walkways.

At times, the entire estate appears as a fortification, emphasised by the detail of narrow, inaccessible slits—a sort of Medieval defence system—running the length of the lift shaft, and which

also rhythmically punctuate a nearby, concrete half wall that circles sections of the estate and cordons it off from the street. One might identify this feature as Goldfinger's signature style which, when measured against the modernist credo of transparency and external legibility, instills a discordant note to the whole of his *oeuvre*, presenting a latent surrealist frame, which is imbued with elements of paranoia and defence.

The Balfron Tower in Poplar, east London, forms a near mirror image of the Trellick Tower. Built in 1968, the Balfron precedes the Trellick and, at 27 storeys high, is also slightly shorter. Various faults which Goldfinger recognised after the construction of the Balfron he attempted to rectify when designing the Trellick; ultimately achieving a more majestic, elongated appearance with the latter building. At a small event dedicated to Goldfinger in the autumn of 2006 one speaker described the Balfron as Trellick's "slightly fatter, uglier sister", an anecdote intended to raise a laugh but which also imprinted an image in my mind of the buildings as 'sisters'.

The comparison of the two models also alluded to a schism much evident within the building. Tenants occupying flats provided by the state have been pitted against those who have purchased their flats outright; a process of gentrification that is quite literally dividing up the building. Approximately 85–90 per cent of the Balfron remains social housing but this will undoubtedly change just as it has throughout other parts of Europe and the world at large. A view of the east facade of the Balfron and its immediate environs reveals the decrepit state of the structure and the various social problems which are now endemic to both towers. A close-up of the Balfron's entrance area highlights the bush-hammered concrete surface treatment and method of construction (much favoured by Goldfinger) that contributes to the uniquely textured and monochromatic appearance of both towers.

On 16 May 1968 Ronan Point—a former housing complex in Newham, east London, that would later come to haunt Goldfinger—suffered a catastophic explosion and effectively stopped the various high-rise schemes (or "streets in the sky") he had planned for the future. On that fateful day, a certain Miss Ivy Lodge's flat unexpectedly exploded as she turned on her gas stove. A large corner section of the tower collapsed to the ground, killing half a dozen tenants and injuring many more. Incredibly, Lodge herself survived; as evidenced from the BBC news footage of the time. The four towers making up the Ronan Point estate would later be imploded; considered unsafe since they too were speedily erected and employed prefab, slab concrete construction as opposed to the labour intensive, poured concrete method favoured by Goldfinger. By the end of 1968, although Goldfinger would go on to build the Trellick Tower, it loomed ominous against the west London skyline; serving as a reminder of the ineffectualities of Ronan Point. (Having gained him the moniker 'Goldprick' and the Trellick 'The Tower of Terror' the Tower became a haven throughout the 1970s and 80s for drug dealing, prostitution and violence, eventually culminating in the present dispute between developers, the Greater London Council and residents.)

A chunk of concrete from Ronan Point (that was allegedly responsible for the death of one tenant) was later hauled off—possibly for insurance and research purposes—to an aircraft hanger near Swindon where it remains to this day. While photographing *in situ* this block-shaped mass of rough hewn, grey concrete—itself reminiscent of modernist sculpture, and inscribed with a series of almost indecipherable scribbles of numbers and letters—I imagined a Rosetta Stone that would pin-point for future generations one of several decisive turning points; signalling the demise of modernism or at the very least a strain of its construction methods.

Aside from being something of an aspiring photographer himself, Goldfinger also had a keen interest in modernist painting and sculpture, having written about and curated a number of exhibitions. He also collaborated with artists, including the sculptor, Helen Phillips, and the architect, Victor Pasmore, who, collectively, took

part in the 1956 This is Tomorrow exhibition at the Whitechapel Art Gallery. While Helen Phillips' name has, for the most part, receded into the past, Victor Pasmore's Apollo Pavilion in Peterlee near Newcastle has surfaced of late as a site of controversy. Although named after the American space mission, this concrete-built pavilion is strictly non-functional, and was constructed to coincide with the commemoration of the new town named after 'Peter Lee', a local hero and coal miner who was instrumental in organising the miners union at the turn of the century. (Pasmore, however, was adamant that it should be an anonymous modernist monument dedicated to absolutely nothing other than itself as pure form.) The pavilion exists today as a kind of inadvertent monument to modernism, not as a failed project but rather an incomplete one, *a la* Jürgen Habermas. It has become an unintended focal point, an abode of unemployed and discontented youth who have transformed its minimal surfaces into a screen for the projection of a communal and generational unconscious, referencing a return to historical attitudes of class unrest and repression and suggesting—no doubt much to the dismay of civic authorities—that all is not well in Peterlee.

The Barbican Estate in London, on the other hand, forms an affirmative counter to the Trellick and Balfron Towers. Built by the architectural team of Chamberlin, Powell and Bon on a former Second World War bomb site, construction began in 1972, yet ten years were to pass before the estate was officially opened by the Queen in 1982. Inspired by Le Corbusier's Unite d'habitation in Marseilles, the Barbican comprises 2,104 flats that house over 4,000 people. Originally estimated to cost between six and eight million pounds, this figure increased to 156 million on completion.

Just as there is an affirmative model to Goldfinger's high-rise projects so, too, there is a negative one in the form of the Thamesmead South estate on the outskirts of east London. A self-contained city in its own right, with a population of some 60,000 people, the estate featured prominently in Stanley Kubrick's dystopic 1971 film, *A Clockwork Orange*, shortly after its construction. Under Kubrick's directorial mode the estate became reconstituted, projected into a near future; bringing modernism to the fore once again. Thus, the very materiality of Brutalism as an architectural style becomes equated with—and transliterated into—the sadomasochistic aesthetics of a misdirected youth culture, embodied within the film by the pathologically brutal Alex and his droogs. Indeed, so hostile was the reception of *A Clockwork Orange,* with its depiction of a future steeped in violence as set in and around London, that the director was compelled to withdraw the film from circulation in England. Although Kubrick did equally identify and project a certain negative unconscious which was, in any case, inherent to much of the modernist project by the 1970s, some 35 years on, while photographing around Thamesmead, I encountered an estate more pathetic and melancholic than harbouring potentially violent undercurrents. Today Thamesmead South seems more exemplary of post-war measures of efficiency and expediency and of a defeated working class and segregated ethnic communities.

In 1939 Goldfinger designed a house at 2 Willow Road in Hampstead for himself and his family. A nearby neighbour happened to be Ian Fleming, author of the James Bond novels who, upon meeting Goldfinger, took an instant dislike to the architect, dismissing him as merely an alleged Marxist; a "Gucci socialist". Fleming went on to lampoon Goldfinger in his 1959 novel by naming one of his most villainous characters 'Auric Goldfinger'. In the film version of the novel, actor Gert Fröbe portrays Goldfinger as the embodiment of pure evil and whose *raison d'etre* is to place the economic stability of the West in jeopardy (he steals from the Fort Knox depository in an effort to further Soviet aims). Goldfinger was naturally upset by this characterisation. As a Hungarian Jew and communist who had fled Nazism and become a British subject in 1947, he interpreted Fleming's gesture as an

anti-semitic attack on his person. Goldfinger subsequently brought a law suit against Fleming, however, he was advised to drop what would have amounted to a costly legal battle when it was made clear to him that Fleming—as a representative of the British establishment—would have won out in the end.

A quintessentially British-style, modernist house, 2 Willow Road was built in 1939 and became a museum in 1992; the first significant modern building in the portfolio of the National Trust. So transparent has the restaging of a semblance of everyday life been at 2 Willow Road that a visitor to the house today may well be forgiven for having thought that its occupants had just stepped out for lunch at one of the many restaurants in the neighbourhood. Curiously, the building was temporarily transformed into a Postmodern abode when, in 2000, Habitat selected it as a backdrop against which to stage a variety of its products. In the catalogue of the same date Goldfinger's own furniture designs, such as his variation on the Safari chair, were vacated from the premises so as to make room for Habitat recreations like the Robin Day sofa upon which a very cosmopolitan, ever so Postmodern, family is seated. Also included are a series of fictional scenarios in which models, including 'Dave the dog', play at being a family while acting out the dilemmas and tribulations of consumer culture.

Toward the end of his life, Goldfinger donated the whole of his archive to the Royal Institute of British Architects (RIBA), amounting to 502 boxes of documents: letters, drawings, models, and memorabilia, including a cluster of receipts for photographic film he had purchased throughout his career—the minutiae of an architect's life in the mid-twentieth century. Goldfinger died in 1987 and, as an atheist, he has no grave. The only marker of his achievements and his life are the documents held by RIBA; a Pharonic-like series of vessels housing a dismembered body (of work).

Reflecting on my six month trajectory in London, the so-called *Goldfinger Project*, from the Barbican Estate, to Thamesmead

South, Ronan Point; perhaps these have proven mere asides. Structures that, due to their very difference, their distinct and separate histories, divergent populations and so on, cannot be measured realistically in relation to one another, much less alongside Goldfinger's comparatively more contained projects. These and other such idle meanderings; the photography of Stieglitz or Frank, Kubrick's *A Clockwork Orange*, James Bond, Habitat may serve—in retrospect—as examples that, by their very eclecticism, illustrate and provide some insight into the underlying ideological premises of the period and thereby become essential in the attempt to build a comprehensive portrait of the Trellick and the Balfron Towers. Two structures, two historical markers, which neither strictly contain nor house the living, but from which the living and life in all its infinite complexities spill out of into a myriad of directions.

Ruptures on the Architectural Grid: Brian Jungen's Treaty Project, Métis Road Allowance Houses and other Models of Inhabiting the 'In-between'
• Candice Hopkins

Brian Jungen is from the northeastern region of British Columbia (BC), an area large enough to hold the states of California, Oregon, and Washington. Like much of Canada, it is sparsely populated and remote. This region marks the beginning of the Alaska Highway, a road over 2,500 kilometres long that links northern BC with the Yukon Territory and Alaska. Completed by the American Army in 1943, the Highway enabled Americans to bring supplies overland to their northern-most state. It also runs directly through Indian Reserve 172, where Jungen's ancestors are from, an area that was ceded in 1899 with the signing of Treaty 8 between the British Crown (now the Government of Canada) and the Aboriginal people living in the area. Upon its completion the Treaty would include the northeastern part of BC to the Rocky Mountains, Alberta and Saskatchewan and up to the Northwest Territories.

Treaty 8 was one of the last of the numbered treaties to be signed in the country. In the early 1890s, there was little incentive for the federal government to seek an agreement as there wasn't yet a significant need for land for settlement. Although there had been talk of valuable resources in the form of oil, gas, and minerals, this was not adequate enough to set the Treaty process in motion. This changed nearly overnight with the discovery of gold in the Yukon Territory in 1896. The Klondike Gold Rush brought forth thousands of people, in the time-span of just a few years, to an area that had never seen as much as a fraction of that. Most prospectors reached the Territory by water and then travelled overland to the interior by the Chilkoot Trail or the White Pass to stake their claims. The trail inland was gruelling both on travellers and the animals they brought with them. (There is an infamous bend in the climb to the summit where, if you look down, you can see the piles of bleached white bones of hundreds of horses who, exhausted and likely starved, voluntarily leapt over the edge.)

This was the easy route, however. Others went over land, up through Alberta, over to BC and then north. Given the urgency and the cultural politics of the day, many had little regard for the Aboriginal people whose land they were passing through. Such a people were understandably restless and wanted protection for their territories and possessions. The government, unfortunately, would not intervene until the Treaty was signed three years later.

Treaty 8, in many ways, has come to represent a site where two conflicting interpretations came to rest; the first based on the understanding that the signing was largely a symbolic gesture signifying peace and friendship (a perspective that has been considered by the federal government as the byproduct of mistranslation) and the other being the surrender of all Aboriginal title to the land in exchange for reserves, government aid and, for some, one-time settlements of 185 acre plots of land or cash. This agreement ensured that there was little or no resistance to future settlement, burgeoning industry, oil and mineral exploration, and the use of the region for travel and the transport of goods.

The concept of property and land ownership, however, was not all that easily understood or rationalised by a people who

Top
View of a street between the tents of the Eighteenth Engineers'
Headquarters and Service Company camp at Whitehorse during
the building of the Alaska Highway, May 1942.
Image courtesy Yukon Archives, Robert Hays Fonds.

Bottom
The Eighteenth Engineers constructing a bridge over
Cracker Creek on the Alaska Highway, June 1942.
Image courtesy Yukon Archives, Robert Hays Fonds.

Opposite left
Brian Jungen
Greater Vancouver, 2007
18 baltic plywood cutouts, wool fabric
320 x 335 x 7.6 cm
Image courtesy Catriona Jeffries
Gallery, Vancouver.
Photograph by Scott Massey.

Opposite centre and right
Brian Jungen
Bush Capsule, along with study, 2000
Plastic chairs, polyethylene,
fluorescent lights
Image courtesy Catriona Jeffries
Gallery, Vancouver.

had developed a fluid and shifting notion of territory, not based on 'ownership' of the land *per se*, but one defined in relation to the environment, its available resources and also to itinerancy, which was enacted through a network of overlapping routes for hunting, trapping and communication. They lived what could be called a 'pluri-local' lifestyle which, to borrow from Stephen Cairns, "consist[s] of one's sense of origin, current location and possible destination".[1] The Aboriginal people who live along the Alaska Highway for example, did not reside in one area, preferring instead to settle farther south in the summer and relocate north to better hunting areas in the winter.[2] The idea that one couldn't continue to have free use over this itinerant route (which could easily stretch for one hundred miles) but would instead 'own' a single plot in a grid measured one mile by one mile was, for obvious reasons, not readily accepted. Land and identity are deeply intertwined and as such are not so easily untangled. Subjectivity, in this sense, was developed in relation to all the shifting elements of the land, not relative to the built environment. It was through the Treaty signing process and its implications that this land (and all the areas of Canada which had been designated as reserve land before this point) shifted from what Henri Lefebvre has called "social space" to "abstract space". Abstract space is "alienated space, universalised and therefore without time. Reified as exchange value by the state, by planners, by capitalist interests, it is an object of instrumentalisation, a way to condition and contain its inhabitants." Social space "complicates the notion of space tied unilaterally to the means of production, appealing instead to its use value and rejecting its representation as necessarily functionalist. Social space is determined conflictually, it is riven at its foundation, heterogeneous and structured around difference."[3]

When asked why he wanted to do a work based on Treaty 8, Jungen replied that it was because the Treaty itself was so bizarre and unfair. The project he is now developing situates itself between these two differing understandings of property and between social

and abstract space. As art historian, Pamela Lee, has pointed out the "very notion of property as a thing to be owned is a relatively recent phenomenon, beginning as late as the eighteenth century".[4]

An aspect of Jungen's project, which will be exhibited in 2008, is the construction of a tent of sorts. Initially installed in his home community on Treaty 8, the artist expects the structure to be used in summer 2009 during the annual Treaty Days Celebration as a site for the distribution of annuities for the Aboriginal people. Each is entitled to five dollars, given out by the Royal Canadian Mounted Police, along with a handshake. Through the building of this structure, which is not a pavilion in the conventional sense as its politics are too riven, Jungen is forming a third space; a structure that physically demarcates the historic meeting point of two nations and also calls attention to the ways in which the distribution of annuities (and other promises outlined by the Treaty) have become a performative gesture. Designed to be ephemeral, the structure does not aspire to historical stability as conventional monuments do: it embraces inhabiting the moment.

Jungen's previous projects often bring together disparate objects. In the past he has furthered the discourse on the readymade by taking apart and resewing Nike Air Jordan trainers into Northwest Coast 'masks' and by re-assembling plastic lawn chairs into massive bow whale skeletons. Here he brings together two different cultures and all the meaning and history invoked in a single handshake. The second part of Jungen's project involves the act of submitting proposals for the possible purchase of various plots of land in the region. He had initially considered filing a lawsuit against the federal government. As curator, Jessica Morgan, has described; the suit would seek compensation for Aboriginal people "who have subsequently left the designated reserves allotted by the Crown in 1900".[5] The process, while of symbolic importance, would take years to come to fruition and would be fraught with enormous legal fees.

Jungen's purchase of this land could be considered akin to Gordon Matta-Clark's *Fake Estates*, an ongoing project where the

artist purchased unusable, diminutive slivers of property between buildings (in some cases less than 30 centimetres wide) often at auctions in New York for very little money. In contrast to the *Fake Estates*—purchased specifically by Matta-Clark because, due to their small size and close proximity to other buildings, they were not developable—much of the land Jungen is interested in buying is unusable precisely because it is too remote and far away from other developed areas. The idea, then, of proposing a shopping mall in Buick Creek, an area near Jungen's reserve, which is home to approximately 25 people, becomes absurd. To quote Lee's writing on Matta-Clark:

> The paradox of buying this unusable land, of submitting without use value to the registers of exchange value, presents a contemporary attenuation of Marx' early thinking on property, when he notes that 'private property has made us so stupid and narrow minded that an object is only ours when we have it, when it exists as capital for us'.[6]

These lands, then, are 'leftover' because they are not (or can not) be legislated for use and they refuse ownership because they are illegible and ambiguous. Jungen's proposal to purchase land in Treaty 8 is also calls attention to the history of the Métis settlement in Canada: comprised by settlers who, because of their heritage, were more often than not left out of the Treaty signing process. The Métis, people, who were of mixed European and native ancestry, quite literally occupied a no-man's land. They didn't have the right to live on Aboriginal reserves and often didn't have the means to purchase land that, up to that point, had been rightfully theirs (an issue that was the cause of some of the most significant rebellions and protests in the formation of Canada). In the provinces of Saskatchewan and Manitoba Métis people increasingly occupied the only area fitting their predicament; slim strips of land bordering

farming communities and Aboriginal reserves set aside for the building of future roads. It was in these road allowances where the Prairie's first squatters came into being; people who, through this illegal act, called into question social and economic systems that didn't serve all of the citizens of the country. The road allowances were formed in the late 1920s, as a result of plans to transfer control of what were called Crown Lands (lands owned by the federal government) to settlers. Through the surveying process and the division of the Prairies into systemised units of measure—acres, in this instance—ten metre wide plots of land were set aside for future roads. These areas, as can be imagined, were too narrow for conventional habitation—their intention being for transportation, not for settlement.

What is significant about the Métis occupation of these spaces was the degree to which they subverted the land from this newly defined purpose. Through the simple act of habitation, these sites were transformed from property into social space.[7] In other words, it was through defining (an)other space, that they rendered a social dimension to the land. If the architectural grid speaks to the rationalisation (colonisation) of space so to speak, the Métis sought refuge in the peripheries of this grid, the in-between, and the non-site. For Matta-Clark, property was only accorded value when it passed into a state of uselessness or ruin. Yet it was only land in this state that the Métis could accord it value. In an act that is part reterritorialisation, part cultural re-appropriation, and part stealthy inversion, the houses that the Métis people brought over to this area, and subsequently transformed, were former trappers' cabins.

For Heidegger, the processes of building and place-making are inextricably linked to the constitution of authentic subjectivity. Perhaps it's not so much the constitution of authentic subjectivity that is brought forth in Jungen's project and the Métis settlements but the meaning found in the transformation, re-appropriation, and resignification of land and the built environment.

Temporary Territories
• Marjetica Potrč

At the Kunst-Werke Cafe

Two weeks ago, on a rainy afternoon, I was sitting in the Kunst-Werke Cafe in Berlin with Kyong Park. We were discussing Balkan cities. The autumn rain was pouring against a glass wall, transforming the pavilion where we sat into a kind of island. At the time I thought, what is it that draws me away from islands and to cities that no one seems to care about and would be afraid to visit? I still remember the e-mails I received, back in the spring of 2003, cautioning me not to go to Caracas. I wondered whether I would be able to tell the stories of a city in crisis and the stories embedded in its architecture? Would people back home understand narratives that, at first glance, did not appear to concern them? Now, looking back at my Caracas experience, I feel that the opportunity to study the city was an extraordinary gift, one that has helped me better understand the cities I love.

Many of my projects started in Caracas: *Dry Toilet,* constructed on site in a Caracas barrio, and the Urgent Architecture exhibition, which I dreamt up with Michael Rush, then director of the Palm Beach Institute of Contemporary Art (PBICA) in Florida. The PBICA exhibition gave body to recent trends in contemporary architecture, such as the emphasis on private space and personal security. For me, the most important thing about this exhibition was the attempt to construct an understandable language out of the apparent madness of cities in crisis. After all, the architecture of such cities tells vivid stories, since reality seems somehow enhanced there.1

The City of Caracas

The city's underground passages were full of people pressing onward, always too close to my body. Above ground, the city weighed heavy. It was noisy and loud, and never slept. It was smelly and dirty. The tropical rain, which unleashed a pure natural energy, was the only thing able to calm things down and give me a chance to breathe.

Caracas is a pagan city full of 'survivors'; individuals who stake their claim to happiness in an apparently collapsing city. Events impose themselves on you easily here, whether crimes, floods or celebrations. I found that, once I had arrived, this dangerous and divided city would not let me go.

I came to Caracas in order to research the informal city, which is one way of referring to the barrios of Venezuela.[1] In Caracas, this informal, climbing sprawl encircles and presses in on the formal city that occupies the valley below. The communities that inhabit the two areas are alien to each other, with different value systems that breed mutual mistrust. They co-exist in close proximity, and continually accommodate each another, but never mix. The divisions in Caracas are unmistakable. I had no problem accepting this fact; the permanence of this division. The finality of such is the only really permanent characteristic of the city. Everything else exists in a flux of decay and expansion in the midst of crisis.

The formal city, once a proud modernist town, is now in decline and fast becoming a modern ruin. It seemed to me that it was losing its body as well as its mind; wildly and without regret. Oversized billboards, sometimes bigger than the houses they were built on, were left empty. The Parque Central building complex—once the pride of Caracas modernism—had deteriorated and was overrun by nature. Built-on additions and vegetation sprouted from its monumental facades. The ground floor shopping mall was deserted, and shop windows barricaded. The elevators did not work. Parque Central was consumed by its own malaise and had apparently abandoned modernism's quest to display the values of functionalism and consumer society. It's demise was almost biblical.

A block away, the Urban Agriculture Co-operative occupied a former public park. Those who lived in the vicinity viewed the

Marjetica Potrč
Hybrid House: Caracas, West Bank, West Palm Beach, 2003
Images courtesy of the artist and Max Protetch Gallery, New York.
Photographs by Michael Price.

urban farm as an invasion of the rural into their urban landscape; the barrios, too, were considered a form of rural architecture, an alien growth in the modernist city. Though the barrios were not as close as the urban farm, they were constantly present. From almost anywhere in the formal city, you could see the outlying hills populated by barrio communities. Who were these people and why did they persist in invading the city with their urban farms and informal marketplaces? They had arrived in Caracas from the rural hinterland and had stayed, becoming the construction workers who built the formal city by day, and their own by night.

The barrios are not planned settlements; they are homes built without permission. These homes are self-initiated structures that have been upgraded and expanded as needs dictate. In Caracas, such barrios are expanding, not decaying, and they exude a confidence in their own body. Theirs is a rural architecture made of tightly interwoven buildings and alleys. The people who live there have prevailed against all odds; their houses growing in size with their families. Such growth is clearly visible from the construction wires that sprout from each rooftop: this ephemeral city is here to stay.

Urgent Architecture

Near the end of my stay in Caracas, I had the seemingly wild idea to compare the structures borrowed from the temporary architecture of Caracas with the West Bank territory in the Middle East; culminating in the project *Hybrid House*. I thought there might be similar strategies of contemporary architecture in both places, and this eventually proved true. Working with Eyal Weizman—the Israeli architect based in Tel Aviv and London—I compiled an archive of case studies that put in perspective the recent architecture of both places. The terms we used to discuss such case studies were useful in explaining facts on the ground, although they sounded rather like a dictionary of

architecture from the distant past or some science fiction future: dynamic mapping, vertical geometry, colonisation and the claiming of land, the appropriation of public space, invasions, temporary territories, and so on. Such were the strategies and direct actions that grew out of extreme urban environments. In both Caracas and the West Bank, public space was eroding and private space expanding. The modernism that Tel Aviv and Caracas are so proud of (and which, in my view, attempted to visualise democracy by creating shared public spaces) was being obliterated. In its place, sharp divisions between public and private space had emerged. Mutually alien communities co-existed in close proximity and had to continually oblige one another; whether Palestinians and Jewish settlers, or the inhabitants of the formal city of Caracas and the barrio dwellers. These are dynamic and hostile territories. Defence architecture takes hold, illustrating an obsessive personal control of territory. In an apparent absence of democratic values, there is a seemingly regressive return to archetypes, such as gated communities and fortress-like houses: the phrase "my home is my castle" is never more prevalent.

A few months prior to this, I put *Hybrid House* forward for inclusion in an exhibition at PBICA, Florida. My work with Eyal had confirmed that both Caracas and the West Bank—on the face of it, very different and unconnected places—developed similar strategies while shaping their environments. Were these strategies just Babylonian murmurings? We proved this not to be the case.

At first sight, the PBICA show looked like a monumental pile of houses and infrastructure gadgetry. It was crucial for me that *Hybrid House* should convey the energy of Caracas, including an overemphasis on communication and energy infrastructure. The gallery space was congested. Despite an apparently wild, uncivilised appearance, the houses referenced in this work are actually put together with great care. Their 'body parts'—and the stories they tell—were analysed, given a name, and reconstructed in the gallery. The first floor of the Caracas house was made with heavy concrete building blocks; a common building material in Caracas barrios. All doors and windows were barred, reflecting the enhanced security found throughout the city. The second floor was built with milk crates—these would be beer crates in Caracas—indicating the kind of recyclable material that is used in barrio structures. A watchtower was placed in the corner of the house to allude to the need for personal surveillance of territory. Most importantly, the house had an extension, or 'extended territory' on the ground; a common strategy employed to enlarge a barrio home. A false facade would be built in front of the house, complete with windows and doors, as a way of declaring one's intention to occupy land. As for the temporary building materials barrio structures use, such as corrugated metal sheets, these eventually become permanent. Here again are parallels between Caracas and the West Bank. In the West Bank, a strategic position on top of a hill allows for personal surveillance of the territory below, while containers—a form of temporary architecture— soon transform themselves into a fortress-like architecture. So, as an afterthought, it seemed a natural idea to install a Jewish-settlement container on the second floor of the Caracas house.

Hybrid House consisted of five structures: a Caracas barrio house, *Dry Toilet*, which the Israeli architect, Liyat Esakov, and I initiated in the La Vega barrio, a Jewish-settlement container, a Palestinian house, and a Palm Beach trailer. These were family-size houses that attempted to portray the determination and the aspirations of settlers who claim their place in the contemporary urban setting.

Caracas: *Dry Toilet*

Dry Toilet was the result of a six month stay in Caracas, where we researched the informal city under the auspices of the *Caracas Case Project*. A dry, ecologically safe toilet was built on the upper part of the La Vega barrio, a district without access to the municipal water grid. *Dry Toilet* attempted to rethink the relationship between infrastructure and architecture in real-life urban practice in a city where half the population receives water from municipal authorities no more than two days a week.

In our collaboration for the *Caracas Case Project*, Liyat and I knew only that we wanted to work inside the informal city and not merely analyse it from a safe distance. It was some time before we could actually walk through the alleys of the barrio. You always had to be escorted there; it was too dangerous to visit alone. With the aid of Raul Zelik, another participant in the *Caracas Case Project*, we made contact with community leaders and were eventually shown around. Most importantly, we were able to discuss living conditions with barrio residents. What became obvious, and most shocking, was the breakdown of the energy infrastructure and the lack of public utilities in the informal city. This was not what we had anticipated, since we all were focused on the fascinating and seemingly precarious architecture of the barrios. We soon realised that the failure of the municipal infrastructure in the barrios was a logical outcome of the houses' construction process. In a planned city, the various forms of public infrastructure are set in place before construction starts. In the barrios, the houses are built first and infrastructure problems dealt with later.

Liyat and I asked a group of barrio residents for their thoughts on self-sustainable energy solutions such as solar panels to provide them with more electricity. They were not interested: self-sustainable energy technologies were relevant only to the 'rich'. Drinking water, however, was another matter since it was provided by the city for only a few hours twice a week. The upper part of the La Vega barrio, where we eventually built *Dry Toilet,* had no access to running water at all. This was a place ruled by necessity.

We wanted to discover if barrio residents could apply their survival strategies to utility infrastructures in a more focused way. Instead of shooting at the municipal water pipes in order to obtain

Opposite left
Marjetica Potrč in collaboration
with Liyat Esakov
Dry Toilet, 2003
Image courtesy the artists.
Photograph by Andre Cypriano.

Opposit right
Marjetica Potrč
Rooftop Room, 2003
Courtesy the artist and the Eighth
International Istanbul Biennial.
Photograph by Muammer
Yanmaz and Orton Akinci.

more water illegally, could they adopt a different approach? Could they reduce their consumption of water? They would certainly use less water if they had a toilet that did not require it. In this way, they could solve the infrastructure problem themselves, independent of municipal authorities.

Dry Toilet caught the imagination of the community; it made sense, after all. It was built by a team of construction workers from the community in La Fila, the upper section of the La Vega barrio, on barrio resident Raquel's 'property' (if you can speak in this way about occupied public land); her house had never had a toilet before. Barrio buildings are self-initiated and self-upgrading structures that function on a small scale. I still wonder why no one had previously thought to apply their strategies—their tropicalism, their non-linear logic—on a more widespread basis.

For Liyat and I, it was important that Hidrocapital, the municipal water company, supported *Dry Toilet*. For the La Vega community, the project provided a long-term sustainable solution for the problem of waste water, radically reducing the community's water consumption. At one point Hidrocapital envisioned building full scale models of the project in every municipality as an educational endeavour. Remember the urban farm in the middle of the formal city? This same co-operative considered erecting a dry toilet on its premises, but eventually decided the contrary out of fear of controversy.

Istanbul: *Rooftop Room*

In 2003, I was asked to create a project for the Eighth International Istanbul Biennial; the title of which was Poetic Justice. At the time, I was deeply involved in the *Dry Toilet* project in La Vega. It became a matter of ethics for me that whatever project I made for Istanbul should be as meaningful as I thought *Dry Toilet* was.

I knew from the start that I did not want to make this project in a public space. I am aware that Europeans are unconditionally committed to such spaces, but this is something I have never really understood. Such dedication to this concept of public space has little to do with what these spaces actually become, that is, territories controlled by special interests. In my view, the European commitment to public space is largely symbolic and is most probably due to the reliance on the social state. One could also look back to the Renaissance, when such spaces became a significant issue along with democracy, to explain such commitment: a public square was intended to be egalitarian, free for everyone.

In contemporary cities public spaces are not only being privatised, but eroded. In Caracas—a contemporary city where what little there is of the social state is dissolving—public space is either lacking or abused. In the informal city, there is no real public space. All public space is privately negotiated, and *vice versa*; private space becomes public only when required. In the formal city, public squares have been invaded by groups of people on a temporary basis; Chavista demonstrators or street sellers, for example. Temporariness, not stability, characterises contemporary Caracas. While the Venezuelan capital might be an extreme example, the West Bank presents an even harsher scenario. There, the temporary condition is sealed behind walls while security measures are pushed to the limit. Both places are telling in their emphasis on private space and personal security. Could they become case studies for European cities, which have been experiencing the gradual consumption of public space by private concerns? (For example, in Liverpool's Paradise Street development, the developer plans to implement a private security programme. If successful, the rest of the city may follow its example.)

For Poetic Justice, then, I decided to make *Rooftop Room*; comprised by a temporary roof built atop a privately owned, flat top house (the house in question belonged to a family in Kustepe, a suburb of Istanbul). The already existing roof was quite large. We

decided to build a 70 square metre tin roof. No plans were drawn up; the construction was agreed on orally and approved by the city. During the Biennial, blue plastic curtains were chosen to encircle the space, and it all looked quite beautiful. A plastic table and chairs —a popular style that has seemingly been around forever—were placed there. I never saw the completed *Rooftop Room* in person, but I later received pictures showing how the family had upgraded the area under the constructed roof.

Essentially, *Rooftop Room* touches on several issues. This was a public project in a private space. In creating it, I diverted money from art to life. The project was not centrally located (Kustepe is an outlying suburb of Istanbul). Surprisingly, Biennial organisers raised no questions either about the dislocation of the project or about the fact that a public project was being implemented in private space that visitors to the Biennial could not enter. By making a temporary project that became permanent, I pointed to the legitimacy of so-called temporary architecture, which is, I believe, the most permanent aspect of contemporary cities.

Liverpool: *Balcony with Wind Turbine*

In 2004, I was invited by Sabine Breitwieser, director of the Generali Foundation in Vienna, to participate in the Third Liverpool Biennial. The result was *Balcony with Wind Turbine*, an installation on the fourteenth floor of the Bispham House tower block. *Balcony with Wind Turbine* developed at the same time as the Istanbul project; the difference was that I first made a research visit to Liverpool before making the proposal. As I perused the city, I was unexpectedly reminded of the work I had done with the *Caracas Case Project*: Liverpool is a shrinking city. Both the *Caracas Case Project* and the *Shrinking Cities Project* examined the informal city, and although I knew that such towns as Detroit, Michigan, and cities in former East

Germany had declining populations, I was not aware that Liverpool did too. From first-hand experience, I could see that Liverpool and Caracas had many things in common (though in differing intensities) such as the privatisation of space, an almost absurd amount of personal security measures, the irrational treatment of space, and the collapse of large scale systems. Of course, Liverpool appeared to be a more balanced city than Caracas, but it was not necessarily less wild (next to London, Liverpool has the greatest number of security cameras per inhabitant in the world).

For *Balcony with Wind Turbine* I originally proposed to attach a bay window to an apartment in Bispham House and upgrade the architectural addition with a windmill to provide energy. I felt such an extension of private space was appropriate in a city that was preparing to transform a public park into a residential gated community with big gardens. *Balcony with Wind Turbine* attempted to point out that tenants do not have to be resettled in order to improve their living conditions and hinted at what a small, customised addition might do. I also hoped it would inspire tenants to be independent of the municipal power grid and generate their own energy.

In the process of implementing the project, which lasted a year and a half, the bay window was transformed into a balcony. The change mirrored a new trend: balconies have suddenly become a desirable feature on residential buildings in Liverpool. As for bay windows, with which Liverpool abounds, I was reminded of the transformations they went through in contemporary Caracas. In this once proud modernist city, bay windows were used to display the interior of a home; now, they hide it. They serve to survey the outside territory from inside the house, just as in Liverpool.

Tent Embassies: Collapsing, Australia and Architecture • Gregory Cowan

In this text I want to discuss tent embassies as examples of an informal architecture that is temporal, mobile and collaborative. The tent embassy is such a marginal spatial phenomenon that, on first consideration, it can barely be recognised as architecture and might equally be regarded as anti-architecture. However, to acknowledge protest architecture as a political tool of active democracy is to understand its value in providing a primordial space for dissent. Georges Bataille's notion of *l'informe*—the informal—is politically very relevant in this case, especially in light of Australia's "Sorry" statement in February 2008.[1]

The activist constructions I consider here have rarely been architecturally theorised. In accord with *l'informe*, protest constructions loosen the symbolic authority of architecture in anticipation of late twentieth century post-Structuralism. This text will argue that such constructions also serve to affect the meaning of architecture and theory in twenty-first century Australia.

Bataille and *L'informe*

Potentially paradoxical, the title *Informal Architectures* illustrates the way in which architecture is often defined by its 'other'. Similarly, the noun construction 'tent embassy' suggests a mobile architecture for a serious diplomatic purpose. If architecture, as read *arche* (significant) *tecture* (construction) is to be understood as being made not literally of matter but process—form may be considered secondary to meaning. Bataille suggests that *l'informe* breaks down the binary thinking of 'form versus content' that dominated modern art. Thus, *Informal Architectures* refers to spaces that are contingent, hypothetical, temporary, mobile, fictional or weak.[2]

> .... formless is thus not merely an adjective with such and such a meaning, but a term for lowering status with its

implied requirement that everything have a form.... Whatever [formless] designates lacks entitlement in every sense and is crushed on the spot, like a spider or an earthworm.[3]

This discussion begins and ends with the Aboriginal Tent Embassy, in Canberra, Australia; the durable 'monument' of a national Aboriginal rights movement. The original, tent embassy, or the 'mother of tent embassies', it is recognised as the site where the term was first coined. An embassy is generally understood to be a diplomatic station for ambassadors in a foreign land. The 'ambassadors' in this case set up camp outside Parliament House in the Australian Capital in 1972; in an attempt to highlight their perceived position as foreigners in their own land; foreigners, because they were citizens with no legal rights to use the land that is their birthright. The emergence of this particular manifestation of post-1968 political activism followed the 1967 referendum that formally precipitated Aboriginal citizenship in Australia. It developed a part of Australian identity, with the informal architecture of the movement playing a critically important background role. The Aboriginal Tent Embassy, Canberra, is a place that, it is suggested, captures the spirit of nomadic Aboriginal architecture (perhaps unconsciously) as temporal, mobile and collaborative. Over 36 years since it was established, the Embassy endures to this day, and is listed in Australia's Register of National Estate.

The Aboriginal Tent Embassy, Sydney—a temporary structure erected form August to October in Sydney during the Olympic Games—builds upon the idea of the Canberra embassy. It helped give rise to the subsequent international embassy at the International Court of Justice at The Hague, in September 2001. There, a plea was made that Australian sovereignty had never been ceded, a message that the Aboriginal Tent Embassy, Canberra, maintains.

This text also addresses the Perth People's Peace Embassy. A protest with no political connection to the Aboriginal Tent Embassy,

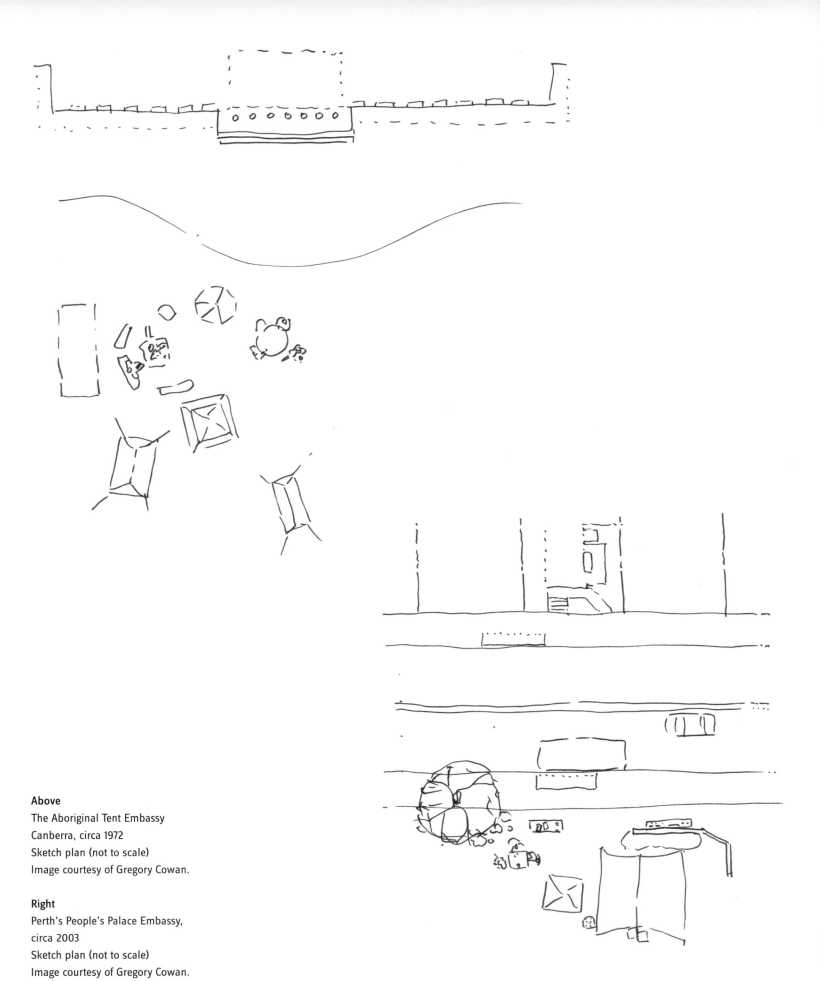

Above
The Aboriginal Tent Embassy
Canberra, circa 1972
Sketch plan (not to scale)
Image courtesy of Gregory Cowan.

Right
Perth's People's Palace Embassy,
circa 2003
Sketch plan (not to scale)
Image courtesy of Gregory Cowan.

Canberra, it gave shape to a grassroots campaign asserting Australian identity, sovereignty and an alternative sense of responsibility for nationhood, on the eve of the invasion of Iraq. The activists responsible for the Perth People's Peace Embassy effectively established a 'temporary autonomous zone' to provide space on 'street level' to debate the Australian government's decision to assist in the invasion of Iraq, and to question the country's political autonomy.[4] This text aims to address the wider relevance of the critical understanding of such embassies and their effectiveness as an architectural tactic for protest culture in Australia.

Nomadic Resistance

A culture of 'nomadic resistance' is the motivation behind the use of temporal, mobile and collaborative architecture in the Australian protest culture sketched out here. From Australia's symbolic political centre in the 1970s—the parliamentary triangle in Canberra—the resistance moved forward in the guise of the Aboriginal Tent Embassy, Sydney, during the Olympic Games. The idea of nomadic resistance by a dissenting minority in a 'pathetic' or 'weak' structure was then extended to the Perth People's Peace Embassy, in 2003, emerging in an arguably audacious (if futile) response to Australian foreign policy; namely, Australia's role in the war in Iraq.

Grassroots protest in Australia has found expression in spontaneous self-built informal architecture. The formal term 'architecture', linguistically Latin in origin, is traditionally embedded in white Western cultural tradition. Attributed to Vitruvius, the word entered the English language in the seventeenth century, and was used by by the British Empire as the agency establishing 'settled civilisation' in Australia.[5] The informal architecture of the tent embassy is not readily recognised from this Eurocentric perspective. Instead, it performs as a kind of 'war machine' in the sense used

by Deleuze and Guattari—autonomous, independent of the state apparatus and nomadic.[6] The outsider has something to say through this device, and their message might create a useful debate with the society from which they have been ejected.

Extending this further, it may be argued that this way of deploying architecture was known also to Vitruvius, in his writing about siege machines.[7] As a form of 'cunning construction', the architecture of the tent embassy harbours a "lament for the loss of movement", as Catherine Ingraham interpreted Vitruvius' description of the war machine in his tenth book on architecture.[8] The tent embassy is remarkable for its conceptual profundity and pragmatism, performing as both message and shelter. It challenges traditional Western notions of architecture as materially crafted and physically permanent 'fortressed' space. The 'weak' and 'pathetic' appearance of the collapsible tent embassy veils the 'content' of this metaphorical architecture; its ironic, powerful meaning.

In a previous text, I have reflected on the situation of Captain Philip's First Fleet of British military arriving and camping in Australia in 1788 in comparison to that of Aboriginal people protesting about being 'foreigners' in their own land in the 1970s. In a mid-1788 diary entry the settler, Watkin Tench, juxtaposes the squalid and unsatisfactory reality of camping in Australia with the romantic image of marquees on an English lawn:

Since our disembarkation, in the preceding January, the efforts of every one had been unremittingly exerted, to deposit the public stores in a state of shelter and security, and to erect habitations for ourselves. We were eager to escape from tents, where a fold of canvas, only, interposed to check the vertical beams of the sun in summer, and the chilling blasts of the south in winter. A marquee pitched, in our finest season, on an English lawn; or a transient view of those gay camps, near the metropolis, which so many remember naturally draws forth careless and unmeaning explanations of rapture, which attach ideas of pleasure only, to this part of a soldier's life. But an encampment amidst the rocks and wilds of a new country, aggravated by the miseries of a bad diet and incessant toil, will find few admirers.[9]

The harsh reality of environmentally sustainable life in the Australian winter was clearly turning out to be less attractive than those summer garden parties in the old country to which the former was always inevitably compared. The bad diet in the colony, despite the unnoticed availability of organic Aboriginal food and the unlimited toil needed to civilise the wilderness of nature, would have been daunting.

The Aboriginal Tent Embassy, Canberra

The Aboriginal Tent Embassy, Canberra, was inaugurated opposite the Parliament House in Australia's capital city in 1972. On 26 January, in response to the then Prime Minister's plans outlined in the Australia Day speech about Aboriginal land rights, activists Michael Anderson, Tony Coorey, Bertie Williams and Billy Craigie drove from Sydney to Canberra in a borrowed car. From the luggage compartment they produced a beach umbrella, which was erected in front of Parliament House, and from this grew a 'sprinkling' of tents. Within hours the Embassy became a tent encampment succeeding, as its 'informal architects' had intended, to alert the world to the plight of the Aboriginal people.

The Embassy is not merely a shelter but a metaphor that communicates a political, social and architectural message; providing a tangible identity for the 'Australian Aboriginal nation', and a case for Aboriginal land rights. It also, idealistically, suggests the environmentally low impact and rent free way of living associated with camping. Following the success of the 1967 referendum leading to formal recognition of Aboriginal people as voting citizens, the formation of a national Aboriginal movement was now possible, along with the freedom to travel nationally. However, the cooperation between people of various culturally and linguistically distinct Aboriginal groups more numerous than those of Western Europe was never effortless, and is still a work in progress.[10] The advent of the Aboriginal Tent Embassy, Canberra, was a milestone in the process of Aboriginal nation building, and the place where the Aboriginal land rights flag was also inaugurated.

The setting is ironic because, although occupied officially for 61 years, Parliament House went by the official moniker 'Provisional Parliament House'.[11] When the new, 'permanent' Parliament House was completed in 1988, the 'Old Parliament House' as it is now known, grew increasingly unpopular.[12] While Australia's national identity was well-established before 1988, its federal parliament building was merely 'provisional' until the two hundredth anniversary of formal colonial arrival/invasion. By occupying the lawn in front of the Old Parliament House—the 'doorstep' of the nation—the Embassy continues to highlight the rights of citizens to peacefully protest and occupy public space.

The use of camping and tents could be regarded as the oldest environmental/architectural tradition in Australia, from the camps of Aboriginal people (an integral part of a holistic architectural nomadology of shelters, windbreaks, fish traps and so on) to the first white 'settlers' and to contemporary global adventure tourism, enduringly popular with visitors from all over the world exercising freedom to 'camp out'. In the Western world (with the exception of Bedouin and other such nomadic tent traditions) tent encampments tend to follow 'formal' military Roman traditions. Camping in Australia seems to reflect an Aboriginal attitude to nature that has parallels among traditionally 'nomadic' peoples all over the world. The symbolism of the architecture has changed considerably with the tactics of occupation.

Gregory Cowan
Untitled
Informal or illegal building is often
regarded as an 'eyesore', yet it challenges
the formal urban architecture, and
therefore the establishment. This
illustration depicts an 'unsanctioned'
construction in Ulaanbaatar, Mongolia,
near the author's apartment.

On 19 February 2002 the local authority objected to a newly erected structure at the Aboriginal Tent Embassy, Canberra, a so-called *gunyah*, and staged a pre-dawn police raid to dismantle the structure. Police watched as contractors "pulled down and removed a six metre high A-frame structure" which had been erected on the original Tent Embassy site over the Australia Day weekend, 24 days earlier.[13]

Aboriginal Tent Embassy, Sydney

The Aboriginal Tent Embassy, Sydney, endured for the duration of the 2000 Olympic Games. There is a dry irony in the contrast between the Olympic tradition from Greek Civilisation and the Embassy in Sydney. The latter was also, quite importantly, a focus for the walks and journeys of its diverse participants before, during and after the Embassy's duration. Reminiscent of the Olympic torch relay, representatives of various Aboriginal groups brought some of their sacred fires to Victoria Park from as far as thousands of kilometres away, retracing ancient Aboriginal walks.

In August 2004 (as has frequently been the case since 1972) the Aboriginal Tent Embassy, Canberra, was denounced by government officials. They proposed to sanitise the area, threatening to replace the lively camp with an alternative 'interactive display'. The campfire would be replaced by a computer screen so that the multiplicity of stories and histories might be consolidated into a singular approved piece of interpretative 'content'; a lifeless monument.

Further protest encampments have sprung up in Australia, especially during the tense period following September 2001. Amid worldwide peace demonstrations in 2001, a Peace Embassy was erected in Melbourne, in front of the State Library of Victoria. Tent encampments such as this are further examples of the spontaneous and ephemeral architecture of political activism.

The Perth People's Peace Embassy

Perth is regarded as one of the world's most liveable cities. As one of the world's most isolated, it is as geographically remote from global political disturbance as can be. The Perth People's Peace Embassy emerged in March 2003 in the wake of the Iraq War after the government became a member of the 'coalition of the willing'. As the antithesis of Australia's war effort, it provided a meeting place for those concerned about humanity in the Middle East.

The Embassy was also constructed in response to geographical landmarks on the site. It was assembled on the grassy verge of Perth Concert Hall, whose low concrete street sign was appropriated as a bunker wall. This verge was also located across from the main urban terrace of the city's American Embassy, exploiting the juxtaposition of the two contrasting Embassies and their sight lines.

As I wrote my notes on 8 April 2003, the Perth People's Peace Embassy had been erected for nearly 20 nights. The City of Perth, as well as the management of the Perth Concert Hall, had been cooperative, making reasonable requests for constraints on their 'tenants'—no recognisable 'tents' and no 'camping' overnight. Ultimately, it seems, they tolerated the democratic use of public space in Perth, and freedom of expression.

Australian Identity

When the Aboriginal Tent Embassy, Canberra, was established in 1972 it was clear that the standard of living for Aboriginal people, along with the state of Aboriginal architecture, travel and landscape management had worsened. The impoverished living conditions of Aboriginal people in the 1960s and 70s starkly contrasted with the affluent non-Aboriginal average. This contrast is reflected in the 'makeshift camp' of the Embassy opposite Old Parliament House.

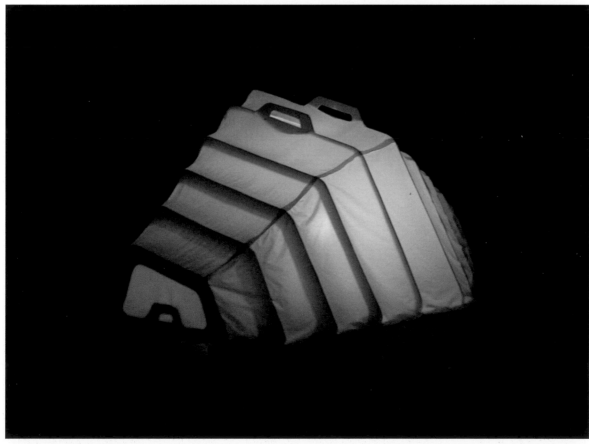

Top
Sophie-Catharine LaFlamme
Floating Frame, 2004
© Robert Kronenburg 2004.

Bottom
Justin Beal
Flat-pack Shelter, 2004
© Robert Kronenburg 2004.

people? And how do heavy, static, inflexible homes restrict human awareness of self, freedom, environment and nature?

It is not just the individual's desires that affect the way that modern architecture is provided, however, but necessity. There is a growing awareness that sustainability and ecological impact are crucial factors in the way we inhabit the world. To protect our long-term future, buildings must be seen as tools that are continually useful and respond to change with minimal reconstruction effort (with its consequent waste of materials and other resources). They must also be finely tuned to our needs in order to be efficient. This means that people should be more aware of the parameters and opportunities of the built environment which they inhabit and, if not physically constructing homes themselves, at least be able to knowledgably influence the sort of homes that are built for them. We all have an intimate experience of our home and the way we use it—it is not something we operate, like a washing machine or a toaster—but rather a building in which we invest time and energy and care for. Few would now argue that 'the house as home' is a less desirable approach to dwelling design than Le Corbusier's famous but misguided statement "a house is a machine for living in".[2]

Portable architecture is a fascinating and important genre in the field of building design. Though the idea of creating buildings that move may at first seem contradictory there are in fact portable buildings that fulfil similar functions to static facilities in every aspect of human activity: dwelling, education, commerce, medicine, industry, entertainment and the military. Portable architecture is invariably commissioned because of its capacity to do things that static buildings cannot. In some cases it is more efficient, more economically viable, more sustainable to build portable. Because of the unique demands that are made on portable architecture it is often innovative in form and construction, using new and lightweight materials, structural strategies, servicing and logistical systems. As a result of the efficiency that is a core factor in its development, portable architecture leads the way in finding new construction strategies of use in convential building than other architecture.

However there are other cultural characteristics of portable architecture that also make it interesting. A mobile building is not subjected to the same restrictions as a permanent one; it can take advantage of sensitive and historic sites where new buildings would normally not be allowed. It can be a surreptitious promoter for avant-garde design in unlikely places. The idea of a movable building has positive associations with freedom of expression and personal liberty. The mobile dwelling denotes the gypsy, the nomad, the seasoned traveller; a simpler lifestyle with fewer restrictions and less baggage. It enables a closer relationship with the environment, by moving with the seasons and providing the opportunity to reside in the natural environment. The possibilities offered by a portable dwelling enables us to connect more readily with the romantic, but nevertheless essential, ideal of living.[3]

The Design Workshop

In the winter of 2000 I was invited to contribute to a new exhibition being curated by the Vitra Design Museum, Weil-am-Rhein, entitled Living in Motion. The exhibition explored the manifestation of flexible design within domestic environments. My previous work, particularly in the area of portable architecture, meant that I could help in the realm of building design (though the curators recognised that to cover the field properly, furniture, decoration, and clothing would also have to be examined). The exhibition and catalogue were hugely popular because the subject triggered a vivid interest in the public.[4]

After the exhibition I was invited to run a design workshop at the Domaine de Boisbuchet, a rural estate not far from Poitiers in the Charente region of France. Vitra has been organising international design workshops in cooperation with the Centre International de Recherche et d'Education Culturelle et Agricole (CIRECA) since 1996 and with partner, Centre Pompidou, Paris, since 1997. Established by Vitra Design Museum director, Alexander von Vegesack, the workshops are run by a wide range of designers from all over the world and attract people from many spheres of life who wish to experience a hands-on approach to design creativity. Each event is created specifically by the designer involved, so the subjects explored, and experiences of those taking part, vary dramatically.

Boisbuchet is a magical place, a remote rural estate with fields, a lake, a wood and—at its centre—an abandoned chateau. The various agricultural and administration buildings that served the estate have been converted to accommodation and, most importantly, workshops with sufficient tools, machinery, and materials to help make real many of the dreams that emerge from the temporary residents' imagination. A huge barn serves as workshop, meeting place, construction space though much of the work is carried out outside.

Though Boisbuchet attracts people who have a special interest in design they are by no means all professionals. Indeed most are either at the very outset of their careers (students) or people who work in other fields and are seeking to extend their experience or change direction. Previous participants in the Portable Architecture workshops have been journalists, furniture makers, graphic designers, accountants, translators as well as architects and interior designers. The Vitra events are international with participants travelling from every continent to take part. Workshops are held simultaneously so cross-fertilisation can take place between the groups as well merging their different experiences. The working environment of Boisbuchet is relaxed yet intensive; designers and participants live, eat and work together in a supportive infrastructure that is perfectly tuned to creative activity.

The Portable Architecture workshop has taken place every summer since 2002, each time setting its participants the same agenda: to create a group of experimental, yet workable, full-size prototype shelters that will explore the formal implications of mobile flexible design. The project's underlying premise is that every person desires to create a personal environment. It thus taps into this innate sense of place-making by enabling participants to create their own 'special place' in the most direct and immediate way possible, while also challenging our perceptions of what a building is and is for.

Most people think of buildings as heavyweight, permanent structures, made at great expensive over an extended period of time. However, truly responsive buildings can be lightweight, adaptable, affordable and portable. The project therefore also deals with the inter-linked themes of mobility and flexibility in architecture and design—crucial issues that also face contemporary designers in their search for appropriate, ecologically aware, building solutions.

The ambition of the workshop is to explore the possibilities of mobile, self-contained environments; ones that are easy to transport, deploy and easy to use, as well as being environmentally sensitive, flexible and reusable. Such environments should also be responsive to change; able to accommodate the individual and also foster the creation of a community of like-minded individuals. Participants are encouraged to design personal, minimal shelters and to develop ideas that respond to their personal desires about life, space and the environment. The resultant architecture should not simply be about shelter but also meaning and expression. Though people are encouraged to follow their desires and be individualistic in their objectives, they are also encouraged to share this information with the group.

Each project begins with a very short presentation briefly illustrating some of the possibilities of mobile and flexible living, just to inspire confidence that this big task—to make a full-size building in five days—is actually possible. This is immediately followed by a group discussion and debate about the practical requirements and constraints of constructing buildings that move. Issues of materiality, strength/weight ratio, movement methods and power sources are identified and explored. We also examine the fundamental reasoning behind the need for mobile buildings (that, in some cases, they simply do the job better than static ones). In the end, however, it is always agreed that each design should also seek to fulfil some fundamental human desire and aspiration (for example, being close to nature or achieving comfort with convenience).

An important part of the early design process is that everyone is encouraged to design only by making models and mock-ups. This is for three main reasons. First, to avoid the preciousness of drawings, which though 'theoretical' become difficult to abandon. Drawing is a relatively easy fluid process; a connection between mind and body, a way to bring ideas into the real world quickly and effectively. However, it is also very easy when drawing (particularly when dealing with innovative ideas) to avoid dealing with difficulties. You can become obsessed with the image, concerned with the outcome rather than the process, creating a wonderful drawing of an unachievable object, which you then struggle to realise in a short period with limited resources. Second, to make the transition to full-size building quick and easy. Models are in effect prototypes. Making a model of a design idea leads to an inevitable engagement with how it is made. If it works in model form it is far more probable that it will work full-size. Participants are encouraged to engage with their modelling materials as representations of full-size materials: string as rope, cardboard as plywood, thin strips of wood as thicker strips of wood. It also helps them to gauge the implications of substituting both materials and construction strategies, and to be responsive to inspiration from the materials themselves. Third, and perhaps most important, to place all design into the group setting. Rather than working in a notebook, which is essentially a private place, everyone works together when modelling (though on separate concepts), sharing materials, tools and workspace. Such an approach encourages

interaction and sharing of problems and successes; the design is out in the open from the very beginning.

By the end of the first day everyone is engaged in the design process. They have a general idea of their objective and have usually worked through several prototypes. Most people could carry on in this mode for a while but it is important to remember that design is not finite once the concept is recognised. Thus participants are encouraged to move into full-size work (or perhaps large scaled prototypes) as soon as possible. By the middle of day two manufacturing has begun for most. This might seem a very quick gestation period, however, it is important to allow the time for further changes to occur to the design during the construction process. Sometimes this happens after full-size mock-ups have been made and tested, or often after the construction of further models. By working through, models construction issues are highlighted early on and so changes in design are not primarily for failures in construction methodology. People may become dissatisfied with what they have created and seek improvement so that it more closely matches their objective, which has also become more focused as the project develops. Sometimes there are material limitations or the materials offer new opportunities not envisaged before. Often, people find the process has left time for improvements and fine-tuning. Participants become deeply engaged with the process and work hard to achieve their goal. The workshop lights stay on well into the night as presentation day approaches.

The objective of completion in just five days seems a difficult one for such an ambitious project but with everyone helping each other with construction tasks (and decision-making) it is very unusual for the deadline not to be met. Different movement strategies, structural systems and materials are often tested for each of the designs and frequent discussions have taken place on an informal basis.

The final presentation takes place as a peripatetic event in the grounds of Boisbuchet. Participants decide on the site where their building will be erected and a walking route is created leading from place to place. The deployment process becomes a performance and is always carried out in front of an audience consisting of the participants from all the workshops, designers and Boisbuchet staff. The dissembled, folded, transported components are mysterious to the audience until they are deployed into their erected state. Once erected everyone wants to experience this new temporary shelter for themselves and the buildings are examined, played-in, pushed and prodded; providing feedback for the creator/builders. Each participant has created a wonderfully personal design, fully constructed and operational that conveys their own response to the agenda of mobile living. That each is so different from the other is testament to the individuality of human nature and ingenuity.

How can the outcomes of the Portable Architecture Design Workshop be quantified? One of its key characteristics is that it is a form of building design in which the element of experience and understanding is accentuated. Mobile buildings are not erected over long periods; they appear quickly, usually within a time period in which people can readily appreciate the process that is taking place. They are erected in unusual sites and leave no or virtually no physical impact when they depart. Portable buildings synthesise the act of performance and event with the process of providing shelter. Portable buildings are lightweight and efficient; the design parameters are so lean that it is generally not possible to add in stylistic features that confuse the buildings' imagery. All these factors help portable architecture to be both intriguing and understandable.

When you see a constructed object being assembled you are at first interested in finding out what it will be like when complete, what it is for. Later this interest enables you to understand more easily how it works. When it is in a place you have previously seen without the new building's presence, it adds a new perspective to the way you view that space. The buildings made at the workshop are the result of a five-day struggle to realise a dream. Along the way the participants acquire new skills, some practical (particularly about materials, structures, what they weigh and how strong they are) some more cerebral (how to communicate personal ideas through form). They experiment with a way of designing that is usually new to them. When the project is complete they have a very limited time to enjoy the fruits of their labours. Typically people work hard up to the last moments before the presentation and then it is over in a few minutes. Most will spend extra time after the presentations talking to others about what they have made, revisiting it during the evening, and relocating it in various places around the estate. Occasionally some will spend their last night sleeping in their building (if that type of shelter was their objective). Not long after the workshop participants have left a new designer will arrive and a new workshop begin. It is the ritual of Boisbuchet that the results of all the workshops are either recycled or burnt. The value of these ephemeral objects is therefore not in a rash of new products appearing in the building market each year but in the experience gained by individuals (both those who have taken part in the workshop and those who saw and experienced its results), the knowledge acquired, but also—like all architecture—portable or otherwise, in the memories of those who experienced them.

Architecture of Motion
• Sarah Bonnemaison and Christine Macy

One would think that architecture as a fine art works solely for the eyes. Instead, it should work primarily for the sense of mechanical motion in the human body—something to which scant attention is paid.[1]

—Johann Wolfgang von Goethe

You can really only talk about space as a result of an experiential body timing its actions.[2]

—Lars Spuybroek

It is not a question of knowing which comes first—movement or space—which molds the other, for ultimately a deep bond is involved. After all, they are caught in the same set of relationships; only the arrow of power changes direction.[3]

—Bernard Tschumi

Introduction

Personal computers, car faxes, laptops, pagers, the Internet, chat lines, cell phones, Blackberries, personal organisers, instant messaging, iPods; over the last 20 years, modes of communication have been changing so rapidly, one leapfrogging over another in quick succession so that once again, our very understanding of self, body, time, mobility and our environment is being redefined. We say "once again", because this happened in an equally dramatic way not so long ago, at the beginning of the last century. At that time, new technologies of transportation and communication—like the train, transatlantic liner and automobile, cinema, wireless and telephone—had artists and scientists, architects and politicians, feel like they were on the brink of wholly new ways of seeing and experiencing themselves in space, and with each other, in the context of modernity.

It is interesting for us to see this parallel and ask what is the same and what is different, between the dawn of the twentieth and twenty-first centuries, in our sense of self in space and time. This is a particularly interesting question for architects, who want to reflect on how people understand and experience space.

Such a line of inquiry brings us back to mobility and perception; the first having to do with space and time, and the second; with our experiences and interpretations of human activity. In this research, we look at the relationship between human activities and architecture. Rather than expecting people to adapt their activities to buildings, we ask how architecture might better support human activities. Would such buildings look different? Would they 'behave' differently? To pursue an answer to these questions we begin, as did the motion scientists of the early twentieth century, with the human body. We start by studying the shape of human activity; in motion and stillness, at work and rest, alone and with others, in crowds and couples, connected by eyes or body language, by voice and the Internet. An architecture that supports activity might begin with exploring the shape of movement.

Capturing Movement in the Visual Field

The pure form of movement becomes an artistic object in its own right.... Movement in space can be experienced as an absolute... disengaged from the performer.[4]

—Siegfried Giedeon

In the second half of the nineteenth century, a number of people began to explore the potential of the camera to see movement in a new way. Photographic inventors such as Etienne-Jules Marey and Eadweard Muybridge developed new techniques that permitted shorter exposure times, trigger releases on the camera shutter, and

Top
Sarah Bonnemaison
Pin-up Board Studies, 2004
Image courtesy of
Dalhousie University.
Photograph by
Sarah Bonnemaison.
Traces from lights attached
to hands and feet on a student
walking up to a board and
pinning up a poster, seminar
at Dalhousie University.

Bottom
Sarah Bonnemaison
Karate, 2004
Image courtesy of
Dalhousie University.
Photograph by
Sarah Bonnemaison.
Light traces of a student
with lights attached to their
hands and feet performing
a Karate move, seminar
at Dalhousie University.

multiple exposures on a single photographic plate. These inventions allowed Marey to capture the trail made by a bird or a person in motion, and other fleeting phenomena such as waves of smoke or turbulence in the air. Muybridge lined up shutter releases in a row to record multiple instants of a movement sequence. Artists like Marcel Duchamp and Umberto Boccioni were fascinated with the unexpected and poetic view of the world presented by these new, seemingly 'objective', technologies of vision.[5] The development of cinema relied on these new inventions, but also produced its own pioneers like Dziga Vertov. In *Man With a Movie Camera*, Vertov followed the path of movement, allowing the viewer to see the effort of a running horse, captured in a close-up shot. The camera could take the viewer to impossible places, and see things the naked eye would never see. It opened up new perspectives on the world, especially in relation to time, speed, and space.[6]

Early modernist architects followed these new technologies of vision closely. They tried to develop architectural analogues to cinema, such as Le Corbusier's "architectural promenade", Eileen Grey's "choreographic architecture", or Moisei Ginzburg's "graph of movement", which enabled the designer to radically rethink architectural envelopes.[7] Influenced by motion-studies scientists Christine Frederick and Frank and Lillian Gilbreth, they traced the movement of housewives in kitchens and stewards in trains and transatlantic liners, in order to design compact, collapsible building components that would support modern lifestyles and needs. These included convertible kitchens, laundries and bathrooms, collapsible beds, desks and chairs, movable railings, operable shutters and screens. They worked at breaking down the rigid exteriors of building facades into planes of solids and voids, into light and shadow, in an effort to see space in a new way—more objective, but also more poetic, or unexpected—above all, more modern.[8]

In our work, we want to revisit this history of experimentation and once again, see what a close investigation of human movements can offer architects in their search for creating forms that respond to human activities. We also want to further develop the idea of tracing movements and the way we go about doing it. The modernists who were recording movement worked within a scientific paradigm. They studied motion in their subject entirely objectively, that is, they believed that they could observe without having any effects on the behaviour of the subject. Marey, for example:

> … always took photographs in order to observe, and he observed in order to measure. Unpredictability did not interest him and neither did invisible or intangible things; there is already so much to do with what can be seen and with what can be measured. But this raises the question of the supplement as a way to shake things up, to effect a counter reading of these photographs with the poetic qualities that these images release in spite of themselves, in spite of the strict rules that produced them.[9]

This excerpt from Georges Didi-Huberman's recent book on Marey suggests a Postmodern critique of the scientific paradigm. Today, those who study human behaviour recognise the impact of the observer on the observed, and the agency of the subject under observation.[10] By invoking Jacques Derrida's concept of the "supplement", Didi-Huberman also declares his interest in the other associations called up by these experiments. They were scientific, to be sure, but also poetic, artistic, disturbing and dream-like. In our revisiting of modernist movement tracings, we want to maintain this Postmodern perspective, and remain critical of the scientific paradigm. We see our effort to map movement as an interactive process that involves viewer, space and performer, like Barthes' active reader, who brings his own interpretations to the text.[11]

To that end, we worked with dancers who got involved with our tracings. Trained in improvisation, these dancers developed movement phrases in response to the demands of our study, and the tools used for translation, whether they were video, drawings, models or mobiles. The results of these collaborations were brought together in a public performance in the summer of 2004.

For the purpose of this text, we can categorise the steps we took in moving from dance to architecture—between tracing movement and generating form—into three lines of inquiry. First, we explored 'line' as a path of movement in dance and a drawn line in architecture. Second, we looked at 'surface'. In dance, this involved working with light, shadow and video projection to add complexity and meaning to the neutral setting of the performance. In architectural terms, our explorations into surface led us to use orthographic projection to map movement onto the surrounding walls (as with projected light), and also to explore the surfaces that could be generated from moving lines in space (like a mathematical surface or volume generated from a line in motion). This study built on our experience in tensile structures. Lastly, by developing performance and installation together, we kept our focus on the relationship between performer, space and audience. "There is no architecture", Bernard Tschumi reminds us, "without event".[12]

Line—The Trace of Movement

> Pictorial art springs from movement, is in itself interrupted motion and is conceived as motion.[13]
>
> —Paul Klee

> It seems that everything—that is to say, every movement—must... create a curve.[14]
>
> —Georges Didi-Huberman

In order to break down the scientific division between observer and observed, we set up an experiment based on contact improvisation, a form of contemporary dance. Contact improvisation is performed by two dancers who maintain a continuous point of contact between their bodies as they move, leaning on and, at times, completely supporting each other. This point between the two bodies is itself constantly in motion, often rapidly, requiring the participants to be fully engaged in the moment or risk losing contact and falling.

We combined this technique of dance improvisation with the practice of contour drawing, a form of line drawing in which the artist traces the external contour of an object with their eyes, and follows this trace with the pencil on paper. The aim is to avoid all preconceptions about what is being drawn. In the contact-contour drawing, the person drawing cannot 'objectively' record the dancer's movements, but is unavoidably caught up in an exchange. As the dancer moves, the drawer must maintain a point of contact with them, and record this movement by drawing a contour line, and maintaining a point of contact with the paper. The drawer leans against and is propelled by the dancer, while continuing to draw. This contact improvisation involves three 'bodies' (dancer, drawer and paper), and two points of contact (the point where dancer and drawer touch, and the point where drawer marks the paper). Here we are reminded of Paul Klee's words: "An activated line, a line moving freely along, is a stroll for strolling's sake. Its performer is a point in transit."[15] The interdependent figure of dancer-drawer actively registers both movement and trace. In one respect, the drawer becomes the instrument of the dancer, recording his or her movement on paper. However this is not a one-way recording, like a seismograph or hydrometer, which (one hopes) objectively records movement as a line. The drawer leans into the dancer, trying to trace a point of contact between the two bodies. Both must pay attention to maintaining such contact, and to all surfaces, including the paper.

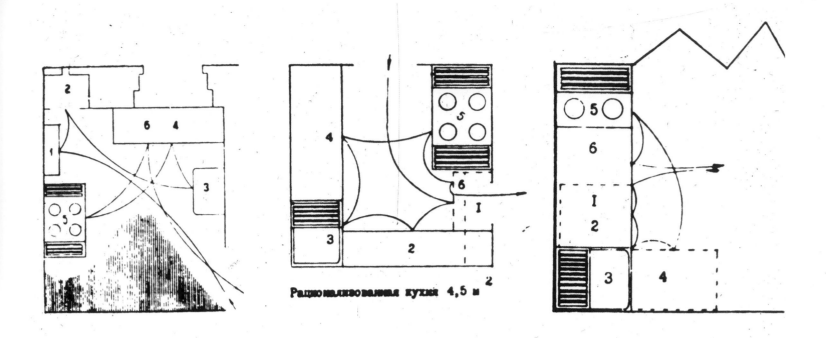

Рационализированная кухня 4,5 м

Surface—Projection with Light, Shadow and Video

Sight can also link the dancer's body and architect's pen. In a subsequent exercise, the artist stayed concealed behind a fabric screen. Again, they trace the line of the dancer's movement, but this time, without physical contact. The attention of the artist is entirely focused on the movement, not on the drawing; the line is generated through the instrument of two bodies, linked by vision. This is a duet, where body and line move in tandem. The drawing appears magically on the stretched fabric.

These exercises focus attention on the connection between feeling and form (to borrow Suzanne Langer's expression), and the necessary relations between movement, the surrounding space, and sensation. Some contemporary architects have been drawn to this almost synesthetic sense of space, going so far as to extend their desire for bodily sensation outwards, to the architecture itself. Lars Spuybroek for example, tells us that "movements can only be fluent, if the skin extends as far as possible over the prosthesis and into the surrounding space, so that every action takes place within the interior of the body, which no longer does things consciously but relies totally on feeling".[16]

Re-enacting aspects of Marey's work with students (who added ideas of their own), we recorded a number of different activities. The traces deposited by everyday activities contrasts with the precision of deliberate movements from dance or martial arts. The light paths are both beautiful and suggestive, artistic objects—as Giedeon suggested—in their own right. The path of light, like the calligrapher's brush, reveals the speed of movement. Where the hand moves fast, the line is thin, but where it slows down, it thickens. A momentary pause becomes a stain of light. In this way, the light tracings open a window onto the more invisible and intangible states of the person moving, recording both perfection of gesture and the nuance of emotion.

As the dancers were lit, shadows of their bodies were transformed, depending on the surface they were cast upon. Like shadows on building facade, they were elongated on oblique surfaces, and fractured when projected onto planes.[17] Projections (of light) allowed us to transform scale and shape. We were reminded of the modernists' interest in de-materialising volume into planes.

The repressed 'other' of motion studies found its outlet in the nineteenth century's fascination with magical scientific effects such as x-rays and electrical light. These inventions made their way into collective entertainments and world's fairs. One device from this era uses two lights positioned in a certain way on a figure to make its shadow disappear. We employed such a device with a group of dancers, creating an animated inkblot of shadow, its centre disappearing into an optical void. Such illusions of light and shadow allowed us de-materialise performers, make them gigantic or grotesque, or vanish altogether.

The choreographer, Rudolf Laban, called the space of movement the "kinesphere". Through projection, one can map the kinesphere onto any architectural setting that surrounds a body. Oskar Schlemmer, who was master of the stage in the Dessau Bauhaus, draws these radiating lines streaming out from the dancer's body until they hit walls, floors and ceiling.[18] It is understood in both Laban's and Schlemmer's depiction of the body in space, that the geometrical coordinates established by each moving body are centred in that body, along its vertical axis of the spine. In a Postmodern rereading of this tradition, the contemporary choreographer, William Forsythe, allows movements to originate from any point in or on the body, effectively dethroning the dancer from their central position. In Forsythe's work, any fragment or point can be understood to generate its own coordinates of

projection, in a process he calls "geometric inscription". "You can use these ideas of geometric inscription", he says, "all over the room and all over your body".[19] In our work, video served an analogous role, de-centring the eye of the observer in the audience, and allowing them to experience multiple, simultaneous points of view.

We avoided using video as a backdrop to the performance, rather, we utilised it to add a dimension otherwise unavailable. Using live feeds, we could project the activity taking place outside the theatre inside, allowing for dancers in two different spaces to perform duets in one visual field. Reshooting the projection of a live video feed, the projected image begins to multiply, as if two mirrors were facing each other. Mobiles created from dancers' movements added to the de-centring and multiplication. As dancers moved with these mobiles, they began to spin and so did their shadows; resulting in a multitude of complex overlapping patterns.

videotaped and its image projected on the back wall. The image of the flickering candle is very large. This is the second technique of creating space; adding scale. When the projected image is filmed with another camera, doubling the image, we have a third technique: multiplication. A dancer enters and performs a movement phrase. They are filmed and their choreography doubled through additional cameras feeding live images. Other dancers enter and the movement phrase is performed by them in unison. Their movements are further multiplied by video, shadows, and mobiles until the whole space becomes a kaleidoscope of motion and traces. These layers of figure and space, of architecture and activity, create a landscape that is inhabited and experienced: a lived space.

Inhabited Space—Performer, Space and Audience

We began with a white box; the equivalent of the blank page. The white box is a quintessentially modernist space, stripped of figuration and—ostensibly—meaning.[20] Our explorations into dance and architecture added shapes, forms, and activities to this neutral space, bringing with them imagery, associations, and meanings.

But only in the performance, for us, does the architectural work come to life. Like Tschumi, we feel that: "There is no space without event, no architecture without programme.... Our work argues that architecture... cannot be dissociated with the events that happen in it."[21]

The performance tells the story of creating that space. It starts in darkness with the lighting of a candle. This is the first technique of creating space; moving from darkness into light. The candle is

Eating Architecture
• Rita McKeough

My installation work first began in the 1980s while Calgary city was being redeveloped. This was during the oil boom when all old houses were torn down and replaced with high-rises and office towers. I wanted to comment on such effects on the city and, in 1981, made a piece for the Alberta College of Art that involved constructing a series of houses and exposing them to the process of tearing down. In so doing I aimed to provide such structures with a 'voice' by introducing sounds from the external world into the gallery. These voices echoed people's experiences in the city while it was being demolished and rebuilt

At the same time I made the installation, *Defunct*, and a number of exterior pieces in spaces such as streets. One of these addressed the bankruptcy experienced by developers in the years just after the boom; the evidence of which was a proliferation of half-finished office towers; concrete shells left standing. I also made several pieces about the quality of those buildings.

Shortly after the boom I made *Skeletal Development* at Banff. This piece explored the notion that, if the demise of the environment continues to happen, there won't be building materials of the same ilk or quantity that we're used to. *Skeletal Development* involved burying all the fragments of a house in Calgary that had been torn down and glued onto two-by-fours painted white. Later I dug them up, and used them to develop an apartment building.

In this work I assumed the role of 'developer'. I transformed the structure into four very tiny apartments—literally 2.4 by 1.8 metres each—inserted into a larger apartment building. The structure became skeleton-like in appearance, as all the wood was bleached white. I wanted to communicate that, without building materials, our living arrangements have to be minimalist—a reality that we will have to come to terms with in the future. Such events during that period in Calgary influenced my work for many, many years.

After *Skeletal Development*, I made a number of works that developed into a piece called *Strucked*. *Strucked* was essentially a motorised house and a bulldozer (within a model construction site), that followed each other around the gallery space while emitting the sounds of human voices. Once more the aim was to create a public arena in which developers had to be accountable and buildings might have a chance of survival. *Strucked* was an attempt to reinstate some kind of possibility and optimism into the situation.

In the midst of all this, I also started researching the history of domestic architecture and its effects upon the domestication of the family unit; particularly in relation to self-sufficiency and isolation from society at large. What I discovered was a traditional model of a family unit that has a myriad of roles embedded in it. The role that troubled me the most was that of women, specifically those that experienced violence in the home. So I started to critically address how the containment of the family affects social dynamics. I also became interested in how domestic architecture affects the use of specific rooms and how this might impact on the development of social roles within the family as a whole.

I conflated such concerns in another house piece at the Stride Gallery in 1985. The house walls became animated, and the structure a kind of prison, which literally revealed its effect on the family. Through this piece, and some of the work that preceeded it, I become more aware of the politics imbedded in architecture, and in gender, and these things became really important to my practice.

I still work from this perspective although—increasingly—the work becomes more abstract, or poetic, than direct. My more recent work is certainly much less didactic, particularly *Long Haul* and *Outskirts*, which are both performances. *Outskirts* was an important and transitional piece for me, and partly came about after the completion of a previous work, *Tower of Silence*, in 2000.

Tower of Silence was also a performance piece and a direct response to the ruins of a traditional Trappist monastery in Winnipeg. In this work I addressed the history of the monks who had lived there. I became particularly interested in the practice of prayer—specifically

Rita McKeough
Defunct, circa 1980
Performance/installation
Images courtesy of the artist.

silent prayer—which they perceived as a resource that individuals who came to them in need could utilise. In my mind, much prayer is about requesting something or asking forgiveness. However this prayer was just given, which I thought was a very nice attitude.

In the making of *Tower of Silence*, Hélène Cixous became very important to my practice. Cixous' *Opera: The Undoing of Women* really influenced my decision to bring music into my work and to address the issues inherent in performance spaces. In *Opera: The Undoing of Women* Cixous discusses the positioning of women in the dramatisation of experience in opera and how the voice might be employed to both neutralise existing narratives and to articulate new ones.

In response, I explored the idea of simultaneously using a sung voice, a spoken voice and gesture in the operatic piece *Boco Lupo*. Bringing these three elements together seemed to me an interesting place to start to hear and understand language a little differently and to explore the residue of anger and its manifestations in the body (as well the chaos that such juxtapositions might entail).

Another Cixous text, *Three Steps in the Ladder of Writing*, really heightened my interest in the power of silence. Cixous discusses the letter 'H' here, and how it can become silent in such languages as Spanish, for example. So I became interested in language, and wanted to use the facade of the monastery to represent this abrupt and, very institutionalised, sense of space. For, although the community that had lived there were very positive in their attitudes, their religion and politics in general are imbedded in a history that is exclusionary of many voices.

Taking Cixous' lead, I built a giant 'H', 12.8 metres tall and 9.1 metres wide, from scaffolding and pushed it right up against the front of the monastery. (To me, that's where the feminism lay in the piece; the 'rubbing' of my H against that historical building.) We performed nine songs altogether. At the same time I made the gesture of digging under the building; descending into the earth in order to come up the other side, in a sense. The other performers climbed to the top of the H. Essentially the piece was about this sense of agency and unique subjectivity that could be articulated by scaling the architectural image of those histories and institutions. For the audience, I think, different things emerged; the quality of the music, for example. They laughed through the whole performance: at the architecture, the performance and the whole drama of the experience. There was this raucous critique—but interest— happening simultaneously.

When I made *Take it to the Teeth* at Glenbow I literally ate the wall. Cheryl L'hirondelle and I spent one hour a day (for 45 days in total) chewing the wall, and removing its surface to reveal speakers that were hidden behind. The sound emitted by the speakers related to the history of the building itself. In so doing the walls became the body (and the speakers, the memory embedded in them).

I responded to the museum itself (which was the largest building I had exhibited in at that time) in a slightly naive but also cautious manner. I was worried about the museum's capability to neutralise my work, so wanted to be present in the piece itself. By gnawing away at the body of the museum, I felt I was able to limit such a threat as well as challenge the institution in general. The process of gnawing was also an attempt to embed my narrative in the space— in the same manner of memory being embedded in the body—by creating a digestive tract through performance.

So, in tasting the wall, I was understanding an experience or memory and deciding whether or not to digest them. Those things that are useful became the nutrients I could extract, and are reconstructed within memory and body. The ones that are repulsive I can reject. The mouth has the ability to be both aggressive and intimate, erotic, and has amazing sensual capabilities. These are all metaphors I tried to address in this work.

Top
Rita McKeough
Tower of Silence, 2000
Performance/installation
Image courtesy of the artist.

Bottom
Rita McKeough
Long Haul, 1992
Performance/installation
(with technical assistance
from Robyn Moody)
Image courtesy of The Banff Centre.
Photograph by Tara Nicholson.

Between the Furniture and the Building (Between a Rock and a Hard Place)
• Jimmie Durham

I want to ask for your help: I want to make a film, and I want to free some stones. For the past couple of years I have been investigating the dictatorial power of architecture in Europe, and such investigations have led to further research into the concepts that support and weigh upon stone. Some materials, innocent in themselves—have been overly scripted—given roles that are too dense. Iron has that problem. (I bet Richard Serra believes everything he's ever been told about iron. He probably thinks that it's hard. Iron! Steel! An art critic in New York wrote of a Serra work that: "It shows us new things about Cor-ten steel." In the first instance, what is Cor-ten steel? In the second, what does a New York art critic know about it and why would we care?)

Cast iron is very brittle and also subject to quick deterioriasation by rust. But cast iron mixed with glass, called Du-iron, is not so subject to either. (There now, I've taught you something new about cast iron, gimme some money! All that heavy, leaden metaphor!)

You needn't think of swords or ploughshares; think instead of steel cable three millimetres thick and three kilometres long, soft and subtle. (You may not believe this but the centre of the earth is molten iron, yet only part of it is liquid. Under our seas is an ocean of liquid iron, with its own currents and tides. In the middle of this ocean floats a large iron ball—molten but solid all the same—due to the weight of the quantity of the stuff.)

I have previously spoken about the English settling in Virginia, but 50 years before this, the Spanish had already arrived as missionaries. They taught us how to make steel and, from that time on, American Indians have been famous knife-makers. (We taught ourselves, though, to find fallen meteors for the best pure iron. We made star patterns in the knife-blades to celebrate that our knives came from the sky.)

Stone suffers from architectural weight; the weight of metaphor, and the weight of history. Last year in Sweden I came across nine pieces of granite that are the perfect illustration of the problems of stone. They were intended to be part of Hitler's oversized Arch of Peace in Berlin. Hitler himself made the original plans and drawings, while Speer polished it and located quarries and carvers in Sweden and Norway. Speer had commissioned the work on the granite stones that I saw. They are beautifully carved, and absolutely massive, quietly waiting for history.

There are similar stones for the same project in Norway and others, from Swedish quarries, actually arrived in Berlin during the Second World War. Those stones were liberated into new slavery by the Soviets, and are now part of the monstrous monument to the Soviet soldier at Treptower Park.

The film I plan to make will not be a documentary, although it will 'document' itself. It will be feature length and of high artistic merit (and therefore 'commercial' in some sense; even if not a 'blockbuster'). We'll find a barge with no engine and, after taking the stones by truck through the forests to the harbour, load and tow them across the Baltic in the direction of Rügen Island and Berlin. We will sink the barge, along with stones, into the Baltic Sea. The stones will be free (and light) as their existence diminishes into the light and cellulose of the film. They will also be eternal—as carved granite cannot be—because they have been transformed into art, and "art is eternal", people say.

So here's the help I need: a film producer and/or hot shot art curator, a director and crew, a lot of money (to get production started) and a barge that will float and sink. Write to me care of the publisher, please.

Katha Pollit (or perhaps it was Barbara Ehrenreich or Barbara Kruger) once said that our century, and modernism, was the age of the phallus. (I'm suddenly reminded of another story here. In the early 1980s I lived with my sweetheart, Maria Thereza Alves. Maria Thereza is Brazilian and the immigration department had misplaced her green card, making her an illegal alien. Every morning she had to stand in a long line at the immigration office next to City Hall in

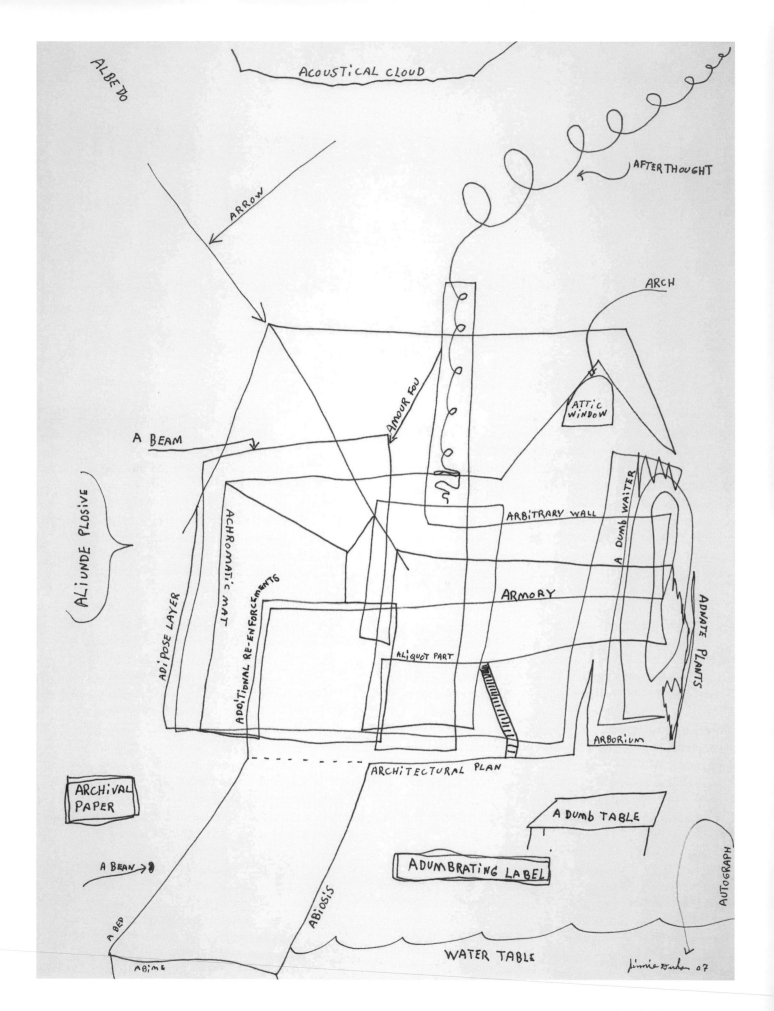

Previous page
Jimmie Durham
*Adventures in Architectural
Planning*, 2007
Ink on paper
57.2 x 65.4 cm
Private collection
Image courtesy of Plug In ICA.
Photograph by Bill Eakin.

Manhattan. Sometimes it would be late afternoon before she got to a desk, only to be questioned suspiciously. Then, as she and dozens of other tired strangers left the building through the back door, they were confronted by a monster: a giant piece of Cor-ten steel named *Tilted Arc* by Richard Serra; seemingly herding up the aliens and pushing them back into the labyrinth of frustration.) If our century is the age of the phallus, of penetrations and thrusts and rockets and fast cars and skyscrapers, the coming age should be seen as the age of the gonad: the age of stored information, of containers and containment.

A True Story

In 1985 a young British sculptor named Nicholas Fairplay came to Manhattan Island to carve stone for the Cathedral of St John the Divine. Conceived by Andrew Carnegie to provide a fitting place to worship it is built atop Morningside Cliff, and faces away from Harlem in the valley below. Beside the cliff there is a high fence and a private police force separating Morningside Heights from Harlem, and a statue of Carl Schurz. (All this was lost on Nick Fairplay. He inadvertently fell in with bad companions; American Indians.)

Document A

On 15 April 1985, Nicholas Fairplay, a British alien claiming to be a sculptor, attended a secret meeting at an apartment on Amsterdam Avenue. Also at this meeting were: Maria Thereza Alves, a Brazilian alien who also claims to be an artist; Flavio Garciandia, a Cuban alien who also claims to be an artist; and Jimmie Durham, a Cherokee who is an active member of the terrorist organisation, AIM. Fairplay left certain documents at the apartment and departed at midday.

Another True Story

Leonard Peltier is an American Indian who is in prison for two life sentences; having been convicted of killing two FBI agents on the Pine Ridge Indian Reservation in 1975. Peltier is innocent. Fairplay carved a perfect likeness of him on a stone section of the front of the Cathedral and American Indian and African heads on other parts of the building. Fairplay told us that when Medieval buildings in England are destroyed it is often discovered that the workers had placed oyster shells between the stone blocks to level them. These shells often have faces and insulting messages carved on them.

In 1997 the Museum of Contemporary Art in Pori, Finland, invited me to do a project. I found a truckload of rocks the size of large potatoes and placed them all over the museum floor. I also arranged these rocks outside the building, on the pavement and into the street. They were not so densely placed that they made a covering; spaced from 50 to 100 centimetres apart. With these 'free' stones I wanted to free up the architecture itself and its agenda for the museum (this was not intended as an attack; the building is quite beautiful and well suited to be an art museum).

As a result, the building looked as though it were getting ready for motion. The interior, especially the reception desk area and the toilets, where no longer so serious and separate. The effect was not theatrical; as such there was nothing to be 'believed' by the way of a narrative. On an interior wall I installed a large map of the world, with a hand-drawn 'route' for kicking stones, not directly to Chalma (the 'Centre of the World' in Mexico), but toward it; from Finland across Northern Russia to Sibera. (Aborginial people in Mexico make pilgrimages to the 'sacred tree' in Chalma. The myth goes that those who give up and try to stop or turn back become stones.)

I'm telling you this partly because a function of this text is that it will act as another 'progress report' on what I call my *Eurasia Project*. This is a self-cancelling project as it has no goal or end.

Four years ago, I moved to Europe from Mexico where I'd lived for almost eight years. It is clearly obvious that Europe is a political entity, not a geographical one. That Europe has no geography was already apparent to me in America, because America is, quite obviously, the best (that is, the worst) part of Europe. But living here on this continent called Eurasia—a single continent that few seem to know or care about—makes Europe acutely 'here' for me and I therefore feel more free of 'Europeness'. I might now be enabled for the first time to 'account for myself', and there might possibly be someone here—like my friend Ken Vos who is half Japanese and half Dutch and says he dislikes those two countries immensely—that I feel I ought to account to.

The other reason I'm speaking of my project in Pori is to introduce the work of a German architect named Thilo Folkerts, whose specialty is landscapes in cities. He made a movable rock garden comprised by a mound of gravel (of a mass equalling four average human bodies) that looks more fluid than either material. Folkerts situates this mound wherever it suits him and shapes and textures it with a rake (after the fashion of Japanese rock gardens). It can change shape and mood in minutes. He has a large collection of photographs of sand and rock formations he encounters in and around Berlin (his "favourite sand piles" he calls them). These are often crowded or 'leaning' against a building and sometimes on street curbs, spilling out onto the road. No boundaries, no shape, but undeniable and accidentally charming non-objects.

Oh, I wish I had thought of these gravel mounds! I would, however, want to bring the gravel pile specifically into art, into the 'art spaces'. (If I made a large pile of very clean, and aesthetically pleasing gravel stones partially cover the reception desk and chair of the catalogues table of a museum, wouldn't that look good? The small stones would be inadvertently scattered by clumsy feet. One might come to rest next to Mario Merz' igloo, another against some giant steel sculpture and lie there awaiting its next collaborative move.)

Having written the word 'collaborative', I see there may be a possibility that Folkert would do a collaborative piece with me. I might, at the same time, try making anti-Folkert work. (Suppose I mixed the gravel with cement and poured it into a mound partially covering the reception desk and table? I could call it *Thilo's Petrified Garden*.)

American theorist Rosalind Krauss said of her show L'informe at the Centre Pompidou in Paris that her first criterion for choosing individual works by the artists in the exhibition was size. She said that large work proved that the artist was serious, and committed. Yeah, really![1]

Caravans Are Cool
• Sean Topham

Caravans or travel trailers as they are also known, are the bane of motorists the world over. The typical caravan is frequently belittled for its lumbering pace and owners often find themselves at the butt of endless jokes and jeers from other road users. In creative circles, too, the caravan is rarely taken seriously as an example of good design. Stylish magazines will give pages of coverage to slick mobile dwelling capsules put forward by architects, artists and other design professionals, but they're unlikely to ever feature the Elddis Avante or Buccaneer Schooner. The two touring caravans are at opposite ends of the range offered by the Explorer Group (a manufacturer based in northern England) and both models have picked up several prestigious awards. The Elddis Avante represents the firm's entry level product while the Buccaneer Schooner is at the top of its range.

Caravan holidays are enormously popular all over the world. Britain's Caravan Club, the first of its kind, had 60,000 family members in the 1970s; in the year 2000 that figure was over 310,000.[1] Caravans such as the Elddis Avante compress many of life's activities into a small box, but that box also has to move.

The relatively large surface area of the caravan is fully exposed to both head and side winds when it is pulled behind a car. This presents an array of problems for the design team who have to keep the trailer light so it can be towed, but not so light that it flips over in a gale. Walls have to be thin to maximise living space but tough enough so as not to disintegrate on impact. Considering the limited amount of space available inside the Elddis Avante there are an impressive amount of facilities on board. Kitchen appliances, bathroom fittings, dining suite and bedding are all there to offer the comforts of home while away from home. This is the key function of this leisure caravan: it is a commercial success because it performs this function very well.

The mobile home—the caravan's close relation—also has a laughable reputation. It is considered by some to be ugly and cheap, yet such dwellings are immensely popular and represent around a quarter of all housing in America.[2] Caravans, recreational vehicles (RVs) and mobile homes are enjoyed by millions of people around the world, but remain ignored or ridiculed as examples of good design. By contrast, recent years have seen more and more architects, and other design professionals, fall in love with the freedom offered by the mobile home. Younger architects are especially keen to fashion living pods, and mobile dwelling units, which take the mobile home to a whole new level. These neat capsules are about making statements in a form that can be communicated easily while also demonstrating new ideas about the domestic environment. No matter how slick or how radical some of these recent portable dwellings appear it is worth remembering that they all owe a great debt to the much-maligned mobile home.

The attraction of caravans, motor homes and mobile homes is that they belong to us all. Their history is not tied to one single discipline. There's a little bit of architecture and a little bit of vehicle design mixed up with a myriad of ideas from a variety of other subjects. Universities offer degrees in the most obscure topics but I've yet to find one that offers caravan design; and that's no bad thing.

The history of the caravan is synonymous with DIY and improvisation. Caravans and other types of mobile home are relatively new phenomena and have developed alongside the introduction of motor vehicles and good quality roads. The earliest recreational caravans were based on the extravagant living vans used by travelling showmen in the nineteenth and twentieth centuries and the lightweight Bowtop wagons that were popular among the Romany population around the same time.

A retired naval officer named Dr W Gordon Stables was one of the first people to take to the road for leisure purposes in Britain. His pleasure caravan was named the Wanderer and, in 1886, he wrote about his travels in the book *The Cruise of the Land Yacht Wanderer*. Stables achieved certain notoriety from his adventures and it wasn't long before other wealthy ladies and gentlemen were